GLOBALISATION, LIBERALISATION, PRIVATISATION AND INDIAN POLITY

GLOBALISATION LIBERALISATION PRIVATISATION AND INDIAN POLITY

(In 8 Volumes)

Economy

(Volume 1)

Editor

PROF. RAMESH CHANDRA

Vice-Chancellor, Bhundelkhand University, Jhansi (U.P.)

ISHA BOOKS

DELHI—110 033

Globalisation, Liberalisation, Privatisation and Indian Polity
(Agriculture, Economics, Environment, Political Science)

Rs. 7000 (Set)

ISBN: 81-8205-015-4 (Set)
ISBN: 81-8205-016-2 (Vol. 1)

Published in 2004 in India by
Isha Books, D-43, Prithviraj Road
Adarsh Nagar, Delhi-110 033

Lasertypesetting by: Varsha Graphics, Delhi
Printed at: Chawla Offset Press, Delhi

Contents

Preface

Globalisation can be defined as a process of growing interdependence between all people of this planet. People are linked together economically and socially by trade, investments and governance. These links are spurred by market liberalization, information, communication and transportation technologies. The phenomenon of globalisation is a rapid-growing movement, a revolution in terms of bringing the world closer and closer.

The process of economic globalisation began to gather momentum in the 1940s, when countries were expected to adjust to the opening up to international trade with convertible current accounts and the International Monetary Fund (IMF). By 1995, several developing countries with different degrees of capital account convertibility became increasingly integrated through capital movements. Globalisation in the information age has seen the integration of finance, markets, nation-states and technologies to a degree never witnessed before—in a way that is enabling individuals, corporations and nation states to reach around the world faster, further, deeper and cheaper than ever before.

International organisations such as World Trade Organisation (WTO), International Monetary Fund (IMF)

World Bank, Organisation for Economic Cooperation and Development (OECD) are the major wire-pullers of process of globalisation. Most of the world's governments and parliaments are signatories to the World Trade Organisation, and members of the International Monetary Fund.

Societies all over the world are experiencing the globalisation of more and more aspects of life, but accompanied by the contradictions of growing inequality within and between countries. Certainly, economic globalisation has led to increased wealth for many in some countries. But it has also led to shattering economic crises, collapse in standards of living, widespread societal and ethnic conflict, social disintegration and greatly increased insecurity for a disproportionately large part of the world's population.

These volumes attempt to provide in-depth and authoritative information about the pros and cons of globalisation. The set describes the impact brought out in various spheres of life such as trade, economy, industries, education, environment, agriculture communication and poverty reduction, in eight volumes. It will prove to be a complete reference material for students, researchers, academics and all the concerned.

Editor

1

Impact of Liberalisation on Economy

Over the last two centuries, the world economy has become substantially more unequal. The last twenty years—the years of the second globalisation—have witnessed some slow down in this secular trend owing to the partial convergence of the incomes per capita of South East Asia, coastal China and part of urban India towards that of the advanced nations. They have also witnessed, however, an increase in the income gap between the advanced nations and all other developing and transitional countries, as well as a worrying reversal of past trends towards lower domestic inequality in many nations. While the debate on the causes of such changes is not over yet, initial evidence shows that they are in part due to the spread of the new 'global market paradigm'. Such paradigm advocates the removal of barriers to international trade in goods and services, the opening up to foreign direct investments, the liberalisation of short-term portfolio flows, the creation of a standardised patent regime regulating technology transfers and intellectual property (now embodied in the

TRIPS agreement of the WTO) and the simplification of all norms on travel, visa, payment systems and so on regulating international exchange.

In contrast, liberalisation of the international labour flows remains off the policy agenda and since the early 1980s migration to Europe has slowed considerably due to the growing legal restrictions. The globalisation of the world economy was preceded and made possible by the liberalisation of domestic markets that began in the early 1980s in many countries. For instance, the rise in foreign investments of the 1990s often consisted in the acquisition by multinational firms of state-owned enterprises and would not have taken place without their prior privatisation and the parallel liberalisation of the labour market that allowed large job cuts in privatised firms. Likewise, the surge in short-term portfolio flows of the 1990s would not have occurred without the liberalisation of the domestic financial markets during the 1980s. Thus, both theoretically and empirically, it is often impossible to separate the effects of globalisation from those of domestic liberalisation and we shall not try to do so in this chapter.

The advocates of 'the global market paradigm' claim that this approach causes a reduction in domestic prices, offers major opportunities for export to the poor nations, channels world savings to countries with low capital accumulation but high rates of return on investment, accelerates the transfer of modern technology to backward countries and—as a result of all this—improves global economic efficiency. They also claim that liberalisation improves global income distribution thanks to the equalisation of factor prices across nations and the convergence of the income per capita of poorer countries with those of the advanced nations. While inequality may worsen in the advanced countries importing labour-intensive goods, it is expected to fall in the poor nations and on the global scale. Against such background, this chapter reviews the trends in global, between-country and within-country inequality over the last twenty years. To place such trends into historical perspective, the chapter first analyses the changes in income concentration during the first wave of globalisation of 1870-1914 so as to emphasise similarities and differences observed over these two periods. The predictions of the standard theory about the changes due to the liberalisation of the world economy often collide with a substantial and growing body of statistical evidence that shows that, over the last two decades, global inequality has risen and that past declines in within-country inequality have been reversed since the early 1980s.

Finally, the chapter explores the possible causes of these changes by emphasising in particular the linkages between liberalisation, globalisation and income distribution. No doubt, the years 1870-1914 witnessed an unprecedented economic integration between the countries of the Old and New World. Thanks to a decline in transport costs and to cuts in the pre-1870 tariff rates, the ratio of exports plus imports to GDP rose steadily in all countries of the Old and New World while commodity prices in the different markets converged sharply—with price gap cuts of 81 percent. Meanwhile capital markets became much more integrated and international lending from Great Britain, France and Germany to the New World and a few Asian countries increased 20 times between the mid 1850s and 1914. Finally, during this period, 60 million of mostly unskilled people migrated from the European periphery to the New World.

The main impact of inequality of these changes is reviewed hereafter to help to put into perspective the impact of the current wave of globalisation. To start with, a massive increase in migration and international trade among the now-developed countries led to a substantial convergence in their average incomes per capita. The wage and income gap between the countries of the Old and New World were reduced markedly, as globalisation increased the relative demand for and the remuneration of the abundant factors and reduced that of the scarce factors. Mass migration from the periphery of Europe to the New World appears to explain most (some eighty-percent) of the drop in the New World-Old World wage gap between 1870 and 1914. Trade expansion accounted for another 30 percent while the capital flows from the comparatively poor Old World to the comparatively rich New World generated a modest disequalizing effect.

Second, globalisation caused a rise in within-country inequality in the rich countries of the New World and a fall in the poor Old World countries. In Great Britain, Ireland and Sweden, the ratio of unskilled wages to farm rents per acre rose following a drop in the supply of unskilled labour due to migration and growing labour demand in the export-led manufacturing sector and to a fall in the prices of agricultural products due to cheap imports. The opposite effects obtained in the New World. Indeed, as predicted by the standard trade theory, free trade drove up the returns to land in the commodity-exporting New World and to labour in the manufactures-exporting Old World. Likewise, migration drove up unskilled wages and down the rental-wage ratio in the Old World but caused the opposite effect in the New World. In addition, as migrants were mostly unskilled, migration caused a reduction in the skilled-unskilled wage differential in the Old World but a rise in the same ratio in the New World.

In turn, the flow of European investments to the New World partially offset the local fall in unskilled wages, as they moderated the decline in returns to a growing supply of unskilled labour, and so retarded the rise in wage inequality, while having the opposite effects in the Old World countries that exported capital. Such trends—the relative decline in the wages of unskilled workers in North America and the relative fall in the incomes of landowners in Europe—were at least partially responsible for the retreat from globalisation during the inter-war period. As similar trends are re-emerging at the end of the 20 th century—the world may retreat again from its drive towards globalisation. Third, convergence of real wages among the countries on the opposite sides of the North Atlantic was accompanied by a sharp divergence between the their wage rate and that of the colonial nations. As observed also over 1980-2000, the globalisation of 1870-1914 remained confined to a limited number of nations and did not manage to integrate into the world economy the now-developing countries. These were fully bypassed by the expansion of trade, capital and modern technology i.e. factors that promote growth and convergence, while migrants from these countries were kept out of the centre by restrictive migration policies and the high cost of the move.

World labour markets were in fact as segmented then as they are today. The limited data on growth for countries such as India, China, Indonesia, Brazil, Mexico and Argentina confirm that—except for the latter country—these economies experienced much lower rates of growth and higher growth volatility than the now-developed countries. The reasons for this divergence are not yet fully understood but have likely to do with domestic factors—such as lack of infrastructure and limited human capital—and international factors such as the global division of labour under colonial rule and asymmetric access to international markets. Fourth, as a result of this growing divergence between the now-developed and the now-developing countries and of the mixed inequality changes within countries, global inequality rose steadily throughout the period 1870-1914.

Changes in Global and between Country Inequality

The global income distribution is the distribution of per capita income among the citizens of the world. It can be decomposed into the distribution of average income per capita between countries (the between-country distribution of income) and the distribution of income per capita within countries (the within-country distribution of income). Most the global inequality suggest that between-country income differences explain 60-90 percent of the total income variation among the citizens of the world (depending on the inequality measure chosen) and that variations in the distribution of income within countries explain the remaining 10-40 percent. Analyses of time trends in global inequality over the last twenty years can be grouped as follows:

A first group of discussions confines itself to the analysis of population-weighted changes in national-currency GDP or GNP per capita converted into US dollars at the market exchange rates. Most of these underscore that while over the last 30 years several East

Asian nations converged towards the average income per capita of the OECD group, the majority of the developing countries further diverged from it and so contributed to a rise in global inequality. Results along these lines were obtained by an UNCTAD, on changes in the population-weighed distribution of average GDP per capita in current US dollars for 124 countries representing 93.6 of the world population. The Gini coefficient of the global income distribution rose from 0.68 in 1980 to 0.74 in 1990 largely because of an increase in the income share of the countries with the richest 10 percent of the world population.

The 1999 Human Development Report which attributes this disequalizing trend to the rapid changes induced by globalisation. The Report analyses changes in the population-weighed distribution of GDP per capita converted into dollars at current exchange rates and finds that between-country inequality rose in recent years as the income gap between the fifth of the world's people living in the richest countries and the fifth living in the poorest ones rose from 30 to 1 in 1960 to 74 to 1 in 1997. The Gini coefficient consistent with these data rose from 0.71 in 1980 to 0.75 in 1995. These analysis make use of market exchange rates to convert GDP/c in national currencies into US dollars and have been criticised because the 'traded sector bias' implicit in this approach raises the estimates of global inequality. They therefore compute a new distribution of between-country income per capita making use of the Afriat true index and find that the Gini coefficient of such distribution rises slightly over time, from 0.615 in 1980 to 0.623 in 1993. By adding a component for changes in within-country inequality, they obtain a Gini coefficient of the global income distribution that appears to have risen from 0.698 to 0.711

(equal to a moderate 1.7 percent increase) over the same period.

Other inequality measures however show bigger inequality increases of between 5 and 8.7 per cent. A second—less numerous—group of discussions is concerned with the distribution of income among individuals, so as to account for changes in income per capita both between and within countries. This is important, as even if between-country inequality rises (falls), world inequality may decline (increase) if within-country inequality falls (rises) in the large countries.

Most of these analyses, however, do not make use of survey data, which alone can provide precise information on the shape of the income distribution, but rely instead on synthetic inequality indexes (such as the Gini or Theil coefficients or quantile shares) and assumptions to estimate the shape of a country's income distribution (the most common being that all distributions are log-normal). The world distribution of GNP per capita at current exchange rates in 46 nations accounting for 68 per cent of the world population over the period 1965-92. They concluded that the world income distribution became more skewed, with the Gini index rising from 0.749 to 0.796 and the Theil index soaring from 1.15 to 1.32.

A decomposition of the latter index showed that between country inequality accounted respectively for 79 and 86 per cent of the world inequality in 1965 and 1992, while within-country inequality declined proportionately. The Gini index rose steadily from 0.64 and 0.72 and the Theil index from 1.51 to 2.14. However, when converting GDP per capita at PPP-exchange rates, world inequality increased between 1960 and 1968 but declined between then and 1989. In the later period, convergence in inter-country income per capita more than offset the increase in within-country inequality. However, when China was excluded from the sample, the decline in global inequality after 1975 was no longer evident.

Table 1

Annual growth rate of GNP per capita: 1960-98 and sub-periods

	1960-98	*1960-79*	*1980-98*	*1980-89*	*1990-98*
World	1.8	2.6	1.0	1.2	0.8
OECD	2.7	3.4	1.9	2.2	1.4
East Asia except China	4.4	4.5	4.2	5.1	3.2
China	5.4	2.8	8.4	7.7	9.2
E.Europe and Central Asia	2.5*	4.2*	-0.8	2.1*	-3.3
Latin America	1.7	3.0	0.2	-1.1	1.9
Middle East & North Africa	—	.0	.1	-0.4	0.7
South Asia except India	2.1	1.5	2.8	3.0	2.5
India	—	1.0**	3.6	3.4	3.8
Sub-Saharan Africa	0.4	1.5	-0.8	-1.1	-0.5

The global Gini coefficients, in fact, fell imperceptibly from 0.645 in 1980 to 0.638 in 1990. This outcome resulted from three offsetting trends: first, a decline in the gap in income per capita between the OECD countries and the fast growing and populous China, India and East Asia; second, an increase in the income gap per capita between the OECD on the one side and low income Sub-Saharan Africa and middle-income Latin America, Eastern Europe and Middle East and North Africa on the other; and, third, the widening of within-country income inequality that affected many countries during those years.

As for the last twenty years, the points to a slow rise in inequality due to a moderate and unstable increase in between-country inequality, and to a rise of within-country inequality. It is worth nothing that this points shows also that within-country inequality declined between 1950 and 1970 and then surged in the subsequent period—a finding confirmed also by the detailed review of the within-country inequality trends carried out. Also this second group of studies suffers from some methodological problems. Indeed, it is impossible to predict the shape of income distribution on the basis of a single statistics (for instance, a Gini coefficient is compatible with an infinite number of Lorenz curves), or it is reasonable to assume that all distributions follow a lognormal pattern.

To solve this problem, a third group of analyses relies on individual income data derived from representative household surveys. This approach allows estimating accurately for each year the shape of the income distribution of each country and, by aggregation, the distribution of world income among its citizens. To the best of knowledge, there are only four studies in this category. The first two comprise only developing countries, while the third includes also the transitional economies. These account for a large share of world output and their exclusion from the analysis affects perceptibly the shape of the global income distribution.

The main problem with this approach is that lack of individual data from household surveys for the earlier years impedes to extend backwards the analysis of changes in global inequality. The approach makes use of

PPP-adjusted survey-derived data on the distribution of income per capita in 1988 and 1993 for 88 countries accounting for 84 percent of the world population and 93 percent of world GDP. Because of their huge size (e.g. rural China represents 18.5 percent of the world population) and of the recent sharp widening of the income gap between their urban and rural areas, the points treats these two sectors of the Chinese, Indian, Bangladeshi, Pakistani and Egyptian economies as separate nations.

The finds that global inequality worsened sharply over 1988-93: the ratio between the average income of the top 5 percent and the bottom 5 percent of the world population rose from 78 in 1988 to 114 in 1993. Meanwhile the Gini coefficient of the world income distribution rose from 0.628 in 1988 to o.670 in 1993 as a result of a surge in both within-country and between-country inequality.

Measurement of the level of global inequality and of the direction of its change over the last two decades is influenced by a number of statistical choices concerning the use of GDP versus income per capita, market versus PPP exchange rates, synthetic statistics of the distribution vs. detailed survey data and the treatment of China, India and few other poor populous countries either as single nations or as two separate urban and rural sectors. This latter choice is particularly important for the 1990s, a period which witnessed a resurgence of the urban-rural income gap in China. In all cases, removing China from the sample raises world inequality. Bearing these considerations in mind, the evidence suggests—on balance - that between the early 1980s and 1993 (no analysis extends beyond that year) global inequality increased - if at a slower pace than during the first wave of globalisation - because of a moderate rise in between-country. In turn, within-country inequality has clearly risen in many countries but its overall impact on global inequality seems to have been less pronounced. The latter conclusion is, however, influenced by the inequality index used. The increase in global inequality was probably more pronounced in the 1990s, a period during which the US and other high-income economies expanded rapidly while rural incomes in India and - to some extent - China grew slowly.

In contrast, during the 1980s, fast agricultural growth in China and India and recession in the OECD countries - caused quasi-stagnation in global inequality in relation to the 1970s.

Changes in Within Country Inequality

The country inequality accounts for most of global inequality and its evolution over the last two decades. However, from a policy perspective, within-country inequality is likely to be more important. There are three reasons for this. First, between-country inequality is path dependent and is not easily modifiable by the policies of a single country save, possibly, the US and China. Second, despite the development of global media and international travel, within-country inequality is much more observable and perceivable than between-country inequality that, for most people, still remains an abstract notion. For this reason, within-country inequality exerts a greater influence on the behaviours of the economic agents than between-country inequality. And, third, most policy decisions affecting the relative income position of the citizens of a country are still taken at the national level. This calls therefore for a greater emphasis on analyses of changes in within-country inequality. This approach is followed in the next sub-section that reviews the changes in income distribution since the end of World War II - and particularly over the last 20 years - in the main non-developed regions.

Inequality Changes by Main Regions

i) *Latin America:* a rise in inequality in the 1980s followed by a further rise or stagnation in the 1990s. In the 1980s and 1990s, inequality in the region was affected by several external shocks, the recessionary adjustments introduced to respond to them, and widespread external liberalisation. In the 1990s, income polarisation did not decline and in half of the cases it worsened further, if at a slower pace than in the 1980s, despite the return to full capacity growth and the liberalisation of the external sector. A review of inequality changes over the 1990s based on 49 representative surveys for 15 countries shows that inequality worsened in eight cases while it stagnated in seven.

The income polarisation of the 1980s and 1990s was the result of fast inequality rises during recessionary spells and slow declines during periods of recovery. As a result, between 1980 and the late 1980s, the labour share declined by 5-6 percentage points in Argentina, Chile and Venezuela and ten in Mexico while such tendency was not reversed in the 1990s. In several countries - as in Chile during the military dictatorship - the fall in the labour share was due also to the regressive changes in labour legislation that relaxed regulations on workers dismissals, restricted the power of trade unions, suspended wage indexation, cut public employment and restricted the coverage of the minimum wage while, at the same time, wealth and capital gains taxes were eliminated, profit taxes substantially reduced and interest rates sharply risen.

Five structural trends emerged in the labour market as a result of these policy changes and of the stagnation of the 1980s and slow growth of the 1990s. First, sluggish growth brought about a slowdown in jobs creation. Second, informal employment (in sectors where low wages are the rule) became much more common. Third, formal sector wages evolved less favourably than GDP per capita. Fourth, minimum wages mostly fell in relation to average wages. Fifth, wage differentials by skill level widened, particularly during the 1990s, in parallel with widespread trade and financial liberalisation. According to Altimir:

> Under these new economic modalities (characterised by trade openness, fiscal austerity, a prudent management of monetary policy, less public regulation of markets and more reliance on private initiative), the pattern of income distribution tends, as suggested above, to be unequal at the very least, and more unequal - in most cases, at least in urban areas - than those [already high] that prevailed during the last stages of the previous growth phase in the 1970s.

ii) *China:* a U-shaped trend in regional and urban-rural inequality. Over the last 50 years, income inequality in China followed a clear U-shaped pattern. At the start of the Maoist reforms in 1953, the nationwide Gini coefficient of the distribution of household incomes stood at a high 0.56. The reforms of the 1950s and 1960s rapidly reduced income polarisation and, by 1975, the Gini index had fallen to 0.26 despite large regional differences in natural endowments. The reforms adopted in agriculture since 1978 replaced the rural communes with an egalitarian family-based agriculture and introduced considerable price incentives for the farmers. The result was a sharp acceleration of agricultural and overall growth between 1978 and 1984. During these years, there was only a modest upsurge in inequality and rural poverty was literally halved, falling from 30.7 to 15.1 percent between 1978 and 1984.

In contrast, inequality rose fast between 1985 and 1990 and very fast after 1990. This increase can be traced to a widening of the urban-rural gap driven by rapid urban-based industrialisation, export-led growth in the coastal area and neglect of the poor interior regions and of agriculture. For example, over 1993-8, the Chinese farmers suffered a 30 percent fall in the price of grains and a tripling of agricultural taxes. Such trends exasperated the urban-rural gap and reduced the pace of rural poverty alleviation which slowed down sharply over 1984-95, the years of the export boom, in relation to 1978-84, the years of agricultural growth.

Public policy was a major determinant of this rise in income polarisation. The fiscal decentralization introduced in 1978 substantially reduced the possibility of the central Government to control regional inequality by means of transfers to poorer provinces. Industrial and export-growth policy - deliberately pursued in a regionally unbalanced manner - plaid an even greater disequalizing role, as it favored the coastal provinces through the granting of special administrative and economic powers, tax privileges and other benefits which facilitated the development of export industries and the inflow of foreign direct investment.

iii) *East and Southeast Asia:* a common if milder and more recent reversal of inequality trends. Countries from this region are well known for having achieved in the past an equitable export-led growth. Yet, since the 1980s, and particularly the early 1990s, inequality rose also in most of the region. In South Korea the Gini coefficient of the earnings distribution declined steadily over time owing to a narrowing of wage differentials by occupation, gender and level of education. Both wage and income inequality rose again, however, in the aftermath of the 1997 crisis. The full-capacity unemployment rose from 1-2 to 4-5 percent between 1995-6 and 1999-2000, while the share of part time and daily workers in the total jumped from 42.5 to 52.5 percent between 1996 and 2000 and the wage spread by employment type widened. As a result, between 1996 and 1999, the labour share fell from 64 to 60 percent while the Gini coefficient of the distribution of earnings rose from 0.29 to 0.32. In Taiwan, income inequality improved steadily between 1964 and 1980 thanks to a rapid expansion of employment among skilled and unskilled workers employed in the domestic and export sector. Over 1980-1993, however, the development of the skill-intensive sectors pushed up again - id moderately - wage inequality, while the share of capital incomes in the total surged in line with the development of large corporations and the escalation of land prices. By 1993, Taiwan reached again the inequality level of 1964. Hong-Kong and

Singapore too show a mild U-shaped pattern, with fairly rapid inequality declines till the late 1970s, followed by moderate rises offsetting half of the earlier falls.

Except for Thailand, the economies of Southeast Asia also follow a pattern of inequality decline between the 1960s and the mid-1980s followed by a rise during the 1990s. In Thailand, the Gini coefficient of the distribution of total income rose steadily (from 0.41 to 0.52) since the 1960s and particularly during the 1990s. Since the mid-late 1980s, this trend is explained by a surge in the share and concentration of non-farm profits linked to the rapid expansion of the globalisation-related finance, insurance, internet and real estate (F.I.I.R.E.) sector in the Bangkok area. In Indonesia, the Gini coefficient of the distribution of income fell from 0.35 in 1964-5 to 0.32 in 1987 thanks to the recycling of the oil rent to the financing of the 'green revolution'. This substantially raised employment and production opportunities in agriculture, reduced rural inequality and fostered rural growth and poverty reduction.

In contrast, the years from 1987 to 1996 - a period characterised by devaluation, tariff reform and financial deregulation - were characterised by the development of the urban-based manufacturing and capital-intensive F.I.I.R.E. sector, a slow down of agriculture, a widening of the urban-rural gap, the retrenchment of rural development programs and, as a result, a rise in overall inequality from 0.32 in 1987 to 0.38 in 1997. In the immediate, the Asian financial crisis of 1997 led to a marginal drop in inequality as middle-high income people employed in the F.I.I.R.E. sector were immediately affected. Shortly after, however, inequality and poverty rose especially fast among the urban poor - due to the recession induced by the crisis, the stabilisation measures introduced to combat it and the differential impact of price rises which affected the poor the most.

iv) *The late liberalizers of South Asia:* By and large, during the post-World War II period, income distribution in the region changed less than elsewhere, though - following the changes of the last decades - it now appears it also followed a mild U-shaped pattern. In India, the Gini coefficient of household consumption expenditure per capita fell from 0.36 to 0.31 over 1951-61 and then fluctuated in the 0.29-0.32 range until the introduction in July 1991 of the first IMF stabilisation and liberalisation programme. In the 1980s, stable inequality, substantial expenditure on rural development and a 4 percent growth in agriculture led by the 'green revolution' reduced substantially rural poverty.

With the gradual liberalisation of the economy in the 1990s, GDP growth accelerated to 5.6 percent. Such growth was, however, highly concentrated in the urban sector, by regions and by income group. While fast urban growth and a moderate rise in urban inequality (whose Gini coefficient rose from 0.34 to 0.36 8) allowed for a decline in urban poverty, rural poverty stagnated owing to slow agricultural growth, cuts in rural development programs and food subsidies and a rise in rural inequality. In sum, the experience of the 1990s points to a moderate rise in both urban and rural inequality, a larger rise in overall inequality due to the widening of the urban-rural gap and a decline in the poverty alleviation elasticity of growth. In Sri Lanka, Bangladesh and Pakistan inequality followed also a mild U-shaped pattern. In Pakistan, for instance, the Gini coefficient declined from .39 to 0.33 during the growth years of 1963-1973 but gradually climbed back to reach 0.41 in 1992-93. As in Bangladesh, the inequality reversal is more pronounced in the rural sector where an initial drop of 7 Gini points was followed by a rise of 12 points.

v) *Sub-Saharan Africa:* falling urban-rural gap, but rising intra-urban and - at times - intra-rural inequality. Conclusions about inequality changes in Sub-Saharan Africa are tentative, as - despite some improvements - there are still few nations with at least two comparable surveys spanning the last twenty years. In the past, inequality was the fruit of a large urban-rural income gap inherited from the colonial era and reinforced by the "urban bias" of post-colonial policy. The 1980s and 1990s were characterised by the massive application of adjustment programs aimed at improving the rural terms of trade and stimulating agricultural exports. These reforms succeeded in liberalising the economy, devaluing the real exchange rate (which fell on average by 30 percent over 1980-1998) and opening up the African economies, as signalled by the rise from 51 to 62 percent in the regional import plus export ratio to GDP. In spite of this, GDP per capita stagnated. Even in the few regional success stories (Uganda and Ghana), the recovery remained fragile while labour-intensive manufacturing exports did not take off. Mauritius is the main exception. It successfully increased textile exports and liberalised the financial sector while experiencing rapid growth, a surge in employment in the export sector and falling inequality.

The impact of policy reform and output stagnation was the hardest in the urban sector that, in several cases, experienced a drop in its terms of trade and large income falls. Rural areas were less affected or gained, as in the case of Uganda. Thus, in most cases, the urban-rural gap was reduced by a process of 'equalising downward'. Intra-rural inequality rose in countries - such as Kenya - characterised by a high land concentration or where the recovery was peasant-based but where the improved earning potential failed to reach the remote areas due to inadequate infrastructure or the collapse of marketing arrangements—as in Zambia. Inequality generally improved in countries such as Mozambique and Uganda caricaturised by a peasant agriculture rebounding from years of civil strife.

vi) A sharp rise of inequality in the former Soviet Bloc. Since 1989, concurrently with the privatisation and domestic and international liberalisation of these economies, income concentration rose moderately in the countries of Central Europe where earnings inequality widened less than expected and a comprehensive welfare state was preserved or even expanded. In contrast, in the former USSR and South Eastern Europe, Gini coefficients rose on average by an astounding by 10-20 points, i.e. 3-4 times faster than in Central Europe. In these countries, the transitional recession and fall in the wage share were extremely pronounced, social transfers declined, their composition and targeting deteriorated and privatisation was less equitable than in Central Europe.

Rising earnings inequality seems to have played a central role in the surge of income inequality. The rise in the wage gap has been attributed to the emergence of "scarcity rents" for professionals such as bankers and other specialists undersupplied during the old system, and to a physiological rise in returns to education following the liberalisation of the labour market. Such explanations, based on standard human capital theory, account however for less than half of the observed increase. Indeed, many educated employees in the public sector continued to receive low wages unrelated to their skills and experience.

Earnings inequality appears to have risen also because of the fall in the minimum wage relative to the average, the expansion of a poorly regulated and inequitable informal sector, mounting wage arrears and a surge in interindustrial wage dispersion favouring politically influential sectors such as mining and power generation. The limited rise in capital incomes reported by the literature is likely the result of the undersampling of the new high-income groups and to the underreporting of their income in the Household Budget Surveys as suggested by the growing discrepancy between the income per capita derived from the national accounts and the household surveys and by the growing concentration of financial assets.

Econometric Anlaysis of within Country Inequality

During the last two decades, inequality increased within most of the countries analyzed and that such rise often represented a reversal of the inequality decline observed during the first two-three decades of the post World War II period. Such result conflicts however with the findings of prior research in this area that has pointed to the broad stability of within-country inequality over the

1950-1990 period. For instance, after fitting linear trends to 49 country data. Examination of the estimation procedure followed in this and similar studies suggest, however, that these conclusions are dependent on the methodology adopted. Indeed, the sample utilised did not include most economies in transition (which experienced a universal rise in inequality in the 1990s), extended only up to 1991-93 (and so missed the disequalizing impact of recent financial crises) and was fitted only with linear trends (i.e. a functional form that does not permit to capture trend reversals).

Finally, the country results were not weighted by population size and GDP-PPP. Cornia with Kiiski tried to overcome the limitations of this literature. They extracted from the November 1998 version of WIDER's World Income Inequality Database (WIID) 770 "reliable observations" of Gini coefficients for 73 countries 9 that account for 80 and 91 percent of the world population and GDP-PPP. These coefficients are derived from fully documented, comparable and representative surveys of the entire economy and refer to "per capita household disposable income" in 52 countries, "per capita consumption expenditure" in nine countries; and "gross earnings" in 14 economies in transition. Each country's time series (that makes use of the same income concept for the entire period analysed) were interpolated with linear as well as quadratic functions (so as to capture trend reversals). For each country, the best functional form was selected on the basis of the most significant t statistics and, as a subordinate criterion, the highest R2.

Inequality was found to have risen in 48 of the 73 countries analyzed, including in large economies such as China, several large Latin American nations, the USA and Russia. Inequality was found to have remained constant in 16 countries including Germany and Brazil, as well as medium or large countries such India, Indonesia and Tanzania.

Only in nine countries there is evidence of a decline in income concentration over the long-term. These include some small countries and a few medium sized ones. Weighing the results by population size and GDP-PPP, strengthens the conclusions. As noted, the November 1998 version of WIID extends only up to 1994-5. Thus, separately moved India, Indonesia, South Korea, Tanzania and the Philippines - all countries that recently experienced inequality reversals—to the 'rising inequality' category. In this way, of the 73 countries in the sample, 53 experienced a surge in income concentration over the last 20 years.

This increase was universal in the economies in transition, almost universal in Latin America and increasingly frequent, if less dramatic in South, SouthEast and East Asia. In sub-Saharan Africa, domestic liberalisation may have improved the agricultural terms of trade but failed to induce - with few exceptions - an expansion of inequality-reducing labour intensive exports.

The observed increase in the Gini coefficients was often substantial. Of the 53 countries with growing inequality, the rise was of between 5 and 10 Gini points in 30 nations (in 9 of them it occurred from initial levels of 0.40-0.45), by between 10 and 20 points in 10 countries and by more than 20 points in a couple of countries of the former Soviet Union. In many countries, greater income polarisation seems to have been driven by both a fall in the labour share (paralleled by a rise in the capital share) and a worsening of the earnings distribution explained only in part by a rise in returns to education. Growing regional disparity and growth concentration in the urban areas were also key factors.

Causes of the recent Changes in Inequality

While the upward impact on global inequality was moderate by historical standards, such increase is perplexing if seen in relation to the predictions of the standard theory and if juxtaposed to the fall in within-country inequality which took place between 1950 and 1970-5 following the adoption of full-employment and redistributive policies in the OECD and socialist economies, and of the land, educational and employment reforms adopted in the East Asian countries, China and - to an extent - India. What factors account for such trend reversals? One can, alternatively, propose three sets of explanations:

i) An aggravation of the traditional causes of inequality? The first—and least plausible - explanation of the recent rise in income polarisation focuses on an aggravation of the traditional causes of inequality such as land concentration.

In developing countries, high land concentration has been and remains a major determinant of rural inequality. Yet, during the last 50 years the share of agriculture in total output and employment has fallen everywhere, while over the 1950s and 1960s land reforms redistributed latifundia and state land to poor farmers in at least 27 countries. As a result, land rents and rural inequality have declined. Second, while countries well endowed with mineral resources are known to have a high income and asset inequality, such 'curse of natural resources' hardly explains the income polarisation of the last two decades, as the mineral rent/GDP ratio has systematically declined since the late 1970s. Third, the same conclusion applies - with some qualification - to an hypothetical aggravation of the 'urban bias'. Indeed, a recent review of such bias in the globalised world economy finds no evidence of systematic change, though the bias appears to have declined in Latin America and parts of Africa and increased in post-1984 China, Thailand and Indonesia.

Finally, greater inequality in the 1980s and 1990s might be ascribed to a worsening in the distribution of educational achievements. Mean educational achievements increased in most countries during the last two decades. Yet, in Latin America, a rise in the average number of years of education was accompanied by mounting educational inequality - as public policy emphasised the reduction of illiteracy (a measure that reduces educational variance) together with a rapid expansion in the number of university graduates (a measure that raises educational variance). Differences in educational achievements thus continue to be a key determinant of wage polarisation in the region while the slow growth in the number of secondary school graduates likely contributed to sluggish growth in manufacturing exports inspite of trade liberalisation.

In Africa and, to a lesser extent, the former Soviet Union the difficulties experienced in sustaining primary education in the 1980s and 1990s and the surge in private secondary and higher education will have a disequalizing impact on the future distribution of human capital. In

Africa, however, two thirds of the population are still engaged in simple tasks so that the impact of growing polarisation in educational achievements on inequality may remain limited for some years. In contrast, the East and Southeast Asian and Middle Eastern educational policy, focused on an expansion of universal secondary education and so helped reducing educational inequality and wage concentration.

ii) *Technological change:* A second - not entirely satisfactory - explanation ascribes the recent rise in within-country inequality to technological change. The latter - it is argued - generates a demand for new skills that chronically outstrips its supply and so creates scarcity rents for skilled workers. International comparisons, however, suggest that whether the relative earnings of educated workers rise depends not so much on technology but on government's investments in secondary and higher education. They conclude that, while technological change does raise the relative demand for educated workers, governments control powerful policies for counteracting the unwanted inequality side effect of technological progress.

When assuming a balanced evolution of the demand and supply of new skills - that new technologies generate an earnings distribution more skewed than that emanating from old technologies. Especially in the service sector and a few industrial branches, new technologies replace unskilled labour with skilled labour and capital embodying new technologies and so affect the labour share in total income and the wage spread. In support of this argument, the World Bank suggests that the shift towards skill-intensive employment observed in the

Western world in the 1970s and 1980s is being matched in a number of developing countries in the 1990s. Yet, this viewpoint does not apply to the many developing countries where either inequality started increasing ahead of this decade of technological modernisation or, as in Africa and Eastern Europe, where low investment rates have impeded a significant technological modernisation. Thus, with the exception of a few middle income countries, the evidence in support of such thesis seems, on balance, weak.

iii) *Domestic and external liberalisation:* The third - and most relevant - set of explanations pivots around the disequalizing impact of liberalisation and globalisation. Standard theory posits that trade liberalisation in poor countries switches production] from non-tradeables and inefficient import-substitutes towards efficient exportables, thus raising the demand for unskilled labour in which the reforming countries are supposed to have a comparative advantage. In turn, capital account liberalisation is expected to raise investment, employment, labor productivity and growth in poor countries with low capital accumulation but high rates of return on investment, with favorable effects on equity and poverty.

The real-life impact of these reforms is, however, more complex and conclusions about their impact depends on the methodology used for their evaluation (cross country regressions, simulations with CGE models, before-after comparisons), the regions analysed and the specific policy mixes considered. Conscious of all this, we first review the literature on the equity impact of the overall reform package, then move to a separate examination of the equity impact of trade and financial liberalisation. Finally, we briefly discuss the impact of those domestic policies that often accompany external liberalisation.

Impact of the overall liberalisation-globalisation package. There are only few review-studies on the distributive effect of these reforms. They focus on six types of economy-wide reforms, i.e. trade liberalisation, capital account liberalisation, domestic financial liberalisation, privatisation, tax reform and labour market reform. The authors found that the overall package has a significant short-term disequalizing effect on wage differentials, the intensity of which, however, declines over time. They also find that the strongest disequalizing impact was due to domestic financial reform, capital account liberalisation and tax reform.

Trade openness had, on balance, no net effect on the wage spread, possibly because its many effects cancelled each other out. The authors tentatively suggests that technological progress - rather than trade - is the channel through which liberalisation affects wage inequality. Broadly similar evidence is provided by a review of the impact of liberalisation during 21 reform episodes in 18 countries during the last two decades. Income inequality was found to rise in cases, remain constant in 6 and improve in two.

Virtually without exception, wage differentials by skill level rose following liberalisation, as a result of a reduction of employment in the modern sector, a rise in productivity and wage concentration by skill within the same, the reallocation of excess labour to the low-paying non-traded sector (informal trade, services and traditional agriculture) and a rise of inequality within the latter. Of the 18 countries analysed, only El Salvador and Costa

Rica managed to reduce inequality on occasion of liberalisation thanks to a surge in the employment of unskilled workers in the export sector. Their regression analysis is carried out on a sample of 32 developing and transitional economies for the years 1980- 95 and suggests that while the reform package had an overall disequalizing effect, this was more pronounced in the economies of the former Soviet bloc, probably on account of their institutional weakness, while it was less pronounced in those with high initial inequality.

The poverty impact of IMF-World Bank reform programs (which comprise macroeconomic stabilisation and structural adjustment measures) Easterly finds that these moderated the rise of poverty during output contractions, possibly because of the cushioning of the crisis through Bank-sponsored, adjustment-related 'social safety nets'. But he also finds that, during spells of economic expansion, Fund-Bank programs reduced the poverty alleviation elasticity of growth in relation to those of 'home-grown' adjustment programs. This would suggest that Fund-Bank programs entail a worsening of income inequality during this process.

For instance, in China - a country with medium inequality and no Fund-Bank program - poverty incidence fell over 1990-2 by 3.8 percent for every point of GDP growth, while in 1995-6 Colombia - a country with high inequality and a Fund-Bank adjustment loan - experienced zero poverty reduction for every point of GDP growth.

Of the six components of the liberal package, capital account liberalisation appears to have the strongest disequalizing effect, followed by domestic financial liberalisation, labor market deregulation and tax reform.

Privatisation of land was found to improve equity and growth in many cases while that of industrial assets and utilities was associated with rising inequality in some regions (Eastern Europe and former Soviet Union) but not always in others (Latin America). The equity effects of trade liberalisation appear to vary from country to country. The impact was favourable in the 1960s and 1970s in East Asia, in a few small countries in recent times and - at the margin - in China and Vietnam, but not in the large Latin America countries, Eastern Europe and most of Africa.

Trade liberalisation: Standard theory predicts that trade liberalisation will improve between-country inequality, within-country inequality in poor countries and, by implication, global inequality (in most cases). Analyses on the 1960s and 1970s seem to support these conclusions. The analyse the determinants of inequality in 35 small and medium developing countries and conclude that the phased removal of trade protection in manufacturing reduces the income of the richest 20 percent of the population and improves that of the bottom 60 percent.

Yet, the last twenty years offer a less encouraging picture than that just presented. Indeed, evidence for the last two decades shows that trade liberalisation widened the wage gap in a broad range of countries including the East Asian exporters of manufactured goods. For instance, wage inequality was found to have increased in six out of seven Latin American countries for which reliable wage data are available, as well as in the Philippines and Eastern Europe. One explanation of this phenomenon pivots around a choice of technologies inconsistent with local factors endowments.

The import of world class investment goods incorporating the latest technological advances by firms operating in the export sector of developing countries leads to a rise in the demand of skilled rather than unskilled labour. A second explanation pivots around the so called 'fallacy of composition' which argues that the historical context under which trade liberalisation took place in the 1990s was very different from that under which it occurred in the 1960s. The Mexican trade liberalisation of 1985-90, for instance, was accompanied by a widening of its wage distribution as the country had to face intense competition from the entry into the world market for low skill manufactured exports of China, Indonesia and other exporters with substantially lower wages than Mexico.

The formal sector of middle income countries no longer has a comparative advantage in labour-intensive exports and either it informalizes its production via a long chain of subcontractors or shifts production towards skill-intensive exports in markets where, however, they face stiff competition from the advanced economies. Third, in the case of low-tech African exporters, trade liberalisation has led to unsatisfactory export growth because of a combination of weak domestic conditions and persistent protectionism in the OECD countries. In a recent review of protectionist tendencies in Northern countries, and in the United States in particular, current trade barriers in the North appear to cost Southern countries billions of dollars annually. While some WTO-governed trade barriers in the North are declining, it appears that there is increasing US resistance to further globalisation via trade and immigration liberalisation. All in all, the predictions of standard trade theory do not seem to hold much in the globalised world of the 1990s.

Alternative theoretical approaches, such as those stressing the imports of world class technology, structural inflexibilities, fallacy of composition, persistent protectionism and a changing political economy of distribution in a world of mobile capital and immobile labour may better explain the recent trends in this area. Standard theory predicts also that foreign trade will reduce between-country inequality.

In a longer-term analysis of the effects of trade, that trade distortions are associated with slow growth and that trade liberalisation would therefore improve income growth in poor countries and their convergence towards the income per capita of rich nations. These analyses are based on weak evidence, proxy trade restrictions through inappropriate variables (such as the openness index and the deviation of domestic from international prices) and omit key factors from the analysis. They conclude that, likely, there is not a clear relation between trade openness and growth. They found that growth in the countries that significantly cut tariff rates or expanded trade volumes was significantly higher than in the non-globalizers.

Since they assigned China and India to the first group, they argue that trade liberalisation triggers also to a decline in between-country inequality. However, been severely criticised for applying suitably arbitrary criteria in the selection of the 'globalizers' and for other methodological problems that bias the final results. When the same test was repeated with an unbiased country selection, there was no evidence that the globalizers grew faster than the other countries. Finally, assigning China and India to the globalizers's club is also problematic. Indeed, the acceleration of growth in China and India started well before trade liberalisation was introduced in the early 1990s. More generally, it is difficult to attribute the recent growth of China, India, Vietnam and other countries to textbook liberalisation.

While these countries adopted some market reforms and increasingly integrated themselves into the world economy, they did so through a highly unorthodox strategy combining export orientation with high tariff and non-tariff protection, public ownership of banking, patent infringements, restrictions on foreign capital flows and a non convertible exchange rate. Furthermore, both income and wage inequality rose markedly in China and to a lesser extent in India in parallel with the growing globalisation of their economy. While export promotion per se generated a favourable impact on equity, it likely entailed the adoption of other policies - such as a regionally unbalanced industrial policy, fiscal decentralisation and a reversal of the rural-urban terms of trade - that generated a strong disequalizing impact. Domestic and international financial deregulation.

Domestic financial sector reform inspired by 'financial de-repression' was one of the first policy changes introduced in developing countries since the mid-1970s. This reform was conducive to private credit expansion, some financial deepening and the creation of bond and stock markets. But it was also often characterised by inadequate bank supervision, a sizeable rise in interest rates and spreads and growing bank failures. The distributive impact of such measures is difficult to capture but the data are suggestive of a negative impact. Indeed, these policy changes, together with the 1982 rise in US interest rates and the IMF policy of demanding large increases in interest rates in crisis countries, fuelled a worldwide rise in real interest rates in the 1980s.

In developing economies real rates often rose by 10-15 points and pushed a number of governments into a 'vicious circle' in which the rate rises augmented the cost of debt servicing, which further pushed upward deficits and indebtedness. Financial deregulation thus led to an increase in the rate of return on financial assets, a rise in the share of GDP accruing to capital incomes and the redistribution via the budget of labor income to holders of state bonds.

Domestic deregulation was followed in the early 1990s by the liberalisation of cross border movements of foreign direct investments, bank loans and portfolio investments. With rare exceptions, these measures - and particularly the liberalisation of portfolio flows - generated a sharp social impact. This is in part due to the 'disciplining' structural effect such liberalisation has on the domestic policy decisions of governments (especially in the field of taxation and redistribution) and on the demands of organised labour, and partly due to the real appreciation of the exchange rate which shifts resources to the non-tradeable sector and encourages subcontracting and wage cuts in the tradeable sector to preserve profit margins.

The impact on inequality is also mediated by the tendency of capital account liberalisation to increase the frequency of destabilising financial crises with real effects. Left to themselves, deregulated financial systems cannot perform well owing to problems of incomplete information, markets and contracts, herd behaviour, panics, weak supervsion and speculation on asset prices. Indeed, such crises have turned out to be costly, in both the short and medium term, as well as disequalizing. Countries that suffered from banking crises over 1975-94 saw their GDP growth rate decline on average by 1.3 percent over the subsequent five years in relation to countries that did not experience banking crises. Their distributional impact is also negative, particularly in countries with weak labor institutions and social safety nets, as underscored by an analysis in Latin America and Asia financial crises raised inequality in 73 and 62 percent of the time while no impact was evident in Finland, Norway and Spain.

Analyses based on micro data show that the impact on inequality is transmitted via differential employment, wages and price effects that affect the lower deciles of the distribution especially hard. In analyzing the price changes of the 1997 financial crisis in Indonesia, price increases had been significantly faster for the poor and for rural households. They conclude noting that '.. the notion that the very poor are so poor as to be insulated from international shocks is simply wrong. Rather, in the Indonesian case, the very poor appear to be the most vulnerable.'

Table 2

Poverty incidence before, during and after a few major financial crises (percentages)

	Before	*During*	*After*
Argentina (87-90)	25.2	47.3	33.7
Argentina (93-7)	16.8	24.8	26.0
Jordan (86-92)	3.0	....	14.9
Mexico (94-6)	36.0	....	43.0

Source: World Bank (2000)

Domestic policy changes accompanying globalisation. As noted at the beginning of this chapter, globalisation tends to be preceded by domestic policy changes that - regardless of their inherent merit - render a country more attractive to foreign investors. For instance, in a world of immobile labor and mobile capital, labour markets are liberalised by relaxing the norms on workers' dismissal, safety at work, minimum wages, social security contributions, unionisation and collective bargaining either in the whole country or in selected export processing zones.

Likewise, policies on corporate taxation, infrastructural development and privatisation may be influenced by the desire to attract foreign investors seeking low-wage, low-tax locations endowed with adequate physical facilities. The distributive impact of these 'complementary policies', however, is seldom factored in the assessment of the impact of open-door policies. While space limitations prevent to deal adequately with this issue, some of the possible linkages are briefly referred to hereafter to illustrate the indirect distributive impact of globalisation.

The liberalisation of the labour market, for instance, is likely to generate a rise in both employment and wage dispersion. The net distributive effect depends on the relative significance of the 'wage inequality effect' and 'employment-creation effect' as well as on the evolving importance of the informal sector. Outside East Asia and China, the experience of last twenty years points to a dominance of the negative effects over the favorable ones. It points to slow employment creation, a surge in the share of informal employment, an almost invariable erosion of minimum wages in real terms and relative to the average wage 13 and slow employment creation. Tax reforms to attract foreign investors may also have had a disequalizing impact.

During the last two decades, tax systems moved away from taxes on corporations and trade and towards indirect taxes. In addition, the progressivity of wealth and direct tax rates was reduced though greater accent was placed on horizontal equity by eliminating exemptions and improving collection. The net impact of these reforms has varied from country to country but the general trend is towards lower tax progressivity. Finally, privatisation-for-liberalisation, most common in Latin America and Eastern Europe, has a had mixed distributive impact.

Privatisation of agriculture has often generated a distributionally favourable impact, as in the case of the dismembering of the communes land in China and of state farms in Armenia and Romania. Privatisation of large industrial assets proved more complex and inequality often rose as institutional reforms in the field of anti-monopoly legislation, competition policy and regulation of privatised utilities and foreign investments has lagged behind. The worst outcomes were observed in the economies in transition where insider privatisation led to rapid concentration of assets in the hands of a small élite of former managers of state enterprises. In Latin America, the acquisition of privatised utilities by multinational firms worsened equity through the low price paid for the assets purchased, the high service prices charged by the privatised utilities, the employment cuts following restructuring and the limited capacity of local regulators to control large transitional corporations.

Today's globalisation shares several commonalties with that of 1870-1914 but also differs substantially from it. While a strongly asymmetric expansion of trade and capital flows characterised both periods, international migration plaid a key role in equalising wages and incomes during the first globalisation but not during the recent one due to the growing restrictions of migration policies in developed countries. Conversely, technology appears to have had a greater impact during the current globalisation than last century.

Finally, the impact of current capital flows to emerging and developing countries - dominated by highly unstable and disequalizing portfolio flows - appears to be far more pronounced now than during the first globalisation. Global inequality appears to have continued growing during the last two decades, though less rapidly than over 1870-1914. The recent rise in globalisation is the result of mutually offsetting trends. On the one side, unprecedented fast growth in Coastal China (and few other East Asian nations) in relation to that of the OECD countries led to a reduction in global inequality, especially in the 1980s. On the other, faster growth in Coastal China and the OECD (the new core of the world economic system) in relation to rural China, rural India and Sub Saharan Africa raised global inequality. Finally, the slow growth or outright stagnation of Eastern Europe, Latin America and MENA relative to the OECD countries also contributed to global inequality, though the comparatively limited populations of these regions moderated this impact.

As during 1870-1914, the current liberalisation and globalisation have led to a selective and asymmetric integration of only a few countries into the core of the world economic system. However - now as then - the majority of the developing and transitional countries has been almost totally bypassed by global integration - despite a considerable opening up of their economies. While over 1870-1914 integration into the world economic core concerned only the nations of the European periphery, the current globalisation has coopted into the core of the world economy most of South East Asia, Coastal China and, possibly, a segment of urban India.

Interestingly, the graduation of these economies into the core of the world system was generally guided by 'home grown strategies' combining elements of market reforms with pragmatic and highly unorthodox policies in the fields of trade, finance, patents and exchange rate. The reasons why large swathes of the developing and transitional world were bypassed by both globalisations remain unclear but cannot only be attributed - as sometimes argued in the literature - to insufficient commitment to liberalisation. For instance, Africa has substantially reformed its macroeconomy and trade policy during the last twenty years but has was simultaneously bypassed more than before by international trade and financial flows. Weak domestic conditions in infrastructure, human capital and institutions, as well systemic problems of fallacy of composition, inadequate access to markets and persistent protectionism of the low tech sectors by the advanced countries are other important factors explaining why some regions lag behind despite profound policy reform. Unlike during the first globalisation wave - when inequality rose in the labour importing New World but fell in the Old World countries exporting labour and manufactured products - the last two decades have witnessed a widespread and symmetric rise in within-country inequality that has involved also the exporters of labour-intensive goods.

There are three possible explanations for this. First, contrary to the experience of the first globalisation, limited migration to the advanced nations - the main source of convergence last century - did not help equalising the distribution of income in the countries of origin. Second, international financial flows have become less stable and more disequalizing than a century ago. And third, inequality was also influenced in a non-negligible way by domestic policy reforms - such as those of the labour market, financial sector, tax reform - which may have been introduced to facilitate the international integration of poor countries but which had unfavorable effects on the labour share and wage differentials.

Finally, the predictions of standard theory about the inequality impact of international trade and capital flows explained more easily the changes observed during the globalisation of last century than during the last twenty years. Indeed, most of the recent evidence on the inequality impact of globalisation contradicts the predictions of standard theory which is unable to capture the effect of other factors such as domestic institutional weaknesses, the complexity of trade and finance in a multi-country multi-goods environment, persistent and rising protectionism in the North and the equity impact of other domestic reforms that are often introduced to facilitate the drive towards globalisation.

Economic Globalisation on Global Climate

According to the Inter-governmental Panel on Climate Change (IPCC), global average temperatures have risen

1.1°F above the pre-industrial average. Twelve of the hottest years in recorded history have occurred since 1980. With higher temperatures, there has also been more energy driving the Earth's climatic systems, which in turn has been causing more violent weather events, such as Hurricane Mitch, which killed 10,000 people and destroyed the infrastructure and economies of two Central American countries in 1998. Scientists expect average world temperatures to rise between 6°F and 25°F over the next hundred years. As a result, if current trends persist, ever-more frequent and severe storms, floods, droughts, dust storms, sea surges, crumbling coastlines, salt water intrusion of groundwater, failing crops, dying forests, the inundation of low-lying land and islands, and the spread of endemic diseases such as malaria and dengue fever are all on the cards. Agriculture worldwide could face severe disruption and economies could collapse. There could also be millions upon millions of environmental refugees - people fleeing from the intruding sea or from the deserts they have left in their wake. Economic globalization is accelerating this highly dangerous phenomenon by expanding industrial activity and universalising the carbon-intensive model of development worldwide. The distancing of producers from consumers and the massive boom in trade precipitated by economic globalization has required a vast increase in greenhouse gas-emitting transport.

Liberalisation of trade and investment around the world has also facilitated the global expansion of industrial agriculture and related food processing industries, which are highly energy intensive and generate vast quantities of greenhouse gasses. It has also stimulated greater consumption of energy-intensive products, such as cars and electric appliances, and the construction of vast fossil fuel-based energy infrastructures. At the same time, governments are prevented from taking adequate mitigating action by three obstacles spawned by economic globalization: the spectacular growth of fossil fuel-related corporations and their consequent leverage over governments; the increase in competitive pressures on domestic industry; and global trade rules policed by the World Trade Organisation. As a result, the climate is changing with very serious implications for us all.

The global economy and the philosophy that inspired its creation by definition necessitate trade over long distances. The central policy prescription of neo-liberalism is that of free trade based on international specialisation according to comparative advantage. Accordingly, all countries should specialise in and export what they do or produce best, and import everything else. The consequence of the adoption of that philosophy by most governments around the world is that diverse local economies supplying their local populations with most of the things that they need are supplanted by economies that produce principally for export abroad and import most of their requirements.

With economic globalization, products that we used to be able to produce ourselves, or foods that were simply unavailable for climatic or seasonal reasons, are now imported year-round. The geographic distance between producers and consumers is thus increased dramatically and goods are transported far greater distances before they reach consumers. The average distance that goods travelled from producer to consumer in the U.S., for example, was 1000 km in 1982. Now that even more local economies have been displaced by regional and global ones, that figure is likely to be even higher. Similar changes have taken place in the process of production. With the liberalisation of investment and trade policy, corporations engaged in manufacturing or food processing are able to locate or farm out the various phases of production at, or to, different sites around the world.

Components are thus shipped back and forth tens of thousands of miles before the product is finally assembled or completed. Hence, as David Korten points out, when Otis Elevator set about creating an advanced elevator system, it contracted out the design of the motor drives to Japan, the door systems to France, the electronics to Germany, and small geared components to Spain. All of these components were then shipped to the United States where they were finally assembled, before being exported around the world - travelling thousands of miles in the process. Similarly, as a study by the German Wuppertal Institute on the distance travelled by various food products revealed, the components of a 150 gram strawberry yoghurt travelled a total of 1,005 kilometres before being put together. The strawberries were imported from Poland, corn and wheat flour from the Netherlands, jam from West Germany, sugar beet from East Germany and the yoghurt itself from north Germany. Aluminium used for the cover travelled 300 kilometres. In this way, economic globalization has stimulated massive growth in the leading modes of international transport for goods, all of which contribute to climate change.

As global trade has expanded, world shipping has grown approximately ten-fold by weight since 1950. Shipping carries 90 percent of the world's trade in goods and the energy demands of the industry are phenomenal: 140 million tons of fuel are consumed each year by ships world-wide; more than the annual consumption of the entire Middle-East. Moreover, shipping is set to increase by about 85% between 1997 and 2010 because of the expected expansion in global trade. Ports such as that of Los Angeles predict a doubling of cargo throughput over the next 25 years.

Such growth will undoubtedly lead to a rise in greenhouse gas emissions. Similarly, world air cargo traffic nearly tripled from 44 billion Revenue ton-kilometres (RTK - the distance each ton travels) in 1985 to 123 billion RTKs in 1997: a 280% increase. Boeing forecasts another tripling in air cargo traffic by 2017. Freight service is expected to continue growing at a rate 2% faster than passenger traffic. The problem with this boom is that transport by air is by far the most energy-intensive mode of transportation: each ton of freight moved by plane uses 49 times as much energy per kilometre than when it is moved by ship. This is particularly damaging because aircraft emissions are high in the troposphere where the air is thinner and greenhouse gases are much more effective at absorbing outgoing infra-red radiation. Water vapour emitted from aircraft, which forms cirrus clouds or con trails high in the troposphere, may also have a considerably greater impact on climate as high clouds are particularly effective at trapping heat.

Freight transport over land has also increased as a result of economic globalization. Europe, for example, has witnessed a tripling of trans-border truck traffic from 400 billion ton-kilometres in 1970 to 1200 billion ton-kilometres in 1997, according to EU estimates. That growth is primarily the result of the liberalisation of trade, which has made trading over longer distances much more viable, and not just the product of greater production and consumption.

Hence, from 1986-1991, the distance over which food was transported in Europe increased by 19%, while it only increased 8% by volume. Similarly, in the U.S., the ton-miles of freight accounted for by rail since 1960 has more than doubled - reaching 1.2 trillion ton-miles in 1994 alone, a year in which the average length of haul was over 800 miles. Truck traffic has experienced even greater growth, especially since NAFTA, to the point where trucks travelled a total of 182 billion miles on U.S. interstate highways in 1994.

The cumulative environmental costs of all such long-distance transport are extremely heavy, and, were they accounted for in the final price of products, would make freight transport on this scale economically unviable. The 15-fold increase in world trade that has resulted from the opening of markets around the world to free trade and investment since 1950 has stimulated significant growth in global demand for fossil fuels. As more and more goods have had to be carried over longer and longer distances, trade transportation has become responsible for the consumption of over one-eighth of world oil production. As that oil is burnt and greenhouse gases are emitted, our climate is being dangerously destabilised.

Industrial agriculture has made the productivity of farmland almost entirely dependent on massive infusions of energy derived from fossil fuels. It is therefore a major contributor to climate change. Already widely adopted in much of the industrialised world, with economic globalization, industrial agriculture is spreading globally, to countries such as China, India and Mexico which until recently have practised far less energy-intensive systems of farming. Their rapid transition to fossil fuel-intensive models of production will therefore dramatically increase global greenhouse gas emissions.

Of all human-created emissions of carbon dioxide, methane and nitrous oxide - the principal greenhouse gases contributing to climate change - industrial agriculture is responsible for 25%, 60%, and 80% respectively. If that is so, it is essentially because industrial agriculture replaces the energy inputs of humans and animals with huge amounts of fossil fuel-derived energy, of which it consumes more than any other industry.

Direct energy, mostly refined petroleum products, is used on farms to power machines for the purposes of plowing, planting and harvesting, fertiliser and pesticide application, and transportation, while electricity is used for irrigation and other purposes. Hence, U.S. consumption of fuels for farm use, for example, in 1993 amounted to 1.4 million gallons of gasoline and 3.5 million gallons of diesel; 11% and 29% respectively of the national total.

Striking as these figures may be, they do not include the even larger amounts of energy consumed off the farm for manufacturing machines, fertilisers and pesticides, and for processing, packaging, and transporting the food after it leaves the farm. Manufacturing each ton of nitrogen, phosphorous and potassium fertiliser, for example, requires between 10 and 72 MJ of primarily fossil fuel energy, and manufacturing and processing food consumed 4.7 percent of total energy in the U.S. in 1991.

Industrial agriculture thus produces a particularly perverse outcome: it is estimated that it causes us to expend many times as much energy to produce food as we actually derive from eating it. And almost all of that energy is derived from burning fossil fuels - emitting large quantities of greenhouse gases in the process. Industrial agriculture is responsible for even more greenhouse gas emissions when we include the consequences of applying 70 million tons of nitrogen fertiliser every year on soils - a process which generates at least 10% of total nitrous oxide emissions.

In addition, industrial farming methods lead to soil erosion, which, in the U.S. alone, is estimated to cause the release of 16 million tons of carbon into the atmosphere each year. Intensive, industrial practices also lead to higher methane emissions in rice and livestock production. Rice fields that are flooded rather than rain fed produce much more methane. Flooding cuts off the oxygen supply to soil, causing organic matter to decompose into methane.

In livestock production, meanwhile, when large numbers of animals are confined in one area, manure is usually stored in huge piles, releasing methane as it decomposes. Emissions are also higher due to the high-protein diet of cattle in feed lots, compared with when livestock eat grass in pastures. It is estimated that intensive livestock production is responsible for 15% of global methane emissions. Conversion from small-scale traditional farming to large-scale industrial agriculture has another important ecological impact: the displacement of people from their land and into cities.

Today, most of the world's population still live in rural communities, where they can provide for at least part of their own food needs. But as small farmers throughout the world are increasingly undermined by imports of industrially-produced subsidised food, the mechanisation and corporatisation of agriculture, and the focus on producing export crops, millions are being displaced from their land to urban areas. In China, for example, agricultural industrialisation caused 10 million peasants to leave their farms in just one year recently, while 440 million more are expected to migrate from the land to China's urban areas in the next few decades.

The implications for global climate are significant because the more cities grow, the more energy is consumed as food and water, building materials and energy must all be transported great distances via vast energy-consuming infrastructures, and as concentrated wastes must be hauled away in fossil fuel-consuming trucks and barges. Industrialised agriculture has clearly proven to be a highly energy-intensive and unsustainable model. To export it to the rest of the world is a recipe for worsening climatic dislocation, yet that is precisely what is taking place.

Because of economic globalization, industrial farming is being practised in more and more countries around the world. With fewer barriers to trade in food - as a result of regional and international trade agreements, such as NAFTA and the World Trade Organisation's Agreement on Agriculture - cheap, subsidised, large-scale industrially-produced food has flooded world markets, making it very difficult for farmers employing traditional, small-scale, less energy-intensive and less subsidised systems of agriculture to compete. As a result, the latter are forced to adopt industrial methods or go bust, as millions have done - in which case, if they do not starve, they are often reduced to buying imported industrial food and selling their land to wealthier farmers who use it to expand industrial production.

Governments are increasingly powerless to protect small farmers from such a fate as the WTO's Agreement on Agriculture and other trade agreements have removed their ability to control domestic agricultural policies. Tools that were once used to secure stable prices for domestic farmers are no longer allowed under WTO rules. Import controls to prevent the flooding of domestic markets; farmer marketing boards to give producers the ability to negotiate collective prices with domestic and foreign buyers; and family farm support programs - are all either forbidden or restricted under WTO rules.

Thus, the world's remaining small, low-energy-consuming agricultural producers are rapidly being replaced with large agri-businesses using industrial practices. Transnational agribusinesses which produce on an industrial scale, such as Cargill and Pepsico, now control seventy percent of world food trade. Cargill alone controls 60 percent of the world trade in cereals.

Furthermore, the reorientation of economic activity towards production for exports that takes place when a country becomes part of the global economy, often following the adoption of an IMF/World Bank structural adjustment program, leads to a vast increase in the production of exportable cash crops - such as coffee, sugar cane and cocoa - grown in monocultures, which require far more high-energy inputs than other varieties. Increased production of cash crops also results from investment liberalisation and privatisation, which open up national economies to foreign agrochemical companies which are able to buy up farming companies and vast tracts of fertile land around the world for that purpose.

The resulting global expansion of industrial agriculture is the cause of growing energy use in the agricultural sector of most countries throughout the world and a consequent increase in greenhouse gas emissions. In Canada, for example, on-farm energy use alone increased by 9.3 percent between 1990 and 1996, and agriculture's share of CO_2 emissions grew 8 percent over the same period.

In developing countries, energy used for agricultural production as a percentage of total commercial energy grew approximately 30 percent from 1972 to 1982; driven by the first 'green revolution' which brought industrial and energy-intensive agricultural production to many developing countries. Since then, energy use in agriculture has increased still further, together with emissions of carbon dioxide, methane and nitrous oxide, with severe consequences for global climate.

As consumer markets in industrialised countries have become saturated, manufacturing corporations have turned to the developing world in search of new consumers. Those corporations have been instrumental in shaping international agreements removing barriers to trade, which, in the absence of an adequate international environmental regulatory framework, facilitate and promote the consumption of carbon emitting products world-wide.

With trade and investment liberalisation, environmentally-destructive technologies such as the automobile and other energy-intensive appliances spread to cultures not yet dependent on such goods. Since the opening of markets to foreign imports, South Korea and Thailand, for example, witnessed annual car growth rates of 25 and 40 percent respectively in the early 1990s. Similarly, the number of cars in Mexico City grew a massive 60 percent between just 1990 and 1993. Such proliferation is significantly increasing the threat of global climate change, as motor vehicles are responsible for a large share of world carbon dioxide emissions. These are only set to increase, as transnational auto companies increase sales to countries that are rapidly liberalising their markets, such as the states of the former USSR that currently have only 1 car per 21 people; India that has one car per 455 people; and China - one car per 1000 people.

Already, as a result of investment liberalisation in China, where people have relied primarily on bicycles, public transportation, and other low-input means of transportation, General Motors (GM) recently signed a $1 billion contract to produce 100,000 mid-sized cars annually. GM has also set up production in Russia, where it hopes to profit not only by producing cheap cars for export but by gaining a larger share of the domestic market. The company is not the only one expanding in this new market - in 1995, over 1 million foreign cars and trucks were sold in Russia and the Ukraine.

The climatic consequences of the global proliferation of the car through economic globalization are disastrous. And the car is but one of a vast array of modern home and office products and appliances, such as washing-machines, clothes dryers, TVs, VCRs, computers, and photocopiers, that require large inputs of climate-changing fossil fuels, and that are now being exported and produced around the world.

International financial institutions - linchpins of the global economy - have directly promoted and financed fossil fuel-intensive energy projects throughout the developing world. Their principal goal is to create the energy infrastructure necessary to integrate developing countries into the global economy; to generate large quantities of cheap energy to fuel expanding manufacturing processes, enable household consumption to rise, and support the vast cities that the globalization of industrial development is creating.

According to the Institute for Policy Studies, the World Bank has financed $13.6 billion worth of energy projects since the Rio Summit in 1992, including 51 coal, oil and gas-fired power plants and 26 coal mines. These projects will emit 38 billion tons of carbon dioxide over their lifetimes, nearly double what was emitted in 1996 by all countries combined.35 Meanwhile, less than 3 percent of the World Bank's energy budget is devoted to renewable energy. Between 1992 and 1998, the Bank spent 25 times more on fossil fuel projects than on renewable energy. Moreover, the immediate beneficiaries of the Bank's projects are G7-based corporations, which have been granted 95% of the contracts, and are the primary consumers of the energy these projects produce.

The Overseas Private Investment Corporation (OPIC) and the Export-Import Bank (Ex-Im) - U.S. export-credit agencies funded by taxpayers which subsidise U.S. commercial interests in developing nations - have also devoted billions of dollars to huge fossil fuel-based energy projects. According to OPIC's own press release, in 1996, over $1 billion was approved for nine American ventures abroad, including 4 power plants. European citizens fund a similar 'corporate welfare' program through the European Bank for Reconstruction and Development (ERBD). Shell, Amoco, Mitsubishi, and Texaco are among the corporations whose overseas investments in energy resources have been subsidised by the EBRD.

The behaviour of these banks is perhaps unsurprising given the assumptions it is based on. The World Bank's charts projecting the world's future energy needs, for example, show a trajectory line that shoots off the graph, indicating expected energy demand for developing countries. Bank officials like to use these charts to shock audiences into believing how badly and rapidly the world needs to exploit all of its available fossil fuel resources. These projections, however, are based on the premise that countries will continue along the same course of export-based, energy-intensive development that the Bank has been pushing for decades.

Accordingly, estimates inflate the expectation for energy needs and ignore localised systems of production and consumption that would significantly reduce overall energy consumption. Energy use, therefore, is over-projected because of the energy-intensive needs of economic globalization and the development model it promotes. By building infrastructures to cater for that expected demand, however, the World Bank and the other multilateral development agencies are playing a leading role in fuelling climate change.

Despite the growing threat posed by climate change, governments are being prevented from taking adequate mitigating action by a number of obstacles spawned by economic globalization, including the increased power of large corporations - particularly those in the fossil fuel industry. By opening new markets around the world to foreign trade and investment, economic globalization has greatly increased the opportunities for corporations to grow, increase their profits, and eliminate or absorb competitors, often through mergers. The fossil fuel sector and related industries have been no exception to this trend. The merger of the two oil giants Exxon and Mobil in 1998, for example, valued at $250 billion, has created the world's third largest corporation and the largest oil company by far. Among many others include the recent merger of BP with Amoco, and Total with Petrofina and Elf Aquitaine. These mergers have been mirrored by countless more in the auto, aircraft and utility industries.

The result of this corporate consolidation has been an unprecedented concentration of financial power in the hands of industries that profit from fossil fuels, to the point where many are now more economically powerful than a large number of nation states. The combined revenues, for example, of just General Motors and Ford - the two largest automobile corporations in the world - exceed the GDP of all Sub-Saharan Africa. This wealth has been used to great effect by fossil fuel-related companies to influence government policy in ways that have resulted in the defeat or watering down of many efforts to mitigate climate change.

The countries with the highest per capita greenhouse gas emissions and which are the most recalcitrant in taking action to reduce those emissions - such as the United States and Australia - are also home to corporations that have spent a fortune funding front groups, think tanks, lobbyists, scientists, economists and above all politicians, to obstruct political attempts to prevent climate change. In the U.S., for example, oil, gas, coal, utility, automobile and other fossil fuel-intensive corporations contributed $63.4 million to both main U.S. political parties between 1992 and 1998. They also spent $30 million lobbying politicians and government agencies in 1998 alone, and $13 million more on television, radio and newspaper advertising in the three months leading up to the Kyoto conference to promote political and public opposition to the resulting treaty.

Millions more have been spent funding corporate front groups, or so-called 'Astroturf coalitions', such as the Coalition for Vehicle Choice and the Global Climate Coalition; think tanks, such as the Competitive Enterprise Institute and the Heritage Foundation; and scientists, such as Robert Balling - the recipient of $700,000 from the fossil fuel industry over the past five years.

The explicit goal of such funding - the extent of which citizens groups could not possibly match - has been to discredit the science of climate change and prevent the changes necessary to prevent its worst effects.

After years of effectively stalling global recognition of the problem, industry groups have successfully fought to limit countless measures to reduce emissions. For example, in the U.S. - responsible for a quarter of global greenhouse gas emissions - Congress voted to bar the White House from requiring car-makers to build more efficient vehicles by increasing automobile fuel economy standards, as a result of corporate influence. Indeed, Congress has tried to destroy what little fuel economy standards are in existence by successfully inserting an exemption for giant sport utility vehicles which now account for one out of every two cars being purchased and which get as little as 14 miles to the gallon.

Congress has also prevented the Clinton Administration from increasing the BTU or energy tax, as well as from increasing the 1999 budget for the development of renewable energy and energy efficient technology to $3.6 billion as the White House requested. It has even rejected the President's policy that fossil fuels produced on public land should be subject to market-based royalty rates rather than the subsidised rate currently in existence.The most significant act of Congressional subversion is the Byrd-Hagel Resolution, passed unanimously by the Senate, 95 votes to 0, in June 1997, which effectively prevents the ratification of the Kyoto Protocol that mandates the U.S. to reduce its greenhouse gas emissions by 7 percent below 1990 levels by 2012. If that were not enough, as the result of legislative efforts by the Right-wing Republican Joe Knollenberg - whose constituency includes Detroit, the capital of the US car industry - and others, new programs designed especially to fulfil the US' Kyoto commitments are now outlawed.

Such political behaviour defies all established scientific knowledge and the public interest, and can only have been taken to satisfy the short-term interests of corporations engaged in activities that are causing the climate to change. To varying degrees of success, the political power of fossil fuel-related corporations is being exercised in similar ways all over the world, including at regional levels such as the EU, and at all the international negotiations on climate change. Economic globalization has given these corporations the financial and political clout to have such influence, with devastating effects.

Another obstacle that governments face in seeking to take action to mitigate climate change is the huge increase in competitive pressures on domestic industry generated by economic globalization. As opportunities for foreign investment increase and as moving manufacturing overseas becomes easier with economic globalization, corporations can pick and choose the regulatory conditions under which they invest. Where local, national or regional environmental regulations are strict, companies complain that they are burdened with extra costs that make them uncompetitive in the global economy.

Countries attempting to take serious measures to protect the environment are thus no longer deemed competitive locations for investment. In such a climate, governments compete with each other to lower or freeze environmental standards to attract foreign investment or to prevent the flight of industries already based in their countries. In a globalized economy, even the threat of relocation is powerful enough to send policy-makers on a deregulatory frenzy or a policy freeze, and attempts to raise taxation or environmental standards become almost impossible. The European Union's failed attempt at introducing a carbon tax in 1992 to reduce carbon emissions provides a clear example. Opponents of the tax argued that it would undermine the competitiveness of European companies abroad, because the tax would not apply to their competitors, who would therefore gain a commercial advantage over them.

In refusing to ratify the Kyoto Protocol, the U.S. Senate has cited similar reasons. The co-authors of the Senate resolution that has effectively blocked the ratification of this treaty, Senators Byrd and Hagel, argued that taking measures to reduce greenhouse gas emissions would damage the U.S. economy, causing an exodus of manufacturing plants to developing countries which are not mandated to reduce emissions under Kyoto.

What opponents of the Kyoto Protocol fail to mention is that industrial relocation would not be possible were it not for the enhanced mobility corporations enjoy as a result of agreements which they ratified and that have reduced or eliminated barriers to trade and foreign investment. Furthermore, given the environmental threats that we face today, the solution to any loss of competitiveness cannot be the freezing, reduction or elimination of environmental protections. If the current global system of free trade and investment is impeding governments' abilities to set and enforce environmental protections, then the economic system itself, flawed as it is, needs to be changed.

Global trade rules policed by the World Trade Organisation also pose a significant threat to national and international efforts to address climate change. WTO rules, for example, could be used to challenge the Kyoto Protocol on a number of grounds.

Under the terms of the Protocol, Parties are encouraged to implement policies and measures aimed at "enhancement of energy efficiency in relevant sectors of the economy" - a key goal of climate change mitigation. An important way in which that may be achieved is by setting energy efficiency standards for consumer products - such as motor vehicles. When that has been attempted by the European Union, Japan and the United States, however, global trade rules have been used to challenge their initiatives, and serious disputes have followed.

In January 1999, Japan announced its intention to introduce legally binding standards for energy efficiency for nine categories of cars on the basis of vehicle weight, in order to meet its commitment under the Kyoto Protocol to reduce its greenhouse gas emissions by 6 percent below 1990 levels. The standards are set based on the most energy efficient vehicle currently commercially available within each weight category - "the top runner" - which in each weight category, happens to be a Japanese car.

The EU, meanwhile, to meet its Kyoto commitment of reducing greenhouse gases by 8 percent below 1990 levels, has forged a voluntary agreement to increase energy efficiency with the European Automobile Manufacturers Association (ACEA). Under that agreement, the manufacturers agreed to reduce carbon dioxide emissions in new cars by 25 percent by 2008 on the basis of fleet averaging rather than specific efficiency requirements on vehicles by category.

The EU and Japan have challenged each other's energy efficiency requirements arguing that they discriminate against imported vehicles - which is forbidden under world trade rules. Because European exports to Japan tend to be in the range of medium and luxury vehicles, they fall into the middle and heavier weight categories which are subject to the greatest percentage of improvements for fuel efficiency.

The EU therefore claims that the effect will be to discriminate against their cars in violation of the WTO's Agreement on Technical Barriers to Trade, which prohibits standards that are discriminatory and more trade restrictive than necessary.48 Japan, meanwhile, claims that EU standards based on fleet averaging discriminate against their vehicle exports, which are primarily higher end vehicles that would need substantial improvements in energy efficiency to meet EU standards.

It remains to be seen if the EU, the U.S., or Japan will mount formal challenges at the WTO, but if they do, the chances of their respective energy efficiency standards' survival are not good, especially given the fate under GATT of the U.S. Corporate Average Fuel Economy (CAFE) standards. Designed to increase energy efficiency, the CAFE standards were challenged by the EU for discriminating in effect against EU auto makers, citing almost identical arguments as the opponents of Japanese and European energy efficiency standards today, even though the U.S. average fuel economy standards were identical for domestic and foreign fleets. A GATT panel, however, agreed with the EU, and, in 1994, overturned the U.S. standards.

The application of carbon taxes - another important strand of any serious strategy for meeting national commitments under the Kyoto Protocol - could also fall foul of WTO rules. By internalising the climate-related costs of using fossil fuels, carbon taxes create an incentive to use less fuel and to develop more fuel efficient production processes.

However, taxing commercial goods at a national level on the basis of how much those goods contribute to greenhouse gas emissions, can place domestic industries at a competitive disadvantage in the global economy - because the tax would not apply to foreign competitors. One way around that problem would be to tax imports based on the energy used to produce them. But under GATT/WTO rules governing "like products", that would be illegal. Those rules prohibit internal taxes on imported products that are "in excess of those... applied to like domestic products,". Any trade discrimination based on the way a product is produced - exactly what carbon taxes are designed to influence - is thus forbidden.

That represents a fundamental conflict between the WTO and the Kyoto Protocol. For while under WTO rules, "like products" cannot be distinguished or discriminated against on the basis of how they were produced or where they came from, the Kyoto Protocol and all three of its flexible mechanisms mandate discrimination between different manufacturing technologies and processes, between signatories and non-signatories, and between higher-emitting developed countries and lower-emitting developing countries.

2

Globalisation and Economic Growth

Post independent India was no different from the rest of the world in adopting a pattern of economic development, best described as state led growth. Significant amounts of direct intervention by the state in projects requiring heavy investments were the norm rather than the exception during this post-war and post-colonial period. The capital requirements of most economies were so large that no entity other than the State was considered capable of harnessing the required resources. Underdeveloped international capital markets, significant trade barriers, and the hangover of sovereignty issues, a legacy of the colonial period, ensured that most nations planned for economic self-sufficiency. Underdeveloped domestic capital markets did not create an environment in which this burden could be shared by the private sector in any significant manner, especially in capital intensive, long gestation investments which are typical in the irrigation, power and transportation sectors.

Unlike some other developing countries, notably those in East Asia, which transited to a liberalized framework in the three decades since 1950, India has been a gradual reformer. Continued reliance on state intervention created a highly regulated economy. The result was the absence of significant levels of competition either from imports or within the domestic economy. Industrial capacity restrictions, prohibitions in foreign trade, high tariff walls, prohibitions on technology transfer, inadequate patent protection, restrictive labour laws and administered interest rates severely limited the scope for the efficiency enhancing impact of markets. The planned and tightly regulated development till the mid 1980s resulted in positive though moderate levels of growth. However growth rates in the 'early reformers' in East Asia were considerably higher as Table 1 illustrates:

Table 1

GDP growth (average % per year); international comparison

	1965-80	*1980-90*	*1990-2000*
China	6.4	9.5	10.3
Korea	9.5	9.7	5.7
Malaysia	7.4	5.2	7.0
Thailand	7.4	7.6	4.2
Indonesia	7.9	5.5	4.2
India	3.7	5.3	6.0

Source: World Development Reports, World Bank.

Not only was economic growth lower in India during the period 1965 to 1980 but unlike the East Asian economies, which aggressively sought export competitiveness for domestic manufactures, India sought self-sufficiency. The insularity of the economy can be gauged from the fact that India's share in world exports reduced from 1.85% to 0.42% between 1950 and 1980.

Post 1985, the Indian economy was gradually liberalized and restructured. Economic reform has been characterized by liberalization and simplification of administrative intervention, phased introduction of domestic and import competition, facilitation of participation by the private sector, public sector reform and reform of the financial system. The results have been positive. During the post 1985 period, the economy grew at around 6% with an increase in real per capita income of around 4 %. The incidence of poverty declined from 44% to 26% and the life expectancy at birth grew significantly from 48 years to 64 years. In the external sector, the period from 1980-2000 was marked by an increase in the share of India's exports in World exports from 0.42 to 0.67% and the restoration of external balance post 1992-93.

The ratio of external debt to GDP declined from 5.5% in 1990-91 to 2.6% in 2000-01. Similarly the profile of external debt became more stable. The ratio of short-term external debt to total external debt declined from a peak of 10.2% in end March 1991 to 2.8% in end December 2000. The level of Foreign Exchange Reserves increased from a level equal to 3 months import in 1990-91 to a level of over 8.5 months of import since 1993-94. By 2000 India's short-term external debt was only 8.5% of foreign exchange reserves, which is much lower than 10% in China, 15.5% in Malaysia, 45.6% in Thailand and 112.6% in Argentina. Macro economic stability and a higher degree of openness have also resulted in an increase in inflow of foreign investment (portfolio plus FDI) from a level of $113 million in 1990-91 to $ 14,294 million in 2000-01, though these are far below the potential inflow. The positive impact of economic reform in India is illustrated in Table 1 by the narrowing of the 'growth gap' *vis-à-vis* East Asian countries during the period 1980 to 1990.

Post 1990 the Indian economy has fared very well in comparison. Economic growth in India averaged 6% per annum during the decade of the 1990's. In comparison economic growth in East Asia, except in the case of China and Malaysia, was adversely affected by the financial crisis in the second half of the 1990's. Differential benefits for the public and private sector from economic reform. The productivity and efficiency of the Indian economy has been a traditional and much analysed concern in India. Usually Total Factor Productivity (TFP) accounts for one half of economic growth. TFP was negative during the period 1959/60 to 1979/80. These are indicators of the structural inefficiency of the Indian economy prior to reform.

Economic reform has positively impacted all sectors of the economy. Annual average growth in this sector increased from 3.9% during the period 1960 to 1985 to 7.2% in the reform period 1985 to 2000. In contrast, annual average growth in the non-agricultural public sector declined from 8.2 to 7.1% of GDP during the comparable periods. The period 1985 to 2000 was characterized by increase in TFP, which should be viewed in association with the higher growth rates in non-agriculture private sector. The 1980's are often called the decade of 'jobless growth' in Indian industry. The overhang of employment, from the 1970's, was used more efficiently and the capital intensity of incremental output increased, driven in part by sticky wages and employment policies, but also by technological requirements.

Economic liberalization provided enhanced and cheaper access to imported capital goods, global technology and global enterprises, all of which facilitated improvement in productivity. Moreover, the pressure of increased competition in the domestic and international market (in the post WTO regime of global competition and falling tariff rates) forced domestic firms to improve the efficiency of their operations through organizational restructuring, improved managerial practices and better capacity utilization. These changes in the macro environment have benefited business in general. As Table 2 illustrates the ratio of PAT to Net sales for private manufacturing increased to a peak of 9.1% in 1994-95 before declining to 6.2% in 1997-98.

Table 2: Profitability of manufacturing (PAT as % of net sales)

	PSE	*Private*
1990-91	-4.5	5.7
1991-92	-5.3	4.9
1992-93	-5.4	4.9
1993-94	-6.9	6.6
1994-95	-2.3	9.1
1995-96	-2.4	9
1996-97	-4.3	7
1997-98	-3.9	6.2

Source: "The lost decade" NCAER study.

PSEs on aggregate continued to make losses in the 1990's. Aggregate loss was 4.5% of net sales in 1990-91. This increased to a peak of 6.9% in 1993-94 before declining to 3.9% in 1997-98. Clearly economy wide reform has benefited both the public and the private sector. In the public sector losses persist. Possibly, the beneficial changes in the macro environment have not been matched by initiatives within PSEs, to increase their competitiveness, perhaps due to complex procedures within PSEs, due to their ownership structure. An important feature of globalization has been the movement of private capital from one country to another so that an economy's growth is not constrained by its own domestic savings.

In 1990 there were 40 countries for which the ratio of FDI to Gross Capital Formation was 5% or more. For India, in that year, this ratio was only 0.2%. By 2000 the number of countries where the ratio of FDI to Gross Capital Formation was 5% or more had more than doubled to 99, while for India this ratio was only 2.1%. Export orientation and the inflow of private foreign capital have played a significant role in the development of the East Asian Countries. At the peak, the foreign capital flow into Malaysia in 1993 was 17.4% of its GDP, while in Thailand in 1995 it was 12.7% of the GDP. In India it has mostly been below 0.5% of its GDP. Globalization has enlarged growth opportunities for developing countries. On average the share of developing economies in aggregate world exports increased from 20.6% in 1988-90 to 29.9% in 2000. Similarly their share in world output increased from 17.9% in 1988-90 to 40.4% in 2000.

Despite overwhelming evidence that market orientation, competition, greater participation of the private sector, export orientation together with freeing of the resource constraint by FDI inflows, provides a reasonable basis for higher levels of economic growth, these growth strategies are not universally accepted in

India. Even today there are endless debates against privatization and there is always an apprehension that FDI will lead to control by external agents. Perhaps these fears are the residual shadows of our colonial past. However those who subscribe to these views forget that the "East India Company" was never intended to invest in India.

The colonial period was marked by the extraction of capital and resources from India and other colonies, to fuel growth in Europe. The process was assisted by the absence of a domestic sovereign authority, which could resist such exploitative extraction. In the globalised world, access to private foreign capital does not imply an erosion of sovereignty. Foreign companies seek investment opportunities in India to enhance their value but in the process such investment creates jobs, adds badly needed infrastructure and provides a functional business link between the economies of the World and India. Such links and commitments are long term in nature and should be differentiated from the flows of "hot money" or portfolio investment, which can be temporary transfers driven solely by arbitrage opportunities. In the recent East Asian crises foreign direct investment was the stable element in the external balance. While to some extent FII investments and foreign lending reduced, FDI flows were consistent.

India cannot afford to starve itself of investment funds simply because the investors are foreign entities. India's low access to FDI as compared to China, Brazil, Poland and a number of South East Asian countries coupled with our lower historical growth rates suggests that there is significant economic value in increasing our access to FDI beyond the existing level of 0.5% percent of

GDP. In fact the low level of domestic savings in India requires a more aggressive approach to utilising foreign savings. As Table 4 illustrates while the rate of private savings, especially in the 1990's is very comparable to the international trend in reforming countries, the rate of saving in the public sector is very low. In fact savings in the public sector as a % of GDP have declined in recent years to negative values of - 1.0%, -0.9% and -1.7% in the period 1998-99 to 2000-01.

Table 3

Structure of domestic savings (% of GDP)

	Period	*Public*	*Private*
Indonesia	1981-88	7.7	14
Malaysia	1981-90	10.3	19.1
Thailand	1980-85	14.3	4.7
	1986-87	8.6	14.6
Japan	1981-88	5.1	15.8
India	1961-70	2.7	9.89
	1971-80	3.7	13.7
	1981-90	3.02	16.16
	1991-00	1.01	22.04

Source: World Bank, Economic Survey data (India).

Savings in the public sector in India have lagged the level of savings in East Asian economies. What is worrying is that there has been no upward trend in public savings since the 1980s. Though a boom in private saving in the 1990's has maintained the investment rate at around 23%, any increase in the investment rate will have to depend on foreign savings.

Higher levels of investment will be key for acceleration of the growth rate to a level of 8%, which is estimated to be the minimum required to effectively tackle the problem of poverty. There is considerable evidence to show that an increase in investment levels sharply increases the rate of economic growth. Increase in productivity coupled with an increase in investment explains the acceleration in economic growth in many developing countries. Table 4 provides an inter-country comparison of incremental investments and increase in economic growth over the period 1980 to 1995.

Table 4

Investment & GDP Growth Rates; cross country comparison (Average % per year)

	Change in investment rate		*Change in GDP growth*	
	1980-90	*1990-95*	*1980-90*	*1990-95*
China	11	15.5	10.2	12.8
Malaysia	2.6	16	5.2	8.7
Indonesia	7	16.3	6.1	7.6
Thailand	9.4	10.2	7.6	8.4
Turkey	5.3	2	5.3	3.2
Argentina	-0.3	5.7	-4.7	16
India	6.5	5.3	5.8	4.6
Venezuela	-5.3	3.8	1.1	2.4
Brazil	0.2	3.5	2.7	2.7
Philippines	-2.1	3.2	1	2.3
Egypt	2.7	-1.5	5	1.3
Poland	0.9	1.1	1.9	2.4

Source: World Development Report 1997.

China, Malaysia (1999-95), Indonesia, Thailand, Turkey (1980-90) and Argentina (1990-95) are examples where a sharp increase in the rate of investment had a positive impact on economic growth. India has had consistent increases in the investment levels with resultant increases in economic growth as well. The low rates of economic growth in Venezuela, Brazil, Philippines, Egypt and Poland can be associated with the negative or low rates of change in investment levels. It has been estimated that India needs to increase its investment rate to 30% of GDP if it is to grow at 8% per year. This is considerably more than what has been achieved in the past. However enhanced savings in the public sector coupled with increased usage of foreign savings can bridge the savings-investment gap in a manner consistent with macro economic stability. FDI is one such stable, potential source of financing, particularly in the context of privatization.

Foreign Direct Investment, Efficiency & Economic Growth

The experience of China, Malaysia and Brazil indicates that FDI inflows are also associated with increases in productivity and competitiveness. Malaysia, whose ratio of FDI to GDP was 4.3% during the period 1975 to 1995, is one of the largest exporter of electronics in the world. Brazil's has attracted $ 30 billion of FDI through privatization of PSEs during the last ten years. China permits unlimited FDI in a number of industries, particularly for the takeover of sick industries. FDI inflows of around $ 40 billion per annum over a number of years have enhanced productivity and competitiveness. Competitively priced Chinese exports provide significant import competition worldwide and are a particular source of concern for domestic Indian manufacturers. China's competitiveness has been enhanced by large-scale privatization of state owned enterprises and rationalization of the labor force, which began in 1995. More than 30,000 companies have been privatized and about 50 million workers have been laid off since 1997 and given VRS at terms, which are 3-5 times worse than the terms for VRS in India.

Fortunately, in the case of India, the scale of PSE restructuring is much smaller than in the case of China. Though employment in central PSEs is around one third of total employment in the central government, the absolute numbers were only 2.18 million in 1999-91 which reduced to 1.74 million by 2000-01. What is significant is that barring the organized private sector, employment levels were stagnant in the 1990's. As table 6 illustrates, of the 1.6 million jobs added in the organized sector 1 million, or two thirds, were added in the private sector during the period 1991 to 2001. This indicates that the private sector has become the major source for incremental employment in the organized sector of the economy over the last decade. In the unorganized sector, which is around ten times larger, it has traditionally been the dominant employer.

Privatization and enhanced access to FDI are the next big frontiers for economic reform in India. In fact the latter is to some extent linked to implementation of the former. International experience suggests that privatization enhances inflows of international private capital. Hence there is a case for making non-discriminatory rules for FDI inflows. Currently, there are additional restrictions on FDI in the case of disinvestment of PSE. This is not exceptional. The Queen of England had to use the Golden share to stop the takeover of National Power of U.K. by Southern Utilities of U.S., only ten years back in the UK. Now of course, London Electricity and Surrey Electricity have been taken over by EDF, France without any public debate. At the best of times privatization is an emotive subject. However it is instructive that other countries have trodden this path before and have found that the economic gains from privatization, justify the pain associated with a break from the past. In a competitive environment, the access to capital for any business entity must bear the test of availability and cost. Hence business entities must be free to determine their own capital mix within non-discriminatory guidelines, which are consistent with the management of our external balance.

Privatisation in India

The imperative for public sector reform

The performance of a very large number of public sector enterprises is disappointing, often owing to reasons beyond their control. Performance is particularly poor in public sector manufacturing industries. Some PSEs have done extremely well, but these are in monopoly sectors like Petroleum, Power and Telecom, where Government determines prices on a cost plus basis. Once these sectors are deregulated, these PSEs are likely to come under severe competitive pressure and may see erosion of their profitability. SAIL 8 is a classic example of a PSE losing profitability when liberalization forced it to compete with imports and domestic private sector steel manufacturers. VSNL is similarly now under tremendous competitive pressure, though since it has been privatized it poses no fiscal threats. MTNL and BSNL face similar challenges, and it is necessary that they be privatised quickly. The deteriorating finances of PSEs, impose fiscal strain on the government in the form of subsidies, equity infusions to finance losses, loans, guarantees and write offs. In comparison, the returns for the Government by way of dividends has been meager. PSE shares have also proved to be less than attractive assets for market participants and institutional investors since they tend to under perform comparable private sector stock. Where public ownership is not dictated by strategic concerns or the need to control market power privatization is the optimum solution, which maximizes welfare gains and reduces the risks for taxpayers.

Disinvestment policy and practice

The policy of the Government on disinvestment has evolved over the last decade. It started with the sale of minority shares in 1991-92, which continued with some modifications till 1999-2000. During this period Rs 18638 crores were realized through this method of market sale of shares.

The policy changed around 31st March 2000 and was announced by the Finance Minister in the Budget speech of 2000-2001 in The Finance Minister had said:

> "Government have recently established a new Department for Disinvestment 12 to establish a systematic policy approach to disinvestment and privatization and to give a fresh impetus to this programme which will emphasize increasingly on strategic sales of identified PSUs."

In accordance with this decision all the disinvestments since 2000 have been strategic sales. Strategic sale is defined as a sale of equity by Government where the management control of the entity is handed over to the strategic partner. Typically the strategic partner is required to purchase an equity stake, which is large enough to ensure a workable majority. This policy has been implemented vigorously.

The Central Government's equity stake, both direct and through holding companies was of the order of about Rs. 80,000 crore on 31st March 2000. The increase in the levels of available PSE stock in the market has resulted in an upsurge in the share prices of disinvesting companies and also in the overall market capitalisation of PSE shares. The market capitalisation of listed PSEs increased by 73.5% i.e. from Rs. 96,063 cr. to Rs. 1,66,672 crore as compared to a 14% increase in total market capitalisation of all BSE listed companies, between January and May 16, 2002.

The market capitalisation in 32 listed public sector companies tracked by BSE has increased in value by about Rs. 70,000 crore in four months. Government shareholding has thus gained about Rs.50,000 crore. If this performance can be improved by initiation of more privatizations, significant benefits would accrue to the economy, Government and financial institutions. This will also catalyse improvement in the performance of our stock markets, which are vital for economic development. The performance of our stock markets is less than satisfactory, with markets growing only by 0.5% against an overall GDP growth of about 6% last year. This is in sharp contrast to Indonesia and Thailand, where the local stock market indices have registered over 30% increase in the last year, even though economic growth has been much lower than in the case of India.

Evaluation of disinvestment strategies

Before the year 2000, the Government had primarily sold minority shares in public sector companies. From 1991 to 1999 through this method of market sale of shares Rs 18,638 crores were realised, an average of Rs 2071 crores per year. The price earning ratio on the basis of the sales value realized by the Government, even in blue chip companies like IOC, BPCL, HPCL, GAIL & VSNL was 4 to 6. In comparison over a two-year period 2000-01 to 2002-03 (till August 2002), more than Rs. 11,315 crore has been realised through strategic sale of Thirty Three PSEs 13 or an average of Rs 4,526 per year. The price earnings (PE) ratio for sales through the strategic disinvestment route has been far higher, from 11 to 89.

The experience gained so far seems to justify the assumption that the strategic sale "discovers" the fundamental, long-term value of the company as opposed to the sale of small lots of shares in the market which get valued on short term considerations linked to the current expectations of the market. The higher sales realizations through strategic sale reflect the control premium, which the investor is willing to pay for managing the company. Three examples will illustrate this proposition. A profitable monopoly like VSNL was sold at a PE ratio of 6 earlier, while the subsequent strategic sale of VSNL in February 2002, despite substantial deregulation of the Telcom industry and erosion of its monopoly status, has yielded a PE ratio of 11.

Shares were sold at a price of Rs. 269 per share. While foregoing the Rights Issue and transferring management control to Suzuki, the Government realised a price of Rs 3280 per share in May 2002. No control premium was charged in 1994. Possibly at that time there was insufficient recognition that the transfer of management control to a strategic investor extracts fundamental value far beyond the current market levels. The Government has now received Rs. 1000 crore as control premium in the case of Maruti. The market sale of the residual stock of the Government of India in Maruti of 66 lakh shares will fetch additional gains for Government. The strategic sale of BALCO in March 2001 was achieved at a PE ratio of 19. In a similar transaction in the private sector, INDAL was bought by HINDALCO at a PE ratio of 11. This indicates, that the sale of BALCO to a strategic partner

During the last two years the Government has sold about 1% of its total equity yielding more than Rs. 11,000 crore. While a simple extrapolation may be misleading and inexact, it indicates that offloading the entire stock of PSE equity held by Government could result in incremental capital resources of about Rs. 10,00,000 crore. In addition to the potential for receipt of such capital gains are the benefits related to reduction in the revenue expenditure of Government. The Government has received around Rs. 11335/- crore from strategic sales. The Government of India's long-term interest rate for market borrowing fell from 12% in January 1999 to 8% in January 2002. The average rate over this period being 10%. Using this average rate for market borrowing, the avoided interest cost of borrowing Rs 11,335 crore is Rs. 1133 crore every year, in perpetuity. As against this benefit, the dividends received by Government on its equity, which has now been sold, averaged Rs. 52.41 crore during the last eight years. However in the case of two companies (PPL and Jessop) of the total sixteen PSEs thus sold, there was an average annual out go of Rs. 126 crore. Thus, the Government lost Rs. 74 crore ever year

(Rs 126 crore out go plus Rs 52 crore equity inflow) due to its majority equity presence in these companies. The sales of part equity in 16 companies would bring an annual real benefit to the economy to the tune of Rs.1133 + 74 = Rs. 1207 crore. Clearly, strategic disinvestment in these sixteen PSEs has proved beneficial for the Governments finances. The case of the public sector hotels is similarly instructive. The total annual loss in hotels during the pre-privatisation period was of the order of Rs. 32.88 crore. This loss would ultimately have devolved to Government. There can be little justification for the average taxpayer subsidizing the inefficient management of a luxury hotel.

BALCO was a profit making company, which paid the Government an average dividend (over eight years) of Rs. 5.69 crore every year on the portion of equity subsequently sold to a strategic investor. The avoided interest cost on Rs 826.5 crores received from strategic disinvestment is Rs. 82.65 crore every year. The net gains for Government are nearly Rs 75 crores per year in avoided interest cost. CMC was a very well managed and profitable company, yet the average dividend was only 0.80 crore per year. The avoided interest cost for Government on the Rs 152 crores realized from its sale is Rs. 15.2 crore · annually.

Maruti Udyog Ltd. gave average returns to the tune of Rs. 13 crore annually through dividends for Government. In comparison the avoided interest cost on the realizations received through the strategic sale of shares is Rs 242 crores per year. IPCL gave dividends on average of Rs. 16.24 crore per year. In comparison the avoided interest cost on the realizations received through the strategic sale of shares is Rs 149 crores per year.

During the period 1991-2000, the sale of minority shares of public sector undertakings has led to realisation of about Rs. 19,000 crore for Government. Most of these shares were bought by Financial Institutions. Unit Trust of India was one such institution, which had picked up substantial quantities of such stock. However the prices of these shares fell in a number of cases, with the result that UTI lost Rs. 5056 crore on an investment of Rs. 6403 crore made by them. With the commencement of the policy of strategic sale there has been a dramatic reversal. The PSE index has increased steadily since then. The market looks favourably on the transfer of management control of PSEs to a private investor as a means of unlocking the inherent business value of such PSEs. The loss to UTI on its PSU portfolio decreased to Rs. 3673 crore by March 1, 2002. By May 16, 2002 the BSE-PSU index had increased from its level of 932.32 on January 8, 2002 to 1662.82. This should allow UTI to recover its loss even further.

Employee Welfare

A fear is often expressed that the employees would lose if companies were privatised. Recent privatizations have shown that these fears are totally unfounded. Privatized companies have not retrenched a single person. Some of the companies are now in the process of restructuring and would accept some voluntary retirement applications. These companies are giving VRS to the employees, at terms, which are normally better than the Government VRS. Shareholders Agreement with private companies normally have a provision that if there is a need for rationalizing the employee strength, the interests of employees would be protected by ensuring VRS, which is better or equal to the Government VRS. In any case linking rationalisation of the employee strength with disinvestment is not appropriate. This is a measure of business restructuring which is needed and has been implemented extensively over the last decade, even in PSEs when employment declined from 2.18 million in 1991-92 to 1.74 million in 2000-01. Very often additional recruitment also takes place in privatised companies and the wages are increased. Some examples will illustrate that fears of unemployment post privatization or deterioration in the terms of employment are exaggerated.

Wages have increased by an average of Rs. 1600 per month per employee in Modern Food Industries Limited post privatisation. Within a month after privatization, the company had been referred to BIFR. At the time of privatization everyone knew that based on its past performance, Modern Food was fast approaching BIFR. Hindustan Lever is now taking measures to financially restructure the company and bring it out of BIFR, at their own expense. Had Modern Foods remained a PSE, the taxpayer would have paid for financial restructuring of the company without any assurance of improvement in the long-term financial viability of the company.

In BALCO, under public sector management, wages had stagnated and had not been increased since April 1, 1999, even though a revision was due. In spite of a loss of about Rs. 200 crore due to the strike after disinvestment, an ex-gratia payment of Rs. 5,000/- was paid to all employees and a long term wage agreement for a period of five years entered into by the privatized management with the employees on October 7, 2001, which guaranteed a benefit of 20% of basic pay to each employee, besides increase in a number of allowances. These are not isolated incidents and upward wage revisions and rationalizations have been made in the other privatised companies as well.

2002-03 is not an easy year for the Indian economy, constrained as it is by the possibility of lower agricultural production and slow industrial revival. Drought conditions in most areas of the country will necessitate larger public outlays for relief and social welfare. It becomes imperative therefore to improve the productivity of our public sector assets and thus add incremental value to the economy. Privatization meets the dual objective of increasing the availability of resources for Government and of enhancing efficient use of capital. It also presents an opportunity to increase the level of investments by bridging the savings investment gap.

Liberalization of the regulations for Foreign Direct Investment, particularly in the context of privatization, is required not only to integrate India with the global economy but also enhance the level of available resources. The experience of other developing countries, in which economic growth and development has outpaced India over the last three decades, suggests that productivity enhancements usually come in association with a significant increase in private investments, coupled with domestic competition and export orientation. The structural changes in the global economy present unique opportunities for the redeployment of the existing public resources in sectors, which are integral to the exercise of sovereignty. These sectors of the economy are often characterized by market failure and significant positive externalities. It is on these areas that Government must focus its resources and leave the contestable areas of the economy to the domestic and foreign private sector.

Russian energy companies seem to be trapped between the ever changing policy of the government, which shapes an unpredictable business climate, and the cash strapped financial situation. The internal Russian market is characterised by nonpayment, barter deals, and a price increase for energy products which lags behind inflation. Investment can rarely be refinanced, wages are not paid. Thus, the internal market is not only unattractive for Russian energy companies, but even makes survival questionable. In addition, redistribution of assets of the companies is still on the way. A closer look at the Russian energy companies' performance is required to obtain a more differentiated picture. While the recent international discussion of the Russian energy sector focuses mainly on foreign investment, exports, and sectoral restructuring; the present chapter sheds some light on a more general tendency of company restructuring: the emergence of a dual structure in the Russian energy sector which differentiates between globalising companies that are faring relatively well on the one hand, and locally oriented ones that are "muddling through" on the other hand. This leads to our hypothesis that globalisation is at present a feasible strategy of survival. Not all of the Russian companies may be able to cope with this challenge. However, some of them will and are already emerging as real competitors of Western energy companies in several regional markets, mainly European ones.

Increasing Globalisation of Energy Enterprises

The globalisation of energy companies is a world-wide

phenomena and it is worthwhile to analyse the strategies of the Russian companies within this international framework. Globalisation is supported by two main tendencies:

1) Internationalisation focusing more inwardly on current business activities, acquiring resources, and building up new facilities in other places of the world, and

2) Orientation towards outwardly directed internationalisation, focusing on diversification into business fields along the value added chain (refineries, filling stations, power plants, linked services), as well as on diversification into "neighbouring" network led businesses (telecommunication, water supply, disposal of waste water, operation of airports, etc.). For Western energy companies, incentives to globalise result from the following reasons:

   — Stagnation or slowly growing traditional markets where existing market shares and profit margins are coming under competitive pressure.

   — Increasing costs of exploration and production of oil and gas reserves (development and application of new technologies) are faced with declining prices of final energy.

The increasing pressure to increase shareholder value in a globalised capital market, where the aim to achieve a high market capitalisation becomes an incentive for mergers or takeovers. In order to cope with these challenges, companies have to reduce operating and transaction costs, to use remaining economies of scale and scope, and to search for new business fields and entrance into new regional markets where higher profit margins can be achieved or value can be added to the traditional business activities. If prices for primary energy are low and prices for electricity declining, higher profit margins could be achieved only in those segments of the value added chain which are closer to the final clients. The portfolio of resources and down stream assets have to be adjusted and optimised. Enhanced asset management would allow for the selection of the best investment opportunities and for the spreading of business risks. Operating synergies can save production and transportation costs.

Technology overhead should be spread over a wider base and organisational overhead is to be reduced. Deficiencies in know-how are to be overcome in order to open up new businesses or to enter into new regional markets. The institutional form for achieving these goals may vary widely. But this is not necessarily the sole opportunity. Resource deposits or concessions may simply be bought and downstream production and distribution facilities may be started from scratch. In addition to these overall incentives for globalisation for the three main energy subsectors—oil, gas and electricity—there exist some more specific incentives. For the oil sector, due to its high level of integration of the value added chain, security of access to oil resources is of crucial importance. Thus, a diversified portfolio of resources would allow for a more easy switch from economically non efficient resources to the more efficient ones. Access to low cost resources, as well as to future operable resources, is a necessary prerequisite for efficient business in the oil product markets, which grant the profit margins within this sector. However, free capital flow into the world-wide most attractive oil resources, i.e. the Arab countries, is still restricted to a certain extent.

For the power sector, which in the past was a market of strong regional monopolies, liberalisation became a critical issue. Growing competition among the incumbents and also with new entrants especially spurs diversification into new business fields where accumulated know how of managing networks could be used. The gas sector is a late comer as far as liberalisation is concerned. Its internationalisation has been spurred by the other energy sectors—oil and power. The energy industry continues to dominate the Russian economy, but it was unable to provide a positive impetus, as had been hoped in the early phase of transformation. In 1998, the energy industry provided almost a third of industrial production, 59% of industrial investment and more than a third of export revenues. Its contribution to the federal budget is said to be 20%. However, all sectors (oil, gas, electricity, coal) have yet to recover from the collapse of the first post-Soviet years.

Energy production and domestic consumption have plummeted by 27% and 33%, respectively, when compared with the 1988 record levels. The slump of primary energy production was marked in the oil and coal industries, whereas nuclear power and gas production contracted less; hydropower even increased production. The output reduction that followed the end of Soviet socialism was the logical consequence of the new economic conditions. The socialist logic of maximising technically possible output was replaced by increasingly serious economic constraints regarding profits and costs. Declining domestic consumption reflects both the inability of industry and households to maintain consumption at increasing energy prices and, to a smaller extent, more efficient use of energy. But this coherence is undermined by the non-payment problem, which remains acute and which represented in 1998 about 48% of all deliveries for gas and 44% for electricity, the remainder largely paid for in barter (only about 15% of all paid supplies of electricity were paid in cash and 16% of all paid gas supplies).

The situation is aggravated by an increase of the internal market prices for energy resources, which lags behind inflation, and the prices for domestic consumers of gas and electricity remaining state regulated. Administrative regulation also is true for access to export pipelines and is often used by the government to carry out political goals. Under these conditions, it is rational for energy companies to reduce output which can not be diverted to exports. Curiously, primary energy consumption contracted less than aggregate economic output, leading to an increase of the energy intensity of official GDP, which already belonged to the highest in the world. Faced with an unprecedented contraction of domestic demand, it appears logical that Russian energy companies sought to develop solvent markets in non-CIS countries. Exports of crude oil and oil products almost doubled between 1991 and 1998, gas exports increased by 50%.

The abandoning of former centralised state trade organisations facilitated the development of individual export strategies by oil companies, whereas gas exports remain the centralised domain of Gazexport, a subsidiary of Gazprom. Electricity exports are marginal for the time being, but likely to rise in the future. In the oil sector, shrinking production of crude oil is not only due to decline of domestic demand and financial inefficiency of domestic supplies, but since Soviet times a couple of negative factors accumulated which now seem to seriously hamper further development of the sector. 'Raubbau'—an entirely unsustainable reservoir management, over-production of fields in the past, and operation on short-term perspectives (negative ratio of production to exploration drilling)—led to the deterioration of the basis of future development in the oil industry. Even if the ratio improved relatively in 1998, it is still much above, for example, the average level in Great Britain.

Production drilling was about 4.3 mln. meters in 1998 (40% less then in 1997) and exploration drilling was about 0.79 mln. meters (22% less then in the previous year). The number of new wells annually put into operation declined from 4,466 in 1995 to 2,500 in 1998. Extremely high exploration and transportation costs from new fields to the external markets put profitability at risk. The downstream business of the oil sector lacks modern technologies which would allow for production of a sufficient share of light oil products granting higher profit margins. The natural gas sector has suffered somewhat less, but it is not certain whether structural weaknesses can be overcome soon. Production fell as a consequence of sluggish domestic demand and constraints on exports, but also due to the gradual depletion of resources. Though the domestic price structure has been modified substantially since 1995, selling gas to Russian consumers is still by and large unprofitable. Whereas in the first half of 1998, domestic prices were on average 55-60% of export prices, this ratio has fallen to about 30% post-devaluation.

The overall payment discipline has deteriorated. It comes as no surprise, then, that exports to non-CIS-countries, the gross sales price of which is estimated at about USD 70/Mcm, remains the only serious option. However, some doubts also exist on the long-term sustainability of this strategy: the reserve base, though still supposed to be the largest of the world, is shrinking, production outstrips reserve additions since 1996. Most large fields are approaching depletion dates. The large E&T programme that was supposed to reverse this trend, Yamal, was put on hold and is facing an uncertain future.

Electricity consumption fell from 1,056 TWh to 784 TWh. Aggregate overcapacity is said to be 20-30%. The average share of cash-income from electricity supply declined from 20-22% before devaluation to 13-15% after devaluation. Exports, as a possible alternative to these internal cash constraints, are restricted by physical capacity and the grid monopoly of RAO EES Rossii, the mainly state owned holding incorporating almost the whole power sector.

Globalisation Tendencies of some Russian Energy Companies

Since privatisation of the Russian energy sector in 1993, the newly emerging energy companies chose different approaches in order to develop their organisational structure and their business strategy under circumstances of an unstable political and economic environment. Some of them tried to develop independently from state influence, thereby relying only on their own potential, others where bought by Russian banks or Financial Industrial Groups, and a third group remained mainly owned by the Federal or regional governments. Some of them have been highly vertically integrated from the very beginning, others are trying to built up an integrated structure or remain disintegrated. In view of insecure domestic revenues from supply to the Russian market being uncertain (non-payment, cash collection problems, remaining state control on prices, unpredictable tax policy), hard currency earnings from exports are the most reliable basis of cash flow and of foreign credit risk securing for the Russian companies. Declining world market prices for oil, and to a smaller degree for gas, undermined the financial basis of the companies.

On the other hand, the devaluation of the Rouble improved the financial situation allowing cost reductions in foreign currency terms and providing opportunities for exports and certain consolidation of finance for some of the companies. However, this was only the case if the company's debts in foreign currency did not overcompensate this advantage. Thus, companies went nearly or really bankrupt if they had been too closely linked to Russian banks, if credits taken in foreign currency exceed exports paid in foreign currency or if the companies were cash stripped because of the non-payments on the internal Russian market. Concerning their business strategy, the existing energy companies can be divided into two main groups, regardless of the specific conditions within the various sub-sectors (oil, gas and power industry).

The first group can be considered becoming Western style companies oriented towards international markets. These companies focus on a high degree of vertical integration, in principle have a consolidated organisational and ownership structure, and try to develop a more or less consistent business strategy. Except for the power utilities (which have no exports), the companies belonging to this group have a positive ratio of export income compared to foreign credits. They managed to maintain their creditworthiness, to attract further foreign investors, and to raise their share prices almost up to the level before devaluation. Internationalisation is a main focus of the business strategies of the companies of this group. The companies belonging to the second group—in principal the larger number of all energy companies—are still muddling through. Their ownership and organisational structure as well as their business strategy remain unclear. For them, devaluation destroyed even attempts to stabilise. They are challenged by considerable structural changes. These companies are either linked with Financial Industrial Groups or remain state owned at the moment. The latter have less of all others principally adapted to the new framework.

Lukoil is one of the prestigious companies at date executing a consistent development strategy where internationalisation of business activities is ranked highly. The company has about 14 bn bbls of domestic audited proven oil reserves and about 60 bln m^3 domestic proven natural gas reserves. In 1998 output of crude oil was 52.9 mln tones (a 4% increase compared with 1997) or 64.2 mln tones if joint ventures and production abroad are included. About 21.1 mln tones have been exported (25.6 mln tones if including joint ventures exports), which was a 29% increase compared to 1997. Thus, supply to the Russian market declined. Production of natural gas and gasoil was about 3.7 mln tones. Lukoil possesses a refinery capacity of about 470 thousand b/d and produced 19.8 mln tones of oil products in 1998, almost one third of which was exported. The company is mainly privately owned, with 33% owned by foreigners and the state holding still about 26%. The performance of Lukoil has much to do with history and the management of the company. The management came from the oil sector (insider privatisation), is engaged in long-term development of the oil company, and has established a strong vertical control of the financial activities of the company.

Inward strategy

The inward strategy focuses on cost cutting as well as on improvement of the structure of vertical integration and the portfolio of reserves. Although many oil companies of the second group also intend to pursue this type of strategy, Lukoil is more successful because of its better starting positions and a more consequent realisation of its goals. Cost cutting was achieved by abandoning 4,500 low-rated and loss-producing high-cost oil wells in West Siberia, where two thirds of its reserves in Russia are concentrated, by reduction of personal, and transferring social liabilities to local authorities. The modernisation of the downstream refining activities is crucial for the development of the integrated oil companies. Contrary to the upstream raw oil business, refining has been less negatively affected by the economic crisis. This is mainly due to market prices allowing for a certain profit margin and spatial segregation of markets.

Improvements in refining are mainly sought in qualitative terms, i.e. increasing the share of unleaded gasoline and low-sulphur diesel fuel. While the basic conversion ratio is currently 65% in Russia, Lukoil already raised refining depth to around 80% in 1997, thus providing additional quantities for export. As Lukoil's own refinery capacities are not sufficient, the company increases its refining basis by setting up „tolling" agreements with other Russian refineries (i.e. Norsi) and acquiring stakes in refineries located close to attractive retail markets (i.e. Central Fuel Company near Moscow, where the company already has a 36% market share of the retail market). In addition, the company built up a new facility for production of lubricants in the Tyumen region with a capacity of about 45 tsd. tonnes/y. Diversification is planned to be extended (chemicals, synthetic fibres). Retail business in Russia is already well developed. The company has 850 filling stations and covers about 12% of the highly competitive Russian retail sales. It invested more then others in modernisation of retail sites (21% modernised) and plans to build a further 500 new retail sites until 2003. Lukoil is also active in diversification into oil transportation. In order to increase independence from export pipeline capacity constraints the company is building up its own tanker fleet including ice-class tankers to operate the northern transportation route to the arctic region (high priced oil product markets) and a Volga river tanker fleet in order to gain control over the distribution system in the Volga region. It acquired a 20% stake in the Novorossijsk sea terminal on the Black sea and a 50.02 % stake in the Murmansk shipping company which owns 13% of the Russian sea fleet.

Outward strategy

Internationalisation is the other focus of Lukoil's business strategy which has been realised with large efforts at all levels of the value added chain, starting with formation of a more international portfolio of reserves, preferably in low cost regions, up to the retail business. The devaluation gave the company additional room for investing into their strategy of diversification and strengthening international integration. Lukoil focuses on risk diversification by diversifying field access with the acquisition of exploration and production licences abroad (about 2.2 bn bbls in the Caspi region (Azerbaijan and Kasachstan), about 3.4 bn bbls in the West Qurnah field in Iraq and smaller reserves in Tunisia and Egypt) while closing of unprofitable wells in high cost West Siberian fields.

For the exploration and production of the Caspian fields Lukoil set up joint ventures with Western companies: with Arco for the Yalama field in Azerbaijan, with Agip for the Karabach reserves and the Shakh-Deniz field, with Chevron and Mobil for the Tengiz field. British Gas, Agip and Texaco are partners in developing the oil and gas condensate field Karachaganak both located in Kasakhstan. The joint venture with Arco—Lukarco—holds a 12% stake in the Caspian Pipeline Consortium which would give Lukoil the right to export from Kasakhstan. As far as the internationalisation of downstream business is concerned, Lukoil gives first priority to the Central and East European countries which are expected to yield greater oil demand growth during the next years than the mature economies of Western Europe. In 1998 these countries have increased shipments through the Druzhba pipeline by 9% to over 1 mln barrels a day. With its activities the company intends to secure its crude supply as well as to expand its position in the more profitable levels of the value added chain in these markets. Lukoil's activities in the refinery sector have been mainly directed to:

— *Romania*—It acquired a 51% stake of the Romanian Petrotel refinery.

— *Bulgaria*—It bids in the privatisation auction for the Bulgarian retail company Petrol AD, which owns 456 filling station in Bulgaria.

— *Ukraine*—It controls a considerable share of the Ukrainian refinery business by means of daughter companies. Luk-Sintez acquired a controlling interest of the Odessa refinery and signed agreements of partnership, among others with one of the most important wholesale companies for oil products in Ukraine— "RUNO". In Krimea, a Lukoil subsidiary supplies crude oil to the Cherson refinery and owns several · modern filling stations.

— *Greece*—Lukoil signed an agreement on building up joint ventures in both up and downstream business with the Greek Hellenic Petroleum, which owns two refineries and 1.100 filling stations in Greece.

— *Croatia*—It has formed a strategic partnership with the Croatian INA company which might lead to the use of the Adria-pipeline for exports of Lukoils crude oil.

Furthermore, Lukoil now owns filling stations and oil storage facilities in Estonia and Lithuania and has retail networks in Romania, Bulgaria, Ukraine, Moldova, Yugoslavia and Turkey. Poland is the next priority. Some of the stations are operated by daughter companies. At present, the retail sites which Lukoil owns in association with a supermarket chain in California seem do be more important for image making and learning about retail marketing in Western countries then for profits. However, in 1998 the company acquired a 50% stake of the US company Neksus Fuel, which constructs and operates filling stations on the property of supermarket chains. The company's creditworthiness did not suffer significantly from the financial crisis in Russia. The eight year loan worth USD 77.3 million handed over by the EBRD in January 1999 to develop the first stage of the Azeri, Chirag and Gynneshli deep water area as well as the USD 150 million three year loan of the Sberbank, which is planned to be used for programmes for the increase of extraction and refining volumes, provide evidence for that. In June 1999 Lukoil made an four year emission of bonds worth 3 bn Roubles.

Of course, the need to internationalise spurred by the non-profitable and low demand Russian internal market is obvious for all of the Russian oil companies, but only those belonging to the first group are achieving success at present. Most of the companies of the second group even did not aim to internationalise. The main reasons for failure and non-awareness are the following: the management of the companies from the second group mainly comes from the Russian financial sector. This, in general, must not be a negative factor of management. The problem for the Russian companies concerned is that the Russian banks which became owner of oil companies via the shares-for-loan deal of the Russian government in 1995 accumulated a huge portfolio of Russian enterprises from very different industrial sectors, the oil companies among them. The banks used the obtained oil companies as cash cows until late 1997. Logic had not dictated the structure of assets which had been acquired at presumably low prices. Many of the combinations failed to maximise logistical synergies. Falling oil prices and the financial collapse of the private Russian banks lead to some rethinking of the banks behaviour concerning the management of the oil companies.

Since the sources of quick money from trading state securities have ended and the market of blue-chips is down, the only source of profit seems to remain the restructuring of the real sector. Thus, at present the banks try to restructure their oil assets. But asset stripping is also still usual, because ownership structures are still questioned. The Rouble devaluation created severe negative impacts for most of these companies as the foreign credit burden was much higher then for Lukoil and Surgutneftegaz compared to their output and export performance.

Especially the Tyumen Oil company and Sibneft have severe liquidity problems. Sidanco has been sued for bankruptcy. The unification of the state owned companies into a national oil company has been debated, whereas the economy of such company and the amount of necessary subventions remain unclear. The companies of the second group are busy with organisational restructuring, which includes strengthening ownership via conversion of holding companies into vertically integrated companies; This is the case with Yukos, Eastern Oil (both managed by the former chief of the liquidated Menatep Bank), Sibneft and Sidanco especially or via consolidation of state ownership. In order to achieve this goal bankruptcy is also often considered efficient.

The flexible spider: Gazprom's diversification and internationalisation Corporate strategies in the gas sector are somewhat easier to identify, due to the monopolistic organisation of the sector. Over 90% of Russian production is covered by Gazprom, the remainder coming from a number of smaller producers, collected by Sibur. According to Gazprom estimates, gas production has not yet hit bottom: a further reduction of the company's output to 543 Bcm and 529 Bcm is expected. In structural terms, Gazprom remains the vertically and horizontally integrated colossus of Russian gas, playing a dominant role in Russian domestic and foreign economics and politics; it is also the largest individual business employer. The conservative approach of maintaining post-Soviet enterprise structures within the gas sector is in sharp contrast to the innovative and proactive strategy of business diversification of downstream activity that Gazprom is pursuing both in Russia and abroad. Diversification is sought in five directions:

— Development of an external resource base, mainly in the Arab Gulf region: For example, Gazprom is a major partner of the National Iranian Oil Company (NIOC) in the development of the gas resources in South Pars;

— Gas-related activities, such as equipment, where Gazprom has been actively acquiring stakes or entire companies not only in Russia but also in Central Europe. Downstream diversification includes petrochemistry, such as the chemical complex in Novi Urengoi;

— Energy-related activities: oil and electricity. With a production of about 10 mn t of condensates, Gazprom is already a considerable oil producer. The oil-only projects at Prirazlomnoye and Astrakhan could make it a 'real' oil producer. Other oil/gas projects, such as Timan-Pechora, might be implemented in the long run. In 1999, Gazprom took the leading role in a petrochemical holding structure, with activities ranging from condensate processing, petrochemistry, and retail business of fuel and gas. Gazprom has also expressed an interest in the power market, as a natural outlet for its gas. It has taken over the Pskov power plant at the Rusisan-Latvian boarder (swap of debt for 72% equity of the company) and is engaging in projects in the Central and Western European markets as well.

— Other industrial activities add to the diversification and internationalisation, e.g. telecommunication, where Gazprom is setting up a country-wide network. Minor activities include agriculture and tourism;

— Finance and banking are the necessary activities of any post-Soviet company facing underdeveloped financial markets. Gazprom holds considerable shares of various well known and important Russian banks like Inkombank, Bank Imperial, PromstroiBank and owns the GazpromBank. The latter is one of the five biggest Russian banks and has subsidiaries in 24 regions.

The most spectacular case of internationalisation is the gas trading business, where Gazprom has developed an extensive network of joint-venture companies all over Europe. The recent opening of the Interconnector between the United Kingdom and Western Europe, in which Gazprom has a stake, means that the company is now able to compete on all European gas market segments itself. The financial markets clearly honor Gazprom's strategy. Even though the company posted an offical 1998 loss of RUR 42 bn (equivalent to USD 1.5 bn), it is one of the most worthy Russian companies with regards to foreign curreny credits.

The Russian power industry has, by its very nature, less incentives and possibilities to internationalise, but has nonetheless undertaken some steps in this direction. A clear sign of this is the search for new markets and/or business in different market segments, the most important one being electricity exports to non-CIS countries. The devaluation of the Russian Rouble has provided a significant advantage for the lowest cost producers, i.e. nuclear power plants: due to the high contents of domestically produced goods and services, average costs fell from about 2 UScents/kWh to slightly above 1 UScents/kWh (this is comparable to an estimated 2 UScents/kWh in the Slovak nuclear power plant of Mochovce). The Russian joint stock company EES Rossii owns the grid, the majority of regional energy supply companies (energos) and more then 35 huge generating utilities, mostly fossil fuel fired. The main export capabilities result from relatively cheap nuclear power energy and are organised within a separate state owned company (Rosenergoatom) and from hydropower. RAO EES is trying to valorise this cost advantage by pushing additional export routes towards Central and Western Europe, in addition to the existing connection between Russia and Finland. Two projects of linking the Russian UPS grid with the Central/Western European CENTREL-UCPTE grid are in the pipeline: i) the 'Baltic Ring' connection between Russia, Lithuania, Kalinningrad and Poland, and ii) the 'Power Bridge' linking the Russian and Ukrainian grids with Western Poland or Hungary. Both programmes would be DC-connections, allowing electricity exchanges in both directions without synchronising the two grids. In a first step, Russia could export about 5 TWh, but capacity could be increased easily once the basic infrastructure is in place. Other export strategies are pursued from regional energos in Siberia with large capacities in hydropower. These are either fully independent or only partially controlled by EES Rossii. The latter gives access to the grid only on a voluntarily basis. Since the cash problems worsened seriously, there are much stronger attempts of EES Rossii to open up for cooperation with foreign partners.

One other field of internationalisation is the nuclear industry. This includes mainly state-owned companies handling all aspects of the nuclear cycle. Co-operation with Western European and U.S. American companies is intensifying. Joint projects have been launched in the engineering of new generation high-pressure nuclear power plants, the treatment of used nuclear fuels (both military and civil), and the stocking of the latter (in Russia). The Western interest in this highly strategic sector is not only economic; one aim is also to increase insight into Russian technology and institutions of the nuclear sector.

Long-term Consequences for the Russian Energy Markets

Russian companies have to compete for international capital with the companies of all other regions of the World with regard to attractiveness of resources and costs and investment conditions. To a certain extent this depends on the general political and economic framework of the country, but to a large extend also on the management culture and openness of the company.

The climate for foreign investors is unfriendly: after several years of debates, in February 1999 the list of fields to be developed under the Production Sharing Agreement was adopted by the Duma, taxation regimes for joint ventures remain unstable, and access to export pipelines has to be negotiated every time. This led to the withdrawal of several foreign firms from joint ventures with Russian companies. However, not all cooperations with Western partners failed. In contrast, the following examples show that the globalising companies are more successful in international partnering then the others. Amongst the most successful joint ventures are those of Lukoil which increased their output since 1996 about 27% and 17% respectively. Another example is Gazprom developing Northern oil and gas fields with Western strategic partners. International co-operation and business activities in international markets create spin-offs in the form of learning effects which should not be underestimated.

The majority of these learning effects are related to business skills concerning marketing where huge deficits of know how in Russian companies have been discovered, but which is of special importance in highly competitive markets like the energy market. Building up brand names combined with high quality of products and services is together with reliability and trust one of the crucial issues. Learning effects are also related to company organisation, organisation of financial flows and relationship to market partners, be that clients or foreign banks or the shareholders. Thus, business experience in foreign markets helps to understand and imitate the comprehensive functioning of competitive markets. Companies acquiring this knowledge will have considerable advantage over their competitors. Both Gazprom and Lukoil are the Russian leaders in that field.

The development of share prices on the Russian stock exchange does not yet fully reflect the 'real' transformation process of the energy companies. This is due to a lack of market transparency, the low liquidity of the stock market, uncertainty about the economics of the reserve figures, and the general economic and institutional instability prevailing in Russia. However, the globalisation of Russian companies also comprises some integration into international financial markets and analysis, thus raising transparency and reliability of the financial indicators. Since the August 1998 crash, the energy industry has fared better than average: the Russian APS Oil-and-Gas Index, that had been around 400 in late 1997, had fallen to an all-time-low of 60 in October 1998, but has somewhat recovered to reach about 350 in July 1999.

A striking difference appears between the recovery of the share prices of the restructuring companies engaging in globalization and consolidation versus those that are only muddling through. Thus, the two oil companies that are succeeding in their restructuring, Lukoil and Surgut, have already reached 9% and 98%, respectively, of their last-years heights. The recovery of other group I-companies, e.g. Gazprom or RAO EES was somewhat less marked, yet they are faring above the average. On the other hand, companies that are 'muddling through' without a clear strategy, are still struggling to re-establish their share value.

The analysis of the behaviour of globalising Russian companies showed that the incentives differ only little from those forcing Western energy companies to globalise. It is mainly the distortion of the internal Russian market instead of the slowly growth of the world market which drives the Russian companies. The pressure on shareholder value has not yet reached the importance as in the West, but plays an increasing role for the Russian 'globalisers'. The characteristics of the strategies to meet th challenges—cost reductions, improvement of vertical integration, and diversification on an international basis—are the same both for the Russian and the Western companies. Thus, those Russian companies which decided to globalise will in tendency become market driven companies like their Western counterparts. The success of the globalising Russian energy companies has some impact on international competition, first of all in Eastern Europe and Russia. When the period of instability of the Russian economic policy comes to an end, the Russian energy market, too, may become more attractive also for foreign investment once again.

Capital is needed for the exploration and development of new oil and gas fields as well as for rehabilitation and modernisation of power plants and energy transportation systems. The wholesale and retail market may as well become attractive if at least prices would no longer be state regulated and the economy would recover. At this time, accumulated know how and improved finances resulting from internationalisation will have prepared the Russian potential global players for the battle over the Russian market. The challenge to adjustment during a deep recession and the experience in highly competitive international markets will force them to much more rapidly run through a process of company innovation then their Western competitors.

Global Russian energy companies would have the best chances, since they would by then have transformed into powerful and belligerent partners and competitors for their Western counterparts. Thus, globalisation of company performance, which could be characterised as learning by a detour outside Russia— would than have a positive impact on the Russian market itself. As far as the Russian energy companies of the second group are concerned there are different scenarios possible.

— In an optimistic scenario, one or two of them might be able to catch up and join the group of the global players. The other will remain of regional importance or become part of the globalised companies.

— In a pessimistic scenario, they will continue to muddle through and lose their economic potential. A re-integration into state companies might be possible, but could hardly be successful because of huge capital needs and empty state budgets on the Federal and regional levels.

— In a potentially realistic scenario, Western energy companies, envisaging the increasing competition with Russian globalising companies on the Russian market, will find it the most successful way to buy a controlling stake of some of the companies of the second group in order to get access to the Russian energy market both in upstream and downstream businesses.

3

Globalisation on Economy and Employment

Globalisation is occurring in a specific situation and conditioned by the existing class relations in the world economy and the different stage of development of countries. It is developing in the interests of international monopoly capital. It is imperialist globalisation. It is based on the principles of Bretton Wood twins -the IMF & WB the WTO controlled by the MNCs of G-7 countries. The decisions in these institutions are taken in favour of these developed nations at the cost of developing ones.

Nearly half the voting power in the WB & IMF rests in the hands of 7 countries. Though all the countries have a scat and vote in WTO, in practice decisions were taken in small groups heavily influenced by Canada, EU, Japan and the US in 2000; 15 African Nations did not have a single trade representative stationed in WTO. The global economy, is rapidly entering a phase where corporate rule is eroding the ability of nation states to regulate capital. The emergence of international finance capital has come to dominate the economy of many countries. In this background, the Structural Adjustment Programme of the Bretton Wood twins followed by India also, consists essentially of the following:

— Radically reducing government spending, 'in order to control inflation and reduce the demand for capital inflows from abroad, a measure that in practice translates into cutting spending in health, education and welfare;

— Cutting wages or severally constraining their rise to reduce inflation and make exports more competitive; liberalizing imports to make local industry more efficient and instituting incentives for producing for export markets, which are seen both as a source of much-needed foreign exchange and as far more dynamic source of growth than the domestic market.

— Removing restrictions on foreign investment in industry- and financial services "to make the local production more-efficient, due LO the presence of foreign competition

— Devaluing the local Currency relative to hard currencies like the dollar in order to make exports more competitive;

— Privatising state enterprises and embarking on radical deregulation in order to promote allocation of resources by the market instead of government decree; another aspect that the assets of state enterprises far exceed the capacity of the capital markets of third world countries. When asset-rich enterprises are suddenly off-loaded into such a market, there is no way preventing foreign capital or its local front organisations from taking over state enterprises; and

— Radical changes in all the legislations that govern economic laws, such as those relating to banking, power, telecommunications insurance etc."

Over ten years of free play of market forces has steered the country's economy in the reverse gear and the economy is presently in a crisis. The GDP growth rate, which was around 7.6 percent before globalisation, had nose-dived to 4.0 percent in 2000-01. According to the Economic Survey 2001-02, the GDP is expected to go upto 5.4 percent in 2001-02, though this optimism is not shared by many including the IMF. Fiscal deficit for 2000-01 is estimated by the Economic Survey to be at 5.5 percent for 2000-01 and 5.1 percent for 2001-02, as against 4.7 percent envisaged in the Union Budget. But according to the latest Macroeconomic and Monetary Development Report of the Reserve Bank of India, the fiscal deficit is estimated a, 5.7 percent of GDP. The revenue deficit is also reported to have exceeded the budgeted level by 16.4 percent. The revenue receipts in 2001-02 were lower by 8.3 percent than the budget estimate.

According to the RBI report, tax revenue in 2001-02 was down by 12.7 percent. In addition, there is already the outstanding of Rs.62,392 crore against -lie corporate houses as on March 31, 2001 on account of Income 'lax, Corporate Tax, Customs Duty and Excise Duty. The very same corporate houses are guilty of not repaying the loans and the interest thereon, amounting to Rs.1,25,000 crore, to the public sector banks. Foreign direct investments, that are wooed without restraint, have only resulted in takeovers and mergers rather than in new productive ventures. The country's industry as such is being restructured by powerful multinationals as to increase the extent of concentration.

Impact of the present form of globalisation on employment is devastating. "The 0.98 percent annual growth rate of employment during the years 1993-94 to 1999-2000 was lower then the annual growth rate of labour force of 1.03 percent, leaving a backlog of 0.5 percent every year. Yet the Economic Survey claims that employment grew by 1.0 percent during 1993-94 to 1999-2000. The employment growth rate in the organised sector during the past two years has alarmingly taken to a negative turn. It was -0.9 percent in 1999 and 0.17 percent in 2000.

The growth rate in the private sector in 2000 was, however, 0.97 percent as against the nagative growth of -0.68 percent in the public sector, says the Economic Survey and concludes that the growth in organised sector employment is now dependent on employment growth in the private sector. The survey has preferred to be silent about the policy thrust on dismantling the public sector, large scale downsizing of the work force through VRS and ban on recruitment. With the present policy thrust on rationalising labour in the name of rightsizing to generate more job losses, the problem of unemployment has since grown to alarming proportions.

The spectre of unemployment, according to an estimate, is coming large over nearly 10 crore people. Incidence of unemployment in age group of 15-29 years in 1999-2000 was 5.4 percent. The unemployment growth has reported to have been 9.2 percent sometime back and the rate should have gone further up by now. About 41 million job seekers in the country though all of them may not necessarily be unemployed, are registered with the Employment Exchanges all over the country and 72 percent of the registered job seekers are less than 30 years of age 69 percent of the Job seekers are educated upto the tenth standard and above. According to official figures, the expected annual addition to the labour force in India is about 8.7 million per over the next 10 years. It is, therefore imperative to accelerate GDP growth to a range between 8%, to 9% to achieve the objective of generating enough additional to provide Productive employment opportunities besides to improve the quality of employment.

The Government of India under the New Economic Policy opened up the path of

— Downsizing (many do this in the name of 'Right Sizing')

— Lean Model production and

— Capital-intensive industrial production

— Unfettered right royal way for the implementation of "Exit Policy".

The result is:

— Over 4 lakh jobs have been lost in the Central Public Sector enterprises alone during the last few years strength down from 2.3 million to 1.7 million). In similar proportion job losses have taken place in the numerous state public sector enterprises also.

— With or without the so-called voluntary retirement / separation schemes, considerable amount of employment losses have taken place in the private corporate sector, both Indian & foreign.

— Over a lakh and twenty thousand have opted out for VRS in (Nationalised) Banking sector lone.

— Even in the sunrise industry viz IT sector thousands of jobs have been frozen on account of the recessionary trend in the western world, particularly USA.

A major industrial restructuring on account of the emergence of capital Intensive industrial growth gave substantially greater room to the industries to carry on their activities as they wished. This changed the entire policy orientation of the pre- 1980s era as the welfare state opted for a market-oriented economy. Liberalised entry of TNCs and the unfettered freedom for big indigenous business groups have jeopardised the interests of the workers adversely affecting the employment opportunities.

The companies have developed various strategies such as transfer of jobs from bargainable / unionised, to non-bargainable / non-unionised categories, off loading of jobs, subcontracting, starting parallel production in unorganised sectors, extensive use of contract labour, productivity coupled with horizontal vertical flexibility, compelling upon acceptance of various management demands", various shop floor level restructuring techniques including multi-trade jobs, siphoning of 'unviable' departments etc.

The virus of VRS is spreading fast. It is infecting many industries in different sectors, spread over the entire country. Some of the major companies resorted to downsizing included Air India, Hindustan Organic Chemicals, Reliance Industries Ltd. (Textile Business), Mumbai Port Trust, Bombay Stock Exchange, ITI, VSNL, HMT, Hindustan Motors, Yamaha Motor India Ltd.. Crompton Greaves, Bajaj Auto, Tata Tea, Glaxo India, Mico, HLL owned Modern Food Industries Ltd., Shipping Corporation of India, SAIL, BHEL, etc.

The Governments plan, policy and the actions should be on following basis:

— "A measure of delinking from the forces of global capitalism and of- linking with the emerging allies in the process of development in the `sub-continent, in the South and globally. State must retain strategic control and direction of the economy, not to act at the dictates of IMF, World Bank, WTO.

— Employment generation should be the single most important criteria for investment policy, although profits and technological updating to be given due weightage.

— Fulfillment of a constitutional obligation ensuring 'Right to Work' should be the overriding function of economic planning.

— Land Reforms as an indispensable instrument for promoting distributive justice, for the employment of the poor and enhancing agricultural productivity.

— Rising of the domestic savings and generation of domestic resources for investment. Foreign investment could be used as a supplement provided 'it goes where we want and not where it wants to go'.

— Public sector reform must be on making it more truly public and efficient, not on unthinking privatisation; liberalisation of public sector from the shackles of excessive bureaucratization and providing functional as well as decision making autonomy to PSEs.

— Investment in social sectors, health, social security & education.

— Fruits of economic development to be shared by all regions & sub-regions.

— Reject corporate and multinational driven technology growth and promote indigenous need based technology growth related to Indian needs and resources endowments;

— South should fight jointly against erosion of national sovereignty, against the conditionalities under TRIMs and TRIPs of WTO.

— A corrupt free governance and transparency in all dealings.

Charter of Social Justice for the sweated wage ordinance is firmly drawn up in part IV of the Indian Constitution. It was the intention of the founding fathers of the constitution that Indian social order must be founded on un-exploitative, just, equitable and ethical basis, that inequality in status and opportunity ram-pant in our society is reduced if not totally eliminated. Article 41 requires that the state should, within the limits of its economic capacity and development, make effective provisions for securing right to work, to education and public assistance in case of unemployment, old age, sickness, disablement, and in other cases of underserved want. Article 43 requires that the "state shall endeavour to secure all workers work, a living wage, conditions of work ensuring a decent standard of life and full employment, of leisure and social and cultural opportunities etc.

Social justice is said to be the signature tune of the Indian Constitution. However, in spite of the constitutional guarantees, ILO conventions and other recommendations since the first National Labour Commission in 1969 onwards, nothing much could be done either to provide a safety net to the deserved or to carry on other social responsibilities. Now the country is in the process of implementing the second generation of reforms, much to the disadvantage of the working people.

Growth with equity as the social objective can only succeed in the long run and that shall be the objective of any planning process. In that objective process safety net, skill development, decent work, minimum free education etc. should found their priority. Just forty countries have signed the fundamental ILO convention No. 102 on Social Security (minimum standards) adopted in 1952. The convention includes the following:

— Medical Care
— Sickness benefit
— Old age payments
— Benefit in the event of occupational accidents and diseases
— Family benefit
— Maternity benefit Invalidity benefit Survivors benefit

India had not signed this ILO Convention. In India, the expected annual addition to the labour force is about 8.7 million per year over the next ten years.But the prevalent situation is that the existing jobs are getting lost. [For example: about 4 lakhs of jobs have been lost in the Central Public Sector enterprises alone during the last Jew years. In similar proportion, the job loses have taken place in the numerous state owned public sector enterprises. With or without voluntary separation schemes, considerable amount of employments have been given up in the established private sector enterprises. Over a lakh and twenty thousand jobs are finished In the Banking sector, as the vacancies caused on account of VRS are not to be filled.

Due to the compulsions of 'downsizing' 'lean model production' and the fast emergence of "Capital intensive industrial development' - all part of the structural adjustment programme, an 'Exit Policy prevails without any appreciable 'Entry Policy'. The first protection against unemployment is a solid policy towards full employment, consisting of macro economic policies at the national and international levels, sectoral, regional and local policies and labour market and training policies. Knowing that the full-employment policies are either not in the thinking or take time to come to fruition, there is an imperative need for specific unemployment protection policies.

The Guiding Principles of Income Security is enunciated in Recommendation No. 67 of the ILO. National Labour Law Association, recommended in 1994 a Wage Guarantee Fund as follows: "In the event of failure of the employers to pay the wages and other statutory dues of their employees due to permanent closure of their establishment or their insolvency the same shall be paid from the Social Security Fund. After payment of the dues the claims of the employers will stand transferred to the fund so that the Fund will be entitled to the collection of the amounts from the employers or the successors as the case may be. It also says that till an integrated social security system is set up it might be necessary to establish a separate Wage Guarantee Fund by collecting contributions for the purpose and the fund might be administered by the ESIC. The rate of contribution may be fixed on ad-hoc basis to begin with at say 0.50 percent of wages and adjusted subsequently on the basis of an actuarial study. The Fund should have wide coverage pooling good and bad risks with no or few exceptions.

In 1969, the National Commission on Labour expressed in favour of adopting a scheme of unemployment insurance. The commission reiterated their recommendation regarding unemployment insurance in dealing with the question of integration of social security schemes: "We believe that it should be possible over the next few years to evolve an integrated social security scheme, which with some marginal addition to the current rate of contribution take care of certain risks riot covered at present. In saying this we are limiting ourselves the benefits of

— provident fund and retirement / family pension and

— insurance against unemployment. In the second case, the insurance will cover only those who were employed and have to face the risk of unemployment."

The Task Force of the Planning Commission had thought of the Unemployment Insurance in the following manner. "A move to a system of unemployment insurance in the organised sector is in our view a desirable institutional development which should be expedited. The scheme should be based on compulsory deduction of contributions from wages, with a corresponding contribution from the employer. Employee's retrenched or otherwise becoming unemployed should become eligible to receive support at a fraction of the wages drawn at the point of unemployment. It would require statutory authority to introduce and would have to be regulated by the Government or some other suitable statutory agency. The feasibility of introducing such a scheme in the organised sector should be expeditiously examined."

The 'generous' unemployment protection systems are found in Australia, Belgium, Denmark, Finland, France, Germany, Iceland, Luxemburg, Netherlands, Norway, Portugal, Spain, Sweden and Switzerland. These countries are characterised by the high level and long duration of their unemployment insurance benefit payments, by extensive unemployment insurance coverage, and by an additional layer of employment protection legislation aiming at greater employment security. The strictness of employment protection system is measured by an OECD index covering different aspects of labour legislation, such as statutory notice periods, procedural inconveniences, the level of severance pay and rules governing unfair dismissal.

In countries with high level systems, unemployment protection consists of various layers of benefits. Unemployment insurance benefits -he first and most important layer, are paid during an initial period of unemployment. With average net replacement rates of more than 60 percent of national average earnings, the level of unemployment benefits in the high-level type. In addition, most high level systems have a second layer of unemployment insurance, usually called unemployment assistance. These schemes cover unemployment workers who have exhausted their entitlement to unemployment insurance benefits and prevent them m from falling directiy into the less generous social assistance schemes.

Canada's unemployment insurance reform, introduced in July 1996 aims to transform the previous old unemployment programme radically by strengthening the link between contribution and benefits. The, objectives of the new policy are three fold

— reduce the cost of providing cash benefits, part of which is to be invested in services to promote re-employment

— lesser dependency and work disincentivesness and

— increase coverage among part time employees.

Many proposals for an unemployment insurance scheme have been announced by the Government, employers and others but they fall short of requirements of the workers during the period of unemployment. Following proposal is suggested after study of Unemployment Insurance Schemes in developing countries.

i) Coverage

— All workers employed in industrial or other establishments having twenty or more employees on their roll.

— Wage / Salary limit should be Rs. 10,000/ - per month.

— The workers must have atleast one year of continuous service out of which they should have made contributions for 6 months.

— Workers who are unemployed due to following reasons shall be excluded from the provisions of the Scheme.

a. Voluntary retirement or resignation.
b. Retirement at age of superannuation.
c. Disabled or invalid workers drawing disability pensions.
d. Lay-off for which compensation is payable
e. Dismissal or discharge from service as a result of disciplinary action for misconduct

ii) Financing

The Scheme shall be financed through contributions by

— Workers : 0.5 percent of wages

— Employers : 1.5 percent of pay roll

— Government : Central or State Governments to meet any deficit on an annual basis.

— For building the initial corpus some of the suggestions made in brainstorming session of Confederation Indian Industry are worth considering. These are:

  a. 10 percent of disinvestment monies.

  b. 10 percent of the net proceeds from sale of land locked up in closed Units

  c. 1 percent of the financial assistance from international financial institutions and other development grants received by the government for restructuring the economy / sectors enterprises.

  d. National Renewal Fund.

iii) Benefits

After a waiting period of seven days an unemployed worker shall be paid:

— 75% of wages for the first 6 months.

— 50 % of wages for the next 6 months.

For implementing the Unemployment Benefit Scheme, it should be entrusted to the Employees Provident Fund Organisation which has 260 Regional / Sub regional / Sub Accounts / Inspectorate offices throughout the country. More such offices can be opened. Moreover the organisation is already building up online service for its subscribers using latest information technology, as per decision of the Central Board of Trustees. Apart from the Unemployment Insurance Scheme, it is suggested that the Central Government / State Governments should draw up and implement Self Employment Schemes on the pattern of Schemes already being implemented by State Government of Maharashtra, Kerala and West Bengal.

The existing schemes and programmes, as admitted by the Government in the SLC/1LC, cover, to the extent beneficial, only one crore workers and not the 37 crore workers employed in the unoganised sector. Within the unorganised sector about 60% are employed in agricultural sector. Home-based workers constitute one of the major segments of the workforce in the unorganised sector. Building & Construction workers is yet another big chunk amongst the unorganised. Barring a few state Governments like Kerala, Tamilnadu, the other states have not even come forward to implement the Construction Workers Act, enacted in 1996.

Inter-state Migrant workers constitute yet another large number amongst the unorganised, who have no security either employment or wage and the relevant Act does not touch the fringe of the issues concerning safety net for them. There are of course, large number of seasonal workers, living below or marginally above poverty level. Almost all of them are unable to contribute or share the cost of any social security scheme, as they have literally no savings.

Scheme like the Krishi Shramik Samajik Suraksha Yojana 2001 supposed to be covering about 10 lakh agricultural workers is just a drop in the ocean. While extending the existing social security net such as EPF, Unemployment Insurance, Health Care, Pension etc. to the unorganised the outlook should be totally different. State cannot just remain a 'facilitator or a regulator" alone. There must be an integrated approach to bring a comprehensive social net, supported by the Government.

Like most European countries, India also has an aging population. At the movement, around 77 million people in India are over 60 years of age. The number will reach 179 million by 2026. More than 65% of women above 60 years are widows. Of those above 60 years, 40% are below poverty line (BPL) and 25% illiterate. The number of people aged 60 and over is rapidly increasing throughout the world in a 'demographic revolution' that could lead to widespread poverty and social exclusion among the elderly.

The Department of Disinvestment had in a document presented to Parliament in November 2000 given the following as the rationale privatisation:

a) "Realising, huge amount of scarce public resources locked up in non-strategic PSEs for deployment in areas much higher on social priority such as public health, family welfare, education and social and essential infrastructure."

   Reality: During the decade since disinvestment started the Government of India collected about Rs 18, 393 crores by selling equity in blue chip PSEs. Almost a trickle had been used for reducing either the internal or external debt; almost nothing had gone augmenting the existing assets by way of revival of such PSEs or modernization of profitable PSEs. Most of the money had gone to meet the revenue deficit on the spacious argument that finances of the Government are fungible. Oil fields Mukta and Panna of Power Purchase Agreement with Enron are just examples to illustrate the kind of privatisation that is taking and to what social priorities they have gone to.

b) "Stemming further outflow of these scarce public resources for sustaining the unviable non strategic PSEs".

Reality: Most of the 'unviable non strategic PSEs were those belonged to the private sector and British MNCs, which were driven to sickness by a combination of loot and mismanagement. Infect, the most profitable ones are being bold / sought to be sold.

c) "Reducing public debt that is threatening to assume unmanageable properties,"

Reality: The fact is that the fiscal deficit had increased as a result of the sale of the equity, because the equity of the most profitable enterprises was sold as a result of which the dividend foregone is more than - lie interest on capital accrued by the sale. For example, between 1992 to 1997, against returns foregone because of the sale of equity in the market (computed on profit after tax) of Rs. 1,78,391 crore, interest saved as a result of transfer of disinvestment proceed was Rs.94,643 crores. The difference of Rs.83748 crores is the extent to which the fiscal deficit had gone up during the years 1992-97 as a consequence of disinvestment. Other similar reasons advanced or rationale shown by the Disinvestment Ministry are dishonest and figment of imagination and deserve to be dismissed with utter contempt.

"National Agenda for Governance" (NAG) released by the ruiing coalition before the last election stated that the 'Government will also expedite comprehensive reforms of PSUs including re-structuring, rehabilitation and disinvestment". But this had not happened. On 19th December 1996, Mr. Murasoli Maran, the then industries minister speaking on disinvestment stated in parliament "We are not doing privatisation. Not changing the ownership at all give you guarantee only a limited exercise in selected PSUs for raising resources." These "guarantees' of the present Commerce Minister have gone with the wind. He was hoodwinking the parliament. He or the Government did not have the political courage to admit that disinvestment is an act of privatisation.

The earlier Disinvestment Commission dealt with 58 PSEs referred to it and gave its decision. In its various reports, the commission

(i) equated control of an enterprise with ownership: 51% of the equity (ignoring that most of the Indian private sector are politically owned but privately managed because of "owners- had an insignificant amount of equity and most of the equity was held by the or the public)

(ii) felt that the ownership of 26% of the equity by the Government provided sufficient leverage to the public interest

(iii) perpetuated the myth that between 51% equity ownership by the and 49% equity lies the difference between being a bonded slave- and being "free", thus a 2% difference in equity would liberate the PSU from the "horrors" of (a) the Government and parliarnentary, (b) accountability to the public audit and vigilance and would a degree of autonomy which alone can enable PSU to become efficient and accountable to the consumer and the market.

(iv) told us to believe that "strategic partnership", "appropriate role in management" are value neutral and simply nothing more than addition of few private individuals as Directors of Boards of PSUs.

(v) made no distinction between Indian and foreign strategic partner,

(vi) committed to the view that the MNCs and their front agencies would not, in due course, corner shares and take over the effective control of profitable blue chip PSUs, particularly those which are public monopolies.

(vii) expected the nation to believe that it is irrelevant whether the public sector or the multinationals occupy the commanding heights" of the economy, and thus rejected the concept of self reliance as an archaic ideology."

Strategic disinvestment presently advanced and perused by the Government is essentially opposed to the Directive Principles of the state policy, under the Constitution of India and it-, obligations on the state. It is an executive decision in the absence o. any law. PSUs are State under Art 12 of the constitution, being instrumentality of the state. Depriving the fundamental right of the workers by an executive order is illegal. The social goals enshrined in the constitution should not be sacrificed.

A new Disinvestment Commission has been constituted by the Government. Earlier Rangarajan Committee recommended 75% of the PSUs shares for disinvestment. Thereafter the Government has decided to go for strategic disinvestment, which is far more than earlier disinvestment proposals. It is virtually privatisation. The Cabinet Committee on Disinvestment had earlier approved disinvestment of 27 PSUs and atleast 13 of them at a fast track within 31st March 2002.

According to the Disinvestment ministry spokesman, the 6 months were hectic and a 3-tier system is working vigorously. Every other day fresh names of CPSUs are added to the list of disinvestment, endorsed by the Cabinet Committee. In the whole process, as admitted by the Disinvestment ministry spokesman in a seminar conducted by the National Labour Law Association in Delhi on the 28-29, September 2001, there is no consultation with the Trade Unions / workers who would be affected and no normal mechanism is expected to be available for this purpose.

Every disinvestment is a private appropriation of public property. We have witnessed in the case of BALCO and Modern Foods, that disinvestment of profit making public sector enterprise is the mother of all scams, allowing cherry picking by the interested private parties. Appropriation of state capital by a bunch of parasites of looters, totally using fraudulent agreements/ arrangements is allowed to take place in the name of strategic disinvestment'. The Minister for Disinvestment is very active in the job assigned to him by the Government obviously under the directives of the world financial institutions. The deficit financing, to the extent of Rs.12,000 crores was sought to be made up through the PSU disinvestment process in last financial year and distress sale was activated. The game of denigrating the PSUs by all vested interests including their promoters - the Government itself and making them sick have reached a peak stage.

Modern Food Industries and Bharat Aluminium Co. Ltd. (BALCO) were privatised in a questionable manner. Modern Food was sold to Hindustan Lever for Rs.150 crore while the value of the prime land under its control at Delhi, Mumbai, Kolkata, Hyderabad. Bangalore, Chennai, Kanpur, Cochin, Chandigarh and other places is estimated to be of value of Rs. 15000 crore at the prevailing market rate. Within a year of its takeover by Hindustan Lever, Modern Food was referred to the BIFR as a sick company. 51 percent of the government's stake in the profit making BALCO was sold for a paltry sum of Rs.551.5 crore to Sterlite Industries, a company debarred from accessing the capital market for two years on the charge of price rigging in the share market. The plant had to be shut down for more than two months as the workers stood firm in resisting the transfer of the plant to a private company.

The 25 percent of the Government's equity in Videsh Sanchar Nigam Ltd. has been transferred to Tatas. A sum of Rs.1884 crore has been realised as proceeds of disinvestment in 7 more PSUs during 2001-02 and 10 more PSUs were in the process of disinvestment by March 31, 2002. 18 more PSUs like Air India, Hindustan Cables. Indian Airlines, Shipping Corporation, MMTC, STC, NALCO and others are on the anvil. There is an all-round opposition and agitation to the proposed privatisation of NALCO. The glaring shortcomings in disinvestment process earned the ire of the Parliamentary Consultative Committee on Disinvestment, which dubbed the Government's disinvestment exercise as immature, lacking transparency." The official white paper on disinvestment makes no mention of the impact of privatisation on economic development and post-privatisation efficiency.

The case of FACT (Kerala) is yet another robbery. If proper valuation is done, it will be more than Rs.6000 crores and the disinvestment proposed is on the basis of the "equity share value only, i.e. the total equity share value is Rs.356 crores and 51% disinvestment of equity shares will fetch Rs.182 crores.

Contrary to the motivated propaganda that public sector was heavily dependent on government for survival, the central public sector establishments have demonstrated their independence by cutting down their reliance on budgetary support which accounts for less than 10 percent of the total plan outlay of Rs.47,526 crore for the year 2000-01.

The Public Enterprises Survey released by the department of Heavy Industries reveals that net profit of the CPSUs increased to Rs.15,653 crore in 2000-01 from Rs.14,331 crore in 1999-2000, reflecting a growth of 9.22 percent. This accounted for a 18.17 percent return on equity as against 17.66 percent in 1999 2000. The total capital employed by the PSUs went up by 19.17 percent from Rs.3,02,867 crore to Rs.3,30,649 Investments in the PSUs went up during the year by Rs.21,369 crore from Rs.2,52,745 crore to Rs.2,74,114 crore registering an increase of 8.45 percent. The combined turn over increased by Rs.69,028 crore from Rs. 3,89,199 crore to Rs.4,58,227 crore, an increase of 18.17 percent. The contribution of the sector to the central exchequer by way of excise duty, customs duty, corporate tax, interest on central government loans, dividend and other levies went up by Rs.4,821 crore from Rs.56,157 crore to 60,978 crore. In contrast, the private sector was guilty of tax defaults of over Rs.62,000 crore. Foreign exchange earnings of the PSUs taken together increased from Rs. 19,737 crore to

Rs.24,772 crore, an increase of 25.51 percent. Despite this performance far superior to the private sector the public sector is systematically maligned through calculated misinformation.

Internationally the examples of Enron, Xerox, World Com etc. and their connected organisations in India have once again proved all is not certainly well with the private corporate sector, instead of learning the proper lessons, the Government of India is yet on the disinvestment spree and privatisation game. It is clear that the structure, vision, goals and systems of the public sector have gone through a whole reformation. Almost at the threshold of the year 2001, the public sector in India is no longer the public sector of the early 1980s or even the late 1980s. Assured of the freedom to operate under new standards of corporate governance now advocated under professional dispensation, the public sector is confident to be globally competitive.

Given the dictates of global competition and need for professional corporate governance, both sectors are slowly but steadily marching towards a convergence. Privatisation, as such, is partly a redundant and partly an obsolete concept. There is a need to be innovative in discovering new models of corporate governance. Given the basis of the foregoing conclusions, and to face the challenges of the new millennium, the public sector has, as it were, to be reinvented with a new vision. The pre-requisites seem to emerge:

- The public sector has to have a vision for itself. The vision shall be of a self-reliant sector with world-class globally competitive and dynamic constituents.
- The public sector to perform shall need total freedom of action within the framework of broad social and

economic policies with total professionalism unimpeded by administrative roadblocks.

— The public sector has to follow best practices with global benchmarks consistent with a Code of ethics and standard values.

Disinvestment and Corporatisation are prelude to privatisation. It is an unabashed attempt to destroy public sector and the worker and their movement are set to resist till the end, despite the declaration of Mr. Arun Shourie that "he will follow Margaret Tachar of Britain dealing with minors strike against privatisation.

Small-scale industries in India are said to be the second largest manpower-employing sector in the country, next only to agriculture. Today the sector accounts for around 95% of the industrial units and is contributing 40% of value addition in the manufacturing sector, nearly 80% of manufacturing employment and about 35% of exports. The sector, according to the Indian Council of Small Industries, provides direct employment to around 180 lakh personnel.For the 10th Five Year Plan the growth rate for the sector has been fixed at 12%. The average annual growth rate in the SSI sector for the period 1980-81 to 1990-91 worked out to be 5.8% and in the subsequent period of economic reforms (1990-91 to 1995-96] worked out to be 4.1%.

In the recent years, the growth rate of the sector, both in terms of output and export has declined. It has been increasingly pronounced that the employment intensity in the small-scale sector has been declining in recent years. The small scale industrialists forum has listed the major problems :

i) inadequate credit flow from banks and financial institutions

ii) inadequate infrastructural facilities

iii) limited opportunities for marketing

iv) low accessibility to raw materials

v) use of obsolete technology

vi) little or no capacity for lobbying and advocacy and

vii) non-implementation of a number of policy measures.

Further, most importantly the SS sector has to face the challenges of competition from opening up of economic globalisation.

Today MNCs play the same role as earlier played by the trading companies in appropriating resources and exploiting cheap labour in the LDCs. The SSIs are threatened in operation even in smaller market because of invasion of branded products through publicity blitz and satellite channels. Since India started to move on the path of liberalisation and globalisation there has been conscious drive to woo foreign investment through numerous concessions. Recent developments including the budget proposals 2002-03 corroborate this fact.

Introduction of special economic zones was designed to open massive foreign investment opportunities and India has decided to allow 100% foreign equity for infrastructural projects in SEZs. Instead of encouraging domestic industries to flourish MNCs are allowed to play freely in a bid to make Indian trade WTO compatible, physical control through QRs is almost attempting to totally dismantle and everything is freely importable. The customs duty has been slashed down to very low or minimal level thereby keeping the customs duty even below the bound rate of import.

In this connection, it is worth mentioning the ILO Recommendation No. 189 concerning General conditions to stimulate job creation in Small and Medium sized enterprises. It speaks of the constraints to the development and growth of efficient and competitive SMEs should be removed particularly those arising from:

a) difficulties of access to credit and capital markets
b) low levels of technical and managerial skills
c) inadequate information
d) low levels of productivity and quality
e) difficulties of access to new technologies
f) lack of transport and communications infrastructure
g) insufficient support for research and development
h) overly burdensome registration, licencing, reporting and other administrative requirements which are disincentives.

A range of potential support which can materially improve SME viability and generate new quality jobs is required such as :

— Business pre-start up, start up and development assistance
— Business plan development and follow-up
— Business incubators
— Consultancy and Research services
— Managerial and vocational skill enhancement
— Promotion and development of enterprise based training
— Support for training on occupational safety & health

- — Access to energy, telecommunication and physical infrastructure such as water, electricity, roads, transportation
- — Assistance in understanding and applying labour legislation, workers' rights, as well as `HR development and promotion of gender equality
- — Support for innovation and modernisation of technology
- — Access to capital markets, credit and loan guarantees
- — Export promotion and trade opportunities in national & international market
- — Quality management, quality testing and measurement
- — Environmental management service."

All these pro active measures will have to be undertaken in order to improve the SSIs.

In the Indian context, the gap between the availability and requirement of working capital was estimated at Rs.71,612 crores in the year 1999-2000. Ironically, 95% of the SSI (tiny) units accounting for nearly 33% employment in the factory sector are not getting more than 3% of their credit requirements inspite of RBI guidelines stipulating 40% advance flowing to SSI sector should be in favour of tiny, village and cottage industries.

Union budget 2002-03 dereserved 50 items hitherto manufactured by SSI sector successfully. This has to be reviewed. Low capacity utilisation has been one of the major problems of small scale sector. Planning commission observed that the overall capacity utilisation in SSI Sector is only 33.35% The number of sick SSI units as of March 1998 were 2.20 lakh and it has increased further. To avert sickness at the incipient stage itself, relief must be granted to the potentially viable sick units as per RBI norms.

Despite the century long struggle by the working class since the first May Day for the existence and recognition of trade unions, many employers in the minimum wage/small-scale/unorganised sector still live in the last century. They oppose the very formation of unions and resort to all sorts of undesirable and unfair practices such as:

— removal of those who come forward,

— brow-beating, transferring or using other methods to silence the activists

— misusing police or engaging local goonda elements etc. A number of management consultants play a harmful role in the process.

In a number of SSIs, even the notified minimum wage has been denied. The enforcement machinery, either being inefficient. indifferent or corrupt, little realises that its primary job is to uphold social justice hence the workers are left in the lurch. The employers lobby in the SSI sector has been canvassing vigorously for exemption of the units employing less than 50 to 100 from all labour legislations. This is being persued or advocated in the name of unhindered growth of SSIs.Some State Governments are favourably inclined to "liberalise" the provisions of laws so as to leave these employers unchecked and unquestioned in so far as the workers' interests are concerned and notified abolition of the so-called "Inspector Raj".

The employers resorted to indiscriminate induction of contract labour to do various jobs of perennial nature. Some SSIs are run only with contractor's workers. It may look strange but remains a fact that in some units the permanent workers were kept idle without work and contractor's workers doing all the jobs, ultimately forcing out the permanent workers.

Globalisation and Economic Crisis

Societies all over the world are experiencing the commercialisation of more and more aspects of life, accompanied by the ugly contradictions of growing inequality within and between countries. Certainly, economic globalisation has led to increased wealth for many in some countries. But it has also led to shattering economic crises, collapse in standards of living, widespread societal and ethnic conflict, social disintegration and greatly increased insecurity for a disproportionately large part of the world's population. The net worth of the world's wealthiest 200 people increased from US $ 440 billion in 1994 to US $ 1,402 billion in 1998, and their assets today are more than the combined income of 41 percent of the world's people.

By and large, those who are already wealthy, socially and politically privileged, or have access to capital, higher education, productive assets (such as land) and other resources (such as technical know-how and hardware) are usually able to benefit from the economic changes brought about by globalisation. But those who are already in lower income brackets, and socially and politically disadvantaged often find themselves much worse off than before since they are compelled to operate in a more aggressive competitive economic environment but without the government and societal supports that they once relied on. The ground for the 1997 economic crisis in East and Southeast Asia was laid through years of trade, financial and capital account liberalisation in varying degrees in countries affected by the crisis. What started as a private sector crisis of illiquidity in the financial sector, quickly developed into a full blown, structural crisis of the financial and real economies, and of the private and public sectors, thanks to the crisis management strategies of the World Bank and the International Monetary Fund (IMF).

According to the World Bank's estimates, by the end of 1998, about 20 million people were added to the 30 million already estimated to be below the poverty line across South Korea, Thailand, Malaysia, Indonesia and the Philippines. The crisis lead to mass unemployment, a sudden rise in poverty levels, severe shortages of food and medicines, drastic cutbacks in all social services, migration from urban to rural areas, soaring crime rates, riots, and social and political chaos.

The already ill prepared public sector was rendered structurally incapable by faulty crisis management to cushion the blows, especially on the most vulnerable populations. It is now widely accepted that women and children absorbed most of the shocks. The standard response by the World Bank and IMF to financial and economic crises is to prescribe more structural adjustments and austerity measures, and this is what they did in Asian crisis as well. Interest rates were increased; publicly provided services and goods were drastically reduced; subsidies and protections for vulnerable sections of the population were dismantled;

public enterprises were privatised; labour markets were deregulated, trade and investment were further liberalised; and domestic commercial entitities in trouble were fragmented and auctioned, usually to foreign buyers.

At a more immediate level, the cost of living rose so quickly and steeply that for people with low incomes or already in poverty, everyday life became a struggle for survival. At a broader level, by dismantling the services and structures on which majority of the population depend to be able to contribute to the national economy, countries handicapped their abilities to pull themselves out of the crisis. Women and men experience economic trends differently in both nature and impact. The impacts of economic globalisation and crises on women need to be assessed in light of women's multiple roles as productive and reproductive labour within the family, their contributions towards overall community cohesion and welfare, and in maintaining the social fabric.

Ideology-in the form of social, cultural and political expectations--and economic pragmatism-in the actual range of tasks that women are expected to perform-interact in complex ways to determine gender relations and roles, which in turn determine the ways in which women are affected by economic policies, trends and crises. For women with access to higher education, professional skills and capital, globalisation has opened up new economic opportunities. But for unskilled women, economic globalisation has often resulted in loss of livelihoods, displacement from traditional occupations, increased migration, and a general erosion of labour and human rights because of new work conditions. These trends are seen more acutely during periods of economic crises. More and more women are migrating on their own, both domestically and internationally, as the primary wage earners in their households and as temporary workers in low-paid jobs.

Following the economic crises in parts of Asia and the former Soviet Union, the trafficking of women and female children has also recorded increases. Research in the 1990s showed that the structural adjustment programmes and austerity measures imposed by the World Bank and the International Monetary Fund (IMF) has affected women more negatively and deeply than men, particularly in lower economic brackets. In most societies, female family members are responsible for providing the crucial care functions that ensure the welfare of their families and communities.

In times of economic crises, women's dual roles as care givers and wage earners acquire heightened importance in ensuring the economic and physical survival of their families. The elimination of public subsidies for health, education and other essential services has resulted in a transference of the "welfare" function of the state onto families, and by extension onto girls and women. This trend has become entrenched as many Southern governments, strapped by debt repayment schedules, have continued to cut back on social spending, thus increasing the burden of caring for vulnerable community members on families. Because of women's traditional roles in most societies as care-givers, this burden has been disproportionately borne by women than men. When public hospitals are privatised or the cost of professional health care goes up, middle to low income families rely more on informal or traditional forms of care. This is usually provided by the female members of households and communities because of their traditional roles as service providers within the home.

As health services are reorganised to increase efficiency and reduce the financial costs of publicly provided medical care, it is the female members of households who pick up the bill through increased costs to their labour, time and resources. When basic education is privatised, or if families cannot afford the rising costs of education and user fees, it is more often girls who drop out of school than boys because of beliefs that boys need formal education more than girls to prepare them for their future roles of social leadership. This in turn has further implications for the type of employment that women are able to find when they move into the wage labour market.

With lower levels of education, women will tend to be concentrated in the lower rungs of the labour market and in jobs that require less formal training or education, and jobs that are easily replaceable. The replacement of manual labour with machines and new technology usually displaces more women than men since women have a larger education gap to cross compared with men in order to learn how to use new technologies. Similarly, increases in the prices of food, fuel and essential services such as water and electricity place extra burdens on females in low income households since women are usually responsible for managing domestic food and water consumption, as well as ensuring the overall health of their families.

Female children are generally expected to perform more housework than male children in most families in any class. In poor families, the labour of girls in cooking, cleaning, child care, and caring for the elderly and sick family members is essential for household maintenance, and also to free up the time of older women who need to find wage labour. However, because the public and private sectors are monetised and care work provided by family members is not, the transfer of costs from the state and the market onto families usually remains hidden and unacknowledged.

Conventional accounts of how economies work and how crises are managed do not pay attention to the centrality of care work in ensuring family welfare and well being, or in how this work subsidises both the state, and the market. Consequently, official processes of crisis management have been more or less blind to the specific needs of women, thus wearing away their capacities, and rights to more balanced and improved lives.

Trade liberalisation has shown to have differential impacts on women and men, which are heightened in times of economic crises. The Asian economic crisis showed that trade liberalisation, when twinned with financial liberalisation can severely exacerbate absolute poverty and inequality. An essential aspect of trade liberalisation is export competitiveness, and much of this competitiveness in Asian and Latin American countries has come from the labour of women.

The development of export processing zones in the 1980s and 1990s in developing countries eager to industrialise was premised on the availability of cheap, docile, unskilled labour willing to work at low wages for long hours. Given a longer history of men's involvement in industrialised production, union organising and political negotiations in the labour market, export processing zones targeted women as the primary workforce, relying on local cultural and social values as domesticating forces. Research shows that no country in Asia has been able to expand its manufacturing capacity without pulling an increasing proportion of women into industrial waged employment.

In the early 1990s, women accounted for more than 43 percent of the manufacturing work force in Indonesia, Malaysia, Philippines, Singapore and Thailand. The manufacturing sector in itself accounted for more than 20 percent of GDP in these countries. In the Thai export sector, women accounted for 90 per cent of the workforce in the canned seafood industry and 85 percent in the garment and accessory industry. Because of the relatively low level of skills required in such employment, women workers are often laid off, or asked to work for lesser wages and reduced benefits during periods of economic crisis. In the Cambodia, Lao PDR and Vietnam, women's labour is considered a significant element of the "comparative advantage" of these countries in export oriented manufacturing.

Governments aggressively invite investors to establish manufacturing bases in their countries in efforts to integrate with regional and global economies. The World Bank's emphasis on promoting small and medium enterprises in these countries is premised largely on using these enterprises as stepping stones to hasten the process of economic integration. While export industries certainly offer women opportunities for employment and income, the unregulated and competitive nature of these regimes also means that women's labour is usually unprotected and dispensable. Few governments have, or are willing to enforce legislation that ensures women workers in this sector with fair living wages, benefits, occupational safety and opportunities for upgrading skills. In times of crisis, it is argued, economic growth must come before labour rights, human dignity and the development of future human potential. An area where the impacts of neo-liberal economic policies and economic crises on women can be clearly seen is the informal sector.

A significant portion of economic activity in Asian countries is not fully counted and does not show up in national census or survey figures, since it is conducted by women in their homes or in small community level production units. These activities include the sale of fruit and vegetables, locally processed food and other goods (artificial flowers, accessories, etc.), subcontracted piece work for factories, and the provision of services such as cleaning, cooking, caring for the elderly, childcare, etc. It is important to note that in many Asian countries, a large portion of informal sector activities are commercialised or "marketised" versions of women's traditional skills of maintaining and reproducing the family and community spheres. While some of these activities are self-owned or self-regulated (i.e., women have reasonable control over production conditions), many are under subcontract arrangements in which women are at the mercy of agents or brokers who determine production and compensation rules. This is particularly the case in production for the manufacturing sector, which is generally organised around contracting agents who receive production contracts from larger agents and then subcontract the work to the women workers. While the informal sector has always been in existence, the Asian economic crisis precipitated its expansion. It is "guesstimated" that many women workers in the formal sector who lost their jobs moved to the informal sector.

A distinguishing feature of such work is that for both cultural and economic reasons, workers do not organise themselves in unions or associations to protect their rights as workers. This is particularly the case in times of crises and economic hardship. Principle contractors are often people known and respected in the community, and take on the persona of "patrons" who bestow favours on community members through economic opportunities. Or, contractors may be from outside the neighborhood or community, and will simply go elsewhere if workers decide to organise and negotiate as a group. The combined effects of years of financial and trade liberalisation, structural adjustment programmes, and increased poverty, unemployment and under-employment of male wage earners because of the economic crisis, have intensified the "distress sale" of women's labour in subcontracted work.

Rising costs of utilities and basic services, and rising household expenditures coupled with a decrease in government subsidies and public provision of essential goods have led low-income families to seek extra income by relying on the labour of female family members. The ability to work in their homes and thus balance the responsibilities of care work with wage earning is a key factor in the increase of women entering the labour force through subcontracted work. Many researchers argue that there is a growing "informalisation" of labour in the export manufacturing sector through the subcontracting of production to unorganised women workers under exploitative working conditions. Such outsourcing of production serve the primary contractors well since they can keep production costs down, and taps into poor women's needs to balance their productive and reproductive responsibilities.

Economic opportunism and profits are served by local culture and tradition, which serve as domesticating forces and ensure a supply of cheap and manageable labour. The expansion of sub-contracted production has increased with the globalisation of production, trade and financial liberalisation, and deregulation of labour markets. On one hand, the informal sector has provided women with much needed income, which in some instances also enhances their status in their families and communities. But at the same time, the inability to organise as a group in such employment makes it extremely difficult for women to negotiate better compensation, working conditions and labour protection for themselves.

Liberalisation in the agriculture sector has affected women in quite particular ways, from losing access to local markets for their products, to dislocation from traditional forms of livelihood, outward migration and geographic displacement. Again, these effects are heightened during economic crises since the squeeze on already limited resources intensifies. Under trade liberalisation agreements (such as in AFTA and the WTO), developing countries are bound to open their markets and import a percentage of agriculture and food products for domestic consumption.

The Asian landscape is dominated by rural economies where at least 50 percent of agricultural and food production is done by women, much of it through small-scale family farms. Local and national food security is dependent on domestic production, which in turn ensures livelihood security for rural families. Obligatory imports of agricultural (especially food) products, accompanied by reduction in tariffs on imported goods and the removal of price controls creates pressure on making local goods "competitive" with imported goods--which are often subsidised in their countries of origin. This negatively affects the food and livelihood security of small-scale domestic producers, leading to increased economic hardship for rural families and a gradual weakening of rural, self-reliant economic structures.

During the Asian economic crisis, countries with a high degree of trade liberalisation were particularly hard hit by the sudden and sharp increases in the prices of basic survival necessities brought about by the devaluation of domestic currencies. In Indonesia, already existing dependence on food and pharmaceutical imports precipitated serious food and health crises, which in turn led to political and social upheaval, and a change in government. In both Malaysia and Indonesia, ethnic tensions reached flash points in the aftermath of the crisis as the anger of desperate mobs was directed at specific business communities. Women again absorbed these shocks by taking on additional wage work, managing domestic consumption and often, by simply "doing without" so that others in the family could survive.

Another crucial sector that is negatively affected by liberalisation and privatisation regimes is natural resources. A huge proportion of rural communities in Asia are subsistence producers who live off common lands and resources, and rely on traditional knowledge of local forests, plants, animals and fish for food and income. Women are usually responsible for meeting the family's daily food and livelihood needs, and are veritable storehouses of knowledge about local bio-diversity and traditional extraction practices. But with commercial harvesting of natural resources for value added production, increase in plantation and monocropping for export markets, and transference of land, water and resource rights to private corporations, bio-diversity, environmental quality and food security are seriously threatened, and local communities are alienated from the very resource base that their survival depends on.

In the aftermath of the Asian economic crisis, many governments have prioritised natural resource based exports as a primary source of revenues. Whether the export of raw timber or the granting of mining concessions, aggressive exploitation of natural resources without concurrent support for resource replenishment and environmental protection will have long term, negative impacts on food security, health and well being of rural families.

The Asian crisis already showed us the complex dynamics of migration by vulnerable groups between rural and urban areas in a bid to survive. With increased migration into rural areas, rural communities faced a squeeze on local natural resources and a general decline in the quality of their livelihoods. To make ends meet, more and more rural people sought wage employment through off-farm work, which often resulted in increased outward migration and family disintegration. And once again, it is largely female household members who have picked up the costs of these trends through increased pressure on their labour, time and capacities.

Economic crises affect women from middle to low income households at an immediate experiential level through: increased household burdens, decreased opportunities for earning decent living wages, reduced access to land and resources, less food and nutrition, fewer opportunities for education and improving their life prospects, weakened health, social alienation and often, deteriorating family relationships. These impacts in turn have longer term implications for the overall capacities of women which, while not visible today, are likely to lead to the longer term dis-empowerment of women. A major challenge for us today is how to formulate, advocate and put into place economic and financial policies that respond to the specific circumstances, priorities and aspirations of women.

The knowledge base that informs national and global policy making is blind not only to gender differences, but also to differences arising from class, culture, race and ethnicity. Some ideas that we could consider are:

— Bring the evidence of the gender-differentiated impacts of financial and economic liberalisation policies to our governments and international bodies, and insist that present and future policies address the root causes of crisis creating circumstances.

— Severely curtail and limit the power of the IMF and the World Bank in the management of economic crises.

— Work with our respective national governments to conduct "gender audits" of economic and financial policies. These audits should form the basis of future policy development.

— Oppose the imposition of World Bank-IMF style structural adjustment reforms, no matter what names they go under.

— Call for governments to immediately put in place appropriate capital controls and freeze further trade liberalisation until suitable protective measures have been developed and put in place.

— Advocate for measures that support women's equitable access to assets, incomes and higher education.

— Formulate and advocate policies that support production and exchange complexes geared towards strengthening local and national markets, rather than feeding distant export markets.

— Advocate for ownership, stewardship and governance of essential natural resources such as land, forests and water at the most appropriate local levels.

— Use the existing international instruments provided by CEDAW, and other appropriate multilateral agreements to advocate for economic and financial policies that are responsive to the diverse needs of diverse social groups.

— Economic and financial policies must serve social, cultural and environmental priorities and not vice versa. One way to do this would be to insist that national budgets are opened up to public scrutiny and changes made to the budget to reflect this prioritisation.

— Democratise economic and financial policy development: too many policies are made behind closed doors by "experts," beyond the oversight of parliamentarians, peoples' representatives and the general public.

4

Liberalisation and Economic Emergence

In medieval times wealth remained mostly idle, inactive and unproductive. This was mainly because of the absence of appreciable trade and commerce. In Europe the Church and the nobility that owned most of the wealth tended to hoard their fortune. But the Crusades that began in Europe in 1095 and intermittently went on till 1291 were actually the beginning of the process of globalisation. The Crusaders going over to the East to fight for the Holy Land came in contact with many commodities they had not seen or used before. This demand for foreign goods gradually led to continuously expanding trade and commerce.

Once the Crusaders wrested control of the Mediterranean route from the Moslems, it became an important trade route between the East and the West. Internal trade also started increasing and goods were bought and sold in terms of money. An economy centering around self-sufficient villages thus transformed into a money economy steadily expanding itself in the context of a world of expanding trade. The Renaissance and the accompanying sea voyages and discoveries of new lands in the 15th century gave a boost to globalisation. At the heart of the process of globalisation were better means of transportation and communication.

The industrial revolution represented a revolutionary improvement in production process by means of the application of technology i.e. of newly invented types of machines-an improvement that brought about a spectacular change in the pattern and structure of the English society. The net effect of all this was a massive influx of wealth by way of profit to the English bourgeoisie. It was a dynamic wealth, which by way of further investment brought about further profit and the revolution in technology, in the form of means of transportation and communication, removed most of the natural barriers to the indefinite accumulation of this wealth. In the old days, when paper notes were invented, they had to be convertible. These were issued by private goldsmiths, and no one would accept them unless quite sure that the goldsmith in question was solid, and could convert the note into money on demand. When governments started printing notes, they had to keep the same promise-or their paper would not be trusted. This was the gold standard.

The gold standard of pre-world war years was a system with high international capital mobility with fixed exchange rates. With the outbreak of World War I, international capital movements collapsed the exchange rate system. The Brettonwoods conference after World War II aimed at rebuilding the world trade and payments system that had been disrupted first by the break down of the gold standard in the inter-war years and also by the trade wars, competition, devaluation and the great depression of the 1930s.

The Brettonwoods system envisaged another periodically adjustable fixed rate system in which all the countries were to be integrated through trade but not capital movements. The US deliberately fostered this system on the world in the late 1940s to forestall another depression and contain communism by putting a premium on markets and information and deemphasising military rivalry. A New International Economic Order (NIEO) was thus created in the 1940s after the Brettonwoods conference. The gold standard collapsed in the 1970s. Once again there was a demand for a new international economic order.

However, the debate for a NIEO in the 1970s was accompanied by a debate for a new world information and communication order (NWICO). The NWICO debate in the United Nations was initiated by the developing countries because they not only wanted to reduce the monopoly of the big five international news agencies but also to get the developed world to make further investments to improve their communication and information infrastructure. The South realised that any state hoping to be fully integrated into the global economy must possess an efficient communications infrastructure with such basics as working telephones and data relay capabilities conducive to data provision and other expanding service industries. So, by demanding increased aid for communications development, the South's goal was to attain the basic resources needed for economic development in a changing global economy.

Communication has been the vital prerequisite and lubricant of international economic changes. There is a positive relationship between the expansion of some forms of international trade and world financial markets, on the one hand, and the ability to communicate efficiently and rapidly, on the other. The international flow of news has always been directly related to transnational economic exchanges, especially trade and investment. A study of the evolution of Reuters illustrates how new information and communication technologies (ICTs), changes in the world economy, and news organisations themselves interact in this policy-making environment.

With the breakup of the Bretton Woods system of fixed exchange rates in the 1970s, dealing in foreign exchange and money was about to expand rapidly. The problem of banks and dealers was how to receive quotations with sufficient speed. Seconds were important, reliance on telephones and telex was unsatisfactory. Reuters decided to install computing terminals in the offices of banks and other foreign-exchange markets. That was the central idea behind the Reuter Monitor Money Rates Service that was started in 1973. Reuters would in this way create an electronic marketplace. Market-makers (contributors) would be able to insert their foreign exchange and money rates into the system. At the press of a button, the rates would be available on a screen to interested parties (recipients) such as banks and international businesses.

The process of globalisation

The initial phase of the process of globalisation was

started in the 1940s, when countries were expected to adjust to the opening up to international trade with convertible current accounts and the IMF, a creation of the Brettonwoods conference, was to provide them financial support when necessary.. After the oil crisis and the breakdown of the fixed exchange rate arrangements in the 1970s, capital movements revived. Even without capital account convertibility, most countries were forced to adjust to increased capital inflows within the framework of a more open world trading system.

By 1995, several developing countries with different degrees of capital account convertibility became increasingly integrated through capital movements and entered the second phase of globalisation. Many developing nations are still in the first phase and adjusting to the problems of opening up to international trade and current payments. The end of the Cold War in the early 1990s, has coincided with the onset of the information revolution.

Globalisation in the information age has seen the integration of finance, markets, nation-states and technologies to a degree never witnessed before-in a way that is enabling individuals, corporations and nation states to reach around the world faster, further, deeper and cheaper than ever before. The Cold War ideas of the clash between communism and capitalism, détente, non-alignment and perestroika are being replaced by free-market capitalism.

The new economic rules revolve around opening, deregulation and privatisation of the economy. The Cold War was about Einstein's mass-energy equation, $E=MC^2$. Globalisation is about Moore's Law, which states that the computing power of silicon chips will double every 18 to

24 months. In the Cold War the fear was annihilation from an enemy you know too well, while the fear in the information age is from anonymous economic and technological forces that are anything but stable. According to Mr Grady Means, global leader, strategic change practice, Price Waterhouse Coopers (PwC), between 1993 and 1996 most of the global corporations across sectors went through the period of consolidation, particularly in telecom and automobiles.

This phase, which followed the previous three years of massive privatisation initiatives in the world, was overtaken by the Internet, which allowed companies to globalise rapidly, helped by very low costs of communications. Every major company must have a global strategy and nations must avoid economic nationalism to be successful in the latest wave of globalisation fuelled by information technology. Austrian economist Joseph Schumpeter's studies argued that an advanced economy is constantly disrupted by "creative destruction"-the perpetual replacement of products and services with more efficient ones-caused by technological innovation.

According to Andy Grove, only the paranoid who are constantly looking over their shoulders to see who is creating something new that will destroy them-and then staying one step ahead-will survive. Other economists talk of long waves in the affairs of nations, 50 to 60 years long, triggered by technological innovation, which if taken at the flood can lead to good fortune.

Water power, textiles, and iron in the 18th century; steam, railways and steel next; petrochemicals, electronics and aviation since 1950 were the earlier technological innovations. The current wave of semiconductors, fibreoptics, genetics and software seems to be underway. Alvin and Heidi Toffler have distinguished between the agricultural, industrial and information revolutions and postulated that nations make war in the same way as they make money.

The dramatic increases in the cost, risk and complexity of technology in many industries render even the largest national markets too small to serve as meaningful economic units by themselves. More importantly the emerging world economy is electronic, integrated through information systems and technology rather than organisational hierarchies.

The digital revolution has "dematerialised" manufacturing and commerce, forced vertically integrated "Fordist" firms to use information technology (IT) so that they can integrate with the international system of networked production. The entry of "electronic" forms of money, in large volumes as explained earlier has added a new dimension to the debate on international money.

India has been pushing for creating a new financial architecture to avoid recurrence of the Asian financial crisis and to address the issues of volatile capital flows besides efforts for making the financial system more resilient and strengthening the capacities for crisis management.

The Indian finance minister speaking at the meeting of the World Economic Forum (WEF) in Davos earlier this year said that in the new era of globalisation, capital flows were playing an enormous role and the flows in the capital account were very large. In such an environment, Brettonwoods institutions like the IMF and World Bank coming to the rescue of countries hit by financial crisis was indeed 'relatively small'.

The Brettonwoods system encouraged countries to help each other enforce capital controls. The IT revolution has coincided with a period in which powerful states have liberalised their external capital controls almost completely.

Economic and Technological Trends

In this information age, information and knowledge are the new sources of wealth. The focus has shifted from material and territory to ideas and technology. The market places higher value on intellectual and human capital than on hard assets like bricks and mortar. Knowledge combines with management skills to produce wealth. Microsoft, with only a relatively small amount of fixed assets, now has a market capitalisation well in excess of Ford, General Motors, and Chrysler combined. Microsoft donates $325 million each year for charitable causes.

In 1981, Infosys Technologies, an Indian software company had $250 to start with. Today it has a market capitalisation of $3 billion, and is listed on the Nasdaq stock exchange in the US. Amazon.com a book selling company on the Internet has a market capitalisation of $30 billion. The powerful economies of Hong Kong (China) and Singapore, countries with virtually no physical assets, demonstrate the growing irrelevance of territory to wealth. Moreover, information is now stolen, and then sold to whomever might be interested. In the US the anti-hacker struggle is led by the US Secret Service, and in the UK by MI5.

Information systems permit distributed production-scale without geographic concentration-and global marketing: designed in the US, chips fabricated in Japan, subsystems built in Taiwan, software written in India, and final product marketed in Europe. Mass production in a single location is disappearing. Companies are in a position to disperse different phases of the industrial life cycle among different countries, depending on local conditions. Under this form of production, producers of IT products are contracting out core functions including production and final assembly itself to contract manufacturers. Such firms are hugely successful in competing against traditional integrated electronics producers. The specialised contract manufacturers had revenues of over $40 billion in 1995. Networked production provides producers with low cost, high speed, high quality alternate sources of supply, available at much reduced demands on their scarce and costly capital. Networked production works best in a tariff free environment.

The defining feature of economic growth in the Information Age is the increasing weightlessness of the output. Production and consumption are shifting away from objects toward information and services. Weightless goods like computer software, financial products, telecommunications, the Internet, entertainment and even management consulting are becoming important.

Production has become increasingly gloablised and competition to the developed nations, especially from the newly industrialised economies (NIEs) has become intense. The defining feature of the information age is the increasing weightlessness of output. The key characteristics of weightless goods like computer software, telecommunications, the Internet, financial products, entertainment and management consulting which accounted for 23 per cent of the US GDP between 1987 and 1994 are:

— Many people can use them at the same time.

— Once the good is produced it can be replicated at low cost.

Another trend today is that the services industry is replacing the manufacturing industry the world over as the fastest growing part of the economy. There is a great opportunity for countries like India because of this shift. Services like medical transcriptions, tele-medicine, bill collections over the Internet, universal libraries, etc which use modern information technologies cost almost 10 times less in India than in advanced countries.

In India almost 40 per cent of our national wealth comes from the service industry. If India can build a good information infrastructure capable of supporting sophisticated, fast and cheap communication technologies, it has the potential to become the Asian hub for all services related activities in the region. There is a potential Rs. 55,000 crore (US$13 billion) market which will provide employment to 1.1 million people by 2008. We should not give away this market to China and South East Asia due to the lack of a proper information infrastrucutre.

There has been a lot of debate the world over about the links between growth and openness to trade. Increased openness affects income by encouraging resource allocation into sectors with a comparative advantage. Moreover, it also affects growth through the direct transfer of technology, the spillover of ideas due to increased personal contacts, the elimination of the duplication of research, the increased size of the market and increased competition.

In a knowledge-based society openness to trade is very significant and countries are moving towards it in order to benefit from all the spillover effects. Moreover, rapid improvements in technology have intensified pressure to open up sectors encased in heavy regulation and protected by their governments.

Some governments insert various conditions in their trade laws in order to deny other countries access to their R&D and their high-technology exports. They have been restricting the export of hi-tech goods and services in the name of national security. The revolution in IT compounds threats to national and international security by greatly facilitating the transmission of information to potential aggressors. However, private markets and enterprises dominate information technologies. Therefore, efforts by the government to restrict their transfer have foundered because of the difficulty in stemming the flow of such technologies and the reluctance to forego the profitable revenue from this largely non-defence trade.

While export controls may be justified in some sectors like encryption software, the use of denial and delaying techniques in other sectors may be counterproductive. Such "techno-nationalism" may also lead to retaliation from the affected countries. Moreover, the US and other developed countries are using skilled manpower from many developing countries like India to develop these technologies. In following the policy of information apartheid with countries like India, the US has to be careful of a "nationalistic backlash" from American Indians (the NASA and the Silicon Valley are full of American Indians). India on its part needs to network with the Indian diaspora in the US to ensure that there is a free flow of technology.

FDI has played an important role in world trade over the last 20 years, and the pattern of FDI in East Asia suggests that it is an important source of technical knowledge and ideas to recipient countries. FDI will help the host country through transfer of technology, modern management techniques and access to better R&D.

Globalisation, technology and trade are closely linked. Technology makes globalisation feasible; trade liberalisation allows it to happen. However, technology-driven globalisation also creates losers, that is those who cannot adapt to the skills. Even these losers use IT to further their cause. Governments have to find a system that is suitable to their country and strike a balance between globalisation, use of information technology and the pace of trade liberalisation.

Many companies the world over have sprung to great size and capital by focussing on standard setting and maintenance. New IT product markets are increasingly characterised by rivalry to set de facto market standards. Microsoft, for example, has been able to make great strides by setting the standards in Windows software for operating systems and Windows NT for networking software.

When a company invests overseas it carries technology with it and usually exports both to and from its home base. Accompanying the flow of goods, services and investment is the flow of propriety technical and marketing information or intellectual property to subsidiaries and suppliers around the world. Unauthorised copying or piracy of compact discs, software packages, trademarks, designer labels, and computer hardware components have to be protected through patents, copyrights or trademarks.

As we are living in a knowledge-based society and a market-based economy, intellectual property must be protected from competitors so that it can be exploited, sold or licensed at the discretion of the owner. This is increasingly becoming a hot topic of discussion amongst trade negotiators and governments at international trade fora.

In the information age very few countries can successfully resist the pressures of globalisation. The pressures of postindustrial capitalism are forcing states to sell government-owned defence industries. Private contractors to look after logistics, commercial satellite pictures for intelligence, dual-use civilian technologies being modified for military use are some of the examples of the privatisation of military functions.

The freely available military goods and services, including skilled manpower to maintain and operate hi-tech weapons after the end of the Cold War, have only reinforced this trend. The contemporary revolution in military affairs (RMA) can be attributed to the rise of information technologies and flowering of capitalism in the world.

Computing power has doubled every 18 months for the last 30 years. The costs of transmission are less than one per cent of what they were in the early 1970s. Communication bandwidths are expanding rapidly, especially with optical fibre cables. Once Internet telephony is legalised in India, the telephone rates will reduce from Rs. 84/- per minute for a call to USA to about Rs. 2/- per minute. Voice communication will be almost free of cost in the next few years. The dramatic cheapening of information transmission has opened the business field to loosely structured network organisations and even individuals.

Individuals, institutions and communities have been linked with one another via computer networks, satellites and expanding public and private telecommunications infrastructures. National markets, regional markets, markets in specific financial instruments or commodities have all become part of global capital markets. Therefore, domestic financial problems in Thailand or Mexico affects markets worldwide and a fall on the Hong Kong stock exchanges sends all the world's stock exchanges falling like dominoes. When one market "catches cold, all the other get sick".

E-Commerce is fundamentally reshaping entire industries, notably financial services, telecommunications services, business and consulting services, travel, and entertainment. It is revolutionary in three respects. Firstly there are many more players. The large corporations and banks are now joined by local retail establishments and households, rather anyone with a few thousand dollars worth of equipment. Secondly, there is a high level of technological change in the information industry. The third revolutionary change is the worldwide availability of information. Consumers can go directly to the producers without going through retailers, wholesalers and distributors. The new intermediaries will be network access providers, electronic payment systems, and services for authentication and certification of transactions. The result would be something approaching the ideal of perfect competition: low transaction costs, low barriers to entry and improved access to information for the consumer.

E-Commerce has thrown up a whole new set of regulatory and tax related issues. Electronic commerce doesn't seem to occur in any physical location but instead takes place in the nebulous world of 'cyberspace'. In the prevalent system, geographic location or jurisdiction determines which authority has the right to tax the income stream arising from the transaction or the sale itself (a sales or value-added tax). In E-Commerce the transactions may be conducted over many geographic locations. Who will get the tax? Where is the transaction taking place?

Effective economic governance in a digital world economy will require increased harmonisation of national legislation and regulations and much more effective and powerful international organisations. The postmodern integrated world economy will require a marked strengthening of international institutions such as the WTO and supranational organisations like the EU. They may well acquire taxation and enforcement powers if territorial jurisdiction is no longer effective.

The Internet is a decentralised computer system available to individuals and small private companies that can participate freely without having to go through the state, a major corporation, or some other institutional structure. This provides the world with an extremely free telecommunications infrastructure, which is why many see the Internet as a symbol of globalisation.

The origins of the Internet can be traced back to the ARPANET (Advanced Research Projects Agency Network)-a network of the US Department of Defence, which was used for scientific and technological research, including military research, and remained far removed from the public until the 1980s. It was only after it began to be used for commercial purposes, that it spread like wildfire.

However, the US maintains unequivocal hegemony over the Internet community. Of the 30 million or so Internet host computers, the US has about 20 million. In the Internet community, a battle is unfolding for hegemony through free economic activity. Both the public and private sectors are taking up the new post-Cold War information trend with enthusiasm. In the information age, hegemony will be established by spreading culture, values and economic activity over the Internet.

In the IT industry the focus is shifting from hardware to software. In 1985, in terms of importance and costs the ratio between hardware and software was 85:15 per cent, but today this has reversed with software at 85 per cent and hardware at 15 per cent. In a world economy that is getting inter-connected at a rapid pace this shift is extremely important. Countries like India, which have a strong intellectual and human capital in the field of software stand to benefit by the increasing importance of software in the information technology industry.

At present India is exporting low level software i.e., the $2 per hour variety. However, the core competence of the Indian software writers is in high-end software exports i.e., the $2000 per hour variety.[40] Indian software exports form 10.5 per cent of the total exports of the country. The value of exports stood at $2.7 billion in 1998-99. If India can target the high-end software this value is likely to increase many times over. By 2003, software exports will overtake all other sectors of exports in India. The National Association of Software and Services Companies (NASSCOM) estimates that the Indian software industry will achieve a target of $85 billion annual turnover by 2008, including $50 billion in exports.

Global Markets: Issues and Trends

One of the important reasons for the end of the Cold War was that it became impossible to continue to operate a closed society in a world economy in which competitiveness was increasingly predicated on access to information and information technologies. China's economic modernisation under Deng Xiaoping and the famous slogan, "never mind the colour of the cat till the time it catches mice", is a recognition of the importance of markets in the world economy.

The recent trade agreement between the US and China which will pave the way for China's entry into the WTO, highlights the importance of markets in national policy making. The globalisation system in the information age is built around three balances. The balance between nation states, the balance between nation states and markets, and the balance between nation states and individuals. The second balance is between the nation states and the global markets.

Information technologies have produced significant changes that are altering the balance of power between these two global domains. The global markets are made up of millions of investors making money around the world with the click of a mouse. This "electronic herd" gathers in key global "supermarkets" such as Wall Street, Hong Kong, London and Frankfurt. The attitudes and actions of the electronic herd and the supermarkets can have a huge impact on nation states, even to the point of triggering the downfall of governments.

The trend today is towards shifting alliances and joint vetures, made possible by computers and advanced communications. Offshore banking encourages widespread evasion of national taxes. Companies are increasingly using the Internet for E-commerce that brings with it its own regulatory problems. The globalisation of financial markets, private capital flows, and the networking amongst international organisations, NGOs and regional organisations are adding many new dimensions to a states' authority to control the economy in the digital age.

While IT may have enhanced the potential mobility of money, it has also given states new tools and mechanisms for asserting their sovereign power and authority in the financial sector if they choose to. Recent US and Australian regulatory initiatives use artificial intelligence (AI) to monitor money flows and look for suspicious transactions that may involve money laundering activities. Various sophisticated software are being used for this purpose.

In addition to the fact that there are monitoring software available, there is a thesis that even weaker states may get technical and legal assistance from the more powerful states in order to enhance the efficacy of international control regimes. The regulatory and law enforcement agencies are also emphasising to the developers of e-money the importance of encryption systems and anti-money laundering systems. Moreover, while capital may not be linked to a physical location in the information age, the same is not true for labour. Therefore, should the changes brought about by globalisation be seen as unjust, a backlash can occur and people will turn to the states for redress.

The nature of the information revolution demands recognition that change has become one of the few constants and that we must accept that literally and figuratively we live in a state of transition. The evolution of information and communication technology, which has only just begun, will probably favour markets over nation-states.

However, there are roles that only the state can perform like collection of tax, meeting the crucial social needs that markets do not value, providing job security, avoiding unemployment, protecting the environment and looking after health care and safety of its population. While globalisation and the focus on technology are important, they do not sound the death knell to the significance of the nation-state. Government policies will play an important role in adjusting to the changes due to technologies.

The industrial revolution and the accompanying advances in transportation and communication converted Great Britain into a global superpower. Technological change was responsible for much of the economic growth in the US between 1909 and 1949. Economists prefer to look at measures of total factor productivity (TFP)-which is usually thought to measure the technological progress-to measure the economic growth of a nation.

In 1952, Japan had a per capita GNP of US$188 in the prices of the day, below that of Brazil, Malaysia, and Chile. Today it has the fourth largest GNP per capita in the world. Much of the growth in labour productivity (output per worker) was driven by TFP growth (technological progress). The highly educated and skilled workforce in manufacturing and the ability to imitate and import technology from abroad helped Japan catch up with the US.

Japan dominates the use of electronic payment systems. Of the total of 150,000 Automatic Teller Machines (ATMs) and 250 million credit cards in eight East Asian economies in 1997, 125,000 ATMs and 225 million credit cards were in Japan. Asia is, however, adopting electronic commerce and payment systems at great speed.

According to Dataquest, the Asia Pacific information technology (IT) market between 1995 and 2000 will grow from US $6.4 billion to US$22 billion. IT penetration in Hong Kong is good, 41 per cent of the adults in Hong Kong own personal computers (PCs) as compared to 52 per cent in the USA. It has one of the finest telecommunication infrastructures in Asia, with 200,000 kilometers of fibre optic cables linked to 1500 buildings. PC banking and video on demand (VOD) facilities have already been introduced.

Asian economies have recognised the importance of E-commerce and electronic payments. They are making the suitable national information infrastructures (NIIs) for this purpose. Singapore has the "Singapore One" network and their "IT Vision 2000" envisages Singapore as an intelligent island. Malaysia's multimedia super-corridor (MSC) project, China's Golden Bridge Network and efforts by Japan, Korea, and Taiwan to build a suitable NII encompass electronic commerce and payment systems by the early 21st century.

The rise of the East Asian Tigers or the newly industrialised economies (NIEs) comprising Singapore, South Korea, Taiwan and Hong Kong can be attributed to many reasons. One explanation is that of openness and export orientation, since these countries have been successful exporters and have also imitated foreign technologies. High saving and investment rates, low taxes, relatively high quality education systems and institutions are some of the other reasons for this success.

The NIEs have attracted substantial amounts of FDI which have enabled them to adopt and adapt foreign technologies. In general, the ability of developing countries to attract FDI seems to depend on whether they follow export-promoting or import-substituting strategies for development. The famous economist, Jagdish Bhagwati has argued that export-promoting countries attract more FDI and that this FDI yields social returns. Lastly, the TFP growth rates in Taiwan, Hong Kong and South Korea, though not miraculous, compare favourably with those of other developing countries and with the OECD.

On the flip side let us see how technology precipitated a financial crisis in the East Asian Region. The continued rapid growth of global trade in goods and services depends on financial flows, and it is here that the instant availability of information has had a particularly dramatic effect. Flashes of data around the world intensify the volatility of currency movements, which can send trade, investment and stock markets in a downward spiral, at least temporarily.

In October 1997, what started as a seemingly localised banking crisis in Thailand spilled over into a chain of events that affected financial markets around the world. The sudden collapse of South East Asia left the biggest and the brightest in the IMF and the World Bank aghast. They called for an implicit faith in the efficacy of market economy, free movement of international capital and an unrestricted and free trade of goods throughout the would. They blamed the "crony capitalism" of

Indonesia and the stranglehold of Chaebols in South Korea; but they had no explanation for the debacle in Thailand and Malaysia. They could also not place their finger on the effects in Hong Kong, Japan and even Singapore.

In a globalised economy, they discovered with feigned wonderment, billions of dollars can be moved at the stroke of a computer key and this fact makes it almost impossible to manage or control its movement. They said that the real culprit was the short-term capital managed by financial intermediaries-commonly referred to as "hot money". At the same time they did not allow imposing any restrictions on the movement of this "hot money", since it went against the basic credo of globalisation.

East Asia still remains an attractive place to do business, with forward looking and innovative companies and well-educated and productive workers. Fundamentally it is the productivity of those workers and those companies that will determine their future, rather than currency crises and bank failures.

While we should do away with restrictions on industries, commerce and finance, we should never do away with regulation. The availability of instant information also makes the markets work better. If the underlying financial and economic conditions are healthy, markets that crash overnight, can also recover overnight, causing little or no damage to trade and investment flows. India today stands at the threshold of the information revolution. The liberalisation of the Indian economy started in 1991, when a comprehensive plan for opening up our markets to the world was started. Global business leaders felt that the momentum of reforms and deregulation were slowing down in 1994.

However the recent pronouncements by the Indian government and the systematic launching of the second phase of economic reforms seems to have rekindled the interest of global business and political leaders in India. Such sentiments have been expressed at the World Economic Summit held at New Delhi in December 1999. India is gearing itself for the revolution in information technology and is aware of the latest economic and technological trends. There are tremendous opportunities for India in this revolution and careful implementation of a futuristic IT strategy can ensure economic security and economic power for India in the first decade of the 21st century.

Capitalist Globalisation on Working Class

Working people of all capitals countries are affected by the 'globalisation' of the economy. But the economy and the working people of the developing countries are worst affected. This process began about one and half decades back. Capitalism developed with its tendency for globalisation. But the present phase of globalisation has come to represent the major changes in the world capitalist economy which have been underway since the last ten or fifteen years. Transitional mobility of capital and its global reach are central of all barriers to international trade and finance. Riding on the wave of trade and capital market liberalisation and assisted by new technological advances, production itself is getting increasingly globalised with different components of a single commodity.

Today's corporate strategies to capture markets maximise profit and outsmart rivals have to be necessarily global character. World sales of foreign affiliates of multinational corporations are now estimated to exceed the world total of exports. Staggering volumes of money crisis cross the globe round the through electronic transfers among interlinked stock markets and financial institutions. These ease and facility with which capitalist globalisation.

Thus the current phase of globalisation is substantially different from all previous records of internationalisation of capital. It is a furious rush for international finance capital to establish its rule of profit all over the world in a situation where capitalism is undergoing a severe from of structural crisis. Starting in 1950's, The World Bank became a major fund giver of development in the third world. After 1972, the fixed exchange rates being abolished. IMF took on much of the management of exploding international debt crisis. And the debt of the third world countries soared, the IMF and the World Bank began to require accepting structural Adjustment Programmes as conditions for new loans. These conditions neatly coincide with the agenda of mobile capital and the cheapening of the costs of production for global corporations by:

— Taking advantage of the on going scientific and technological revolution and thus using high tech in production displacing human labour.

— Radically reducing Government spending, a measure that in practice translated into cutting spending in health, education and socials welfare.

— Reduction of labour by drastic downsizing of industrial and government departments.

— Cutting wages or severely constraining their rise to inflation and make profits more competitive

— Liberilising imports and removing restrictions on foreign investment in Industry and Financial services

— Devaluation of local currency

— Privatisation of state enterprises and radical deregulation and to leave the economy to market forces

— Using the entire process for intensifying the exploitation of labour and maximising profits

— Changing labour laws in favour of the capitalists and obviously against the labour.

Now, most Third World Countries governments abandoned the pursuit of more just international economic order and instead acceded to virtually any condition in exchange for loan renewals. Similar 'shock therapy' plans were imposed on the ex Communist countries as a pre condition for loans and adjustments. In 1994 another international organisation World trade Organisation (WTO) came into being as a result of the protracted Uruguay Round of multilateral negotiations.

The WTO redefined 'free trade' to mean the right to Multinational Corporations to go where ever they want and do whatever they like with as little interference as possible from any one. Such 'freedom' for Corporations means restricting the freedom of governments and citizens. These new institutional Trinity - IMF, World Bank and WTO now set the rules and conditions with each individual nation must operate to serve the Corporate Agenda, which means an Agenda against the common masses.

With the set back of socialism in former Soviet Union and the East European countries, the balance pf forces, albeit temporarily, shifted towards capitalism. The capitalist world is no longer to make concession to the working people out of fear of socialism. The concept of a welfare state was given a good bye. Reaganiasm and Thacherism launching a strong officensive against the working class, employees and all other sections of the toiling people in a bid to tide the structural crisis replaced the concept of welfare, capitalism is suffering from. The capitalist class demands a 'free market economy' claiming that the economy must be free from any government intervention. Not even the poor should receive help.

The Government should cut health care, education and even food subsidies and privatise the government-controlled enterprises and reduce workforce by in discriminately introducing new technology. Added to this was the crazy search for cheap labour and raw materials by the Multinational Companies in order to maximise profits. This led the multinationals not only to open new units in the developing countries, but even to relocate the existing units to distant developing countries where cheap labour and raw materials are abundantly available. Thus the workers and the common masses of the advanced capitalist countries had to face twin dangers of reduction of the existing work by the use of computer, automation, etc and also because of relocation of the existing industrial units to Third World countries.

The basic concept of globalisation of economy is the liberalisation and privatisation. Although the economic theory underlying much of the current interest in privatisation may be traced back to Adam Smith's economic theory. It is only recently that the free market economic theory has been repackaged and adopted to the language of the contemporary economic and political discourses. The growth of public sector and the concept of a welfare state primarily arose in the second World War period to a great extend as an attempt to counter the spread of influence of soviet socialism in the rest of Europe. It also owes to a considerable extent to the Keysian theory of increased public expenditure in order to raise employment potential and purchasing power of the people.Public enterprises were thus conceived basically as instruments of economic development.

After the end of the War and the defeat of fascism, when liberation of the colonies started taking place, most of the ex colonial countries followed the path of building public enterprises and many also went ahead with economic planning to a certain extent in soviet models. But with the onset of recession and the consequent deepening pf structural crisis of capitalist economy, the privatisation campaign was started by Reagan Administration in the 1980's in the United State and followed by Great Britain embarking upon a privatisation spree. Some if the huge Government Corporations including British gas, British Telecom and British Airways were privatised. Privatisation started in other Western European countries also notably in Germany, France and Italy.

Thereafter in the developing scenario of heavy debt burdens of the developing countries, when the World Bank and IMF granted loans under conditions of introducing Structural Adjustment Programmes in the developing countries, privatisation pf Public enterprises became a major condition set forth by these international financial institutions. This was purported to drastically reduce Government's interference in the economy, to reduce Government's fiscal deficit and overall to promote a private sector culture. As a result, the Asian Countries, Indonesia, Philippines, Singapore, Thailand and Malaysia and then India and all other countries in the sub continent, in Latin America, in some African Countries. In a word in the entire developing world, privatisation became the moving force of new economic philosophy, dictated by World Bank- IMF.

Globalisation of which dismantling of public enterprises, cultivating a private enterprise, culture and reducing public expenditure are the main motive forces, is hunting the common people in all countries pf the world including the developed capitalist countries. But the impact on the Third World including the former socialist countries is most devastating. Cuts in health care have led to more sickness and ill health. While multinationals spend millions of dollars on advertising to sell their products, every three seconds a child in the world dies, most in the developing countries.

Since the mid 1980, developing countries send money every year to the developed capitalist countries than they receive. Most of this is interest payment on debts going to the World Bank. IMF and other Western Financial Institutions. This the moneylenders get richer and the borrowers poorer. The growing inequalities, that this globalisation is creating has been sharply pointed in Human Development Reports also. The 1996 Report pointed out, during the process of liberilisation adjustment and privatisation, concern for the poor was pushed to the background. The 1998 25 years ago' while 'consumption per capital has increased steadily in industrialised countries over the past 25 years'. It further points out, the poorest 20% of the world's people are deprived of basic consumption needs.

Of the 4.4 billion people in developing countries, nearly three-fifth have no access to clean water, A fifth of children do not attend school to grade 5, the Report then pointedly mentions, inequalities in consumptions are stark... Globally, the 20% of the world's people in the highest income countries account for 86% of total private consumption expenditures, the poorest 20% muniscule 1.3%. From the UNDP Report 1998, it becomes clear that globalisation is playing havoc in the developed capitalist countries also. The report point out human deprivation are not just are found in all industrialised countries... The new human poverty index (HPI-2) shows that some 7.17 % of the population in industrial countries of poor... The United States, with the highest average income of the countries ranked, has the highest population share experiencing human poverty.The Report points out, 'human deprivations are not just the lot of poor people in the developing countries. More than 100m people in rich nations suffer a similar fate. Nearly 200m people are not expected to survive to age 60. More than 100m are homeless and atleast 37m are without jobs, other experiencing a state of social exclusion'. What a horrifying situation capitalist globalisation has created even in the developed industrialised countries of the world.

Earlier the World Bank described the present state of growth as jobless growth. Now the ILO Report 1998 mentions that presently there are thousand million jobless or under employed people in the globe and by the end of the year 1998, the situation will further worsen.

The ILO report further points out that one third of the current workforce of the world are either jobless or partially employed. The reports also mention that as a result of the present Asian economic crisis, more than 10m people have been rendered jobless in the current year.

The then Director General of ILO Mr Michael Hansen has mentioned that the underemployment situation pf the world would turn more seriously grave form the present grave from the present grave situation. The report points out that the unemployed situation has worsened than it was during the great depressions of the 1930's. The ILO report of 1998 deals with unemployed situation in different countries of the world. The average unemployment level in all the developing countries has reached figures higher than 8% of the labour force.

In these countries there are 120m people official registered as unemployed and over 700m people who are underemployed. In the 24 developed countries (OEDC countries), youth unemployment grew from 11.6% in 1990 on the average to 13.4% in 1997. In Spain youth unemployment is staggering 39% while in France it is 28.1%. In the advanced west European countries, the average unemployment is in double digits. As for the advanced west European countries, the average unemployment is in double digits.

As for India, currently the number of urban registered unemployed has reached the staggering figure of 40m. The rural unemployment, according to certain estimates will come around another 60m. The latest World Bank report 2000-2001 and World Labour report by ILO also estimate that one third of the world work force remain unemployed. Thus is the ultimate result of globalisation on the employment situation of the world.

Today workers of the world are passing through an unprecedented difficult period. Never before, the jobs of the workers and employees have been so jeopardised and the workers have been rendered so completely unsecured. The World Bank- IMF dictated structural adjustment programmes after about a decade of putting into practice have proved to be definitely anti worker. Our Trade Union International is concerned primarily with the public service employees.

The public employees in general either in the developing countries have become direct victims of the neo-liberal economy and the structural adjustment programme. The basic concept of neo-liberal globalisation is privatisation and drastic cut in public expenditure. In the scenario of heavy debt burdens of the developing countries, the IMF- World Bank dictated structural adjustment programme was based on the basic condition of privatisation of public enterprises, even of public services and drastic cut in social security measurers like health care, education, housing, pensionary benefits etc. and all reduction of staff.

As the reforms dictated by the IMF-World Bank are implemented and Public Sector industries are closed down or privatised, thousand of workers and employees are rendered unemployed. The banking, insurance and the entire financial sector employees are hard hit as the governments in the developing and developed countries are taking middles steps for privatisation. Workforce in this sector is being hastily reduced and there is no new employment. Moreover, deepening economic crisis is also resulting in banking crashes as is evidence in Japan recently and in some other South East Asian Countries.

Privatisation of other government departments and enterprises are also taking place in different countries. Right from Telecom, Postal service to railway service are being privatised. Many of the government departments in several countries are either being privatise or simply being closed down. Casualisation of staff increase in home based workers, steady reduction of regular and permanent employment in the public service are the order of the day in all developing and developed countries.

The public employees have therefore started resisting this onslaught. The strikes of the public employees in France, Spain, Portugal, South Africa, India, South Korea and massive mobilisation of the employees in various other forms of struggle around the globe right from the Latin American countries like Brazil, Argentina, Columbia to South Asian Countries like Japan, Philippines, Indonesia, etc. against cut back, redundancy, retrenchment indicate a growing mood of resistance pf the employees against this new economic regime.

The situation in the former socialist countries like Russia, other CIS countries and the eastern European countries seems to be the worst. Not only rampant privatisation and sharp reduction of staff, even non-payment of salaries to the existing employees are new phenomenon in these countries. Unfortunately, the governments in various countries particularly in the developing countries are desperately trying to stall these rising struggles through draconian anti worker measurers.

In some countries like South Korea, anti employee enactments have already been made. In India, retrograde amendments to existing labour laws are on the agenda of the government. Moreover, many member states have not yet implemented some if the basic conditions of recommendations of the ILO in regard to the rights of the workers. Some member states have not even ratified the convention no. 87 (1948) (concerning freedom of association and protection of the of the right to organise) and the convention of no. 98 (1948) (concerning application of the principles of the right to organisation and to collective bargaining) Most worrying is the fact that many member state have not yet ratified the convention no. 151 (1978) concerning protection of the rights to organise and procedure for determining conditions of employment in the public service.

In developing countries the situation is becoming alarming. As the reforms demanded by the IMF are implemented and public sector industries are closed down or privatised, thousands of workers and employees are rendered unemployed. Present even the government departments are either be partially abolished or the government activities are being surrendered to indigenous or multi-national capitalist.

The Banking, Insurance and the entire financial sector employees are hard hit as the governments in the developed and developing countries are taking hasty steps for privatisation. Workforce in this sector is being drastically reduced and there is no new employment. Moreover, the deepening economic crisis is also resulting in banking crashes as evidenced in Japan recently and this is rendering thousand of financial sector workers jobless. In India, the government is desperately trying to privatise the banking and insurance sector against which the employees of this sector are struggling. The public sector workers, especially in the financial sector and also in the government sector workers, especially in the financial sector and also in the government sectors along with other sections of the working class have to bear the burden of this globalisation and they are suffering.

In countries like Bangladesh, Pakiston, Srilanka, Nepal and India, the situation is becoming precarious. In India alone since 1991 about 1m workers have been rendered jobless because of the closure of industries, reduction of staff and dismantling of the public enterprise. In India Insurance sector has been opened up to private capital, indigenous and foreign despite stiff resistance by the trade unions in the insurance industry. In the banking sector private banking including foreign private banking is being encouraged and the nationalised sector of the banking is being curtailed. Now the government is thinking of VRS in the nationalised banking sector.

Many of governments departments also, like telecom has been corporatised threatening the jobs of the employees and closing the possibilities of further recruitment. Of late, threatening the jobs of the employees and closing the possibilities of further recruitment. Of late, the government of India has announced 10% cut in staff strength in all departments besides setting up a commission for downsizing of the government departments. Earlier the government of India announced 74% disinvestments and privatisation of public sector. Other public utility services like Medicare is also under privatisation. Corporate hospitals because of reduction of health budgets. Similar is the situation in education field also where private educational institutions are being encouragement at the cost of government-funded education.

Working people all over the capitalist world are being severely attacked and against this attack, resistance of the working people is also developing in all countries. This spate of struggle encompasses all the contingents of the world. Right form Brazil, Mexico, and Central West European countries, down to the South and East Asian countries working people's struggles are breaking out.

The December, 1995 historic strike in France with its waves Germany, Spain, Italy and other European countries, the December 1997 militant upheavals in South Korea, the mass upsurge in Indonesia, working class resistance in Japan against consumption tax and increased expenditure of medicare, against unemployment, the general strikes in India, workers resistance in Bangladesh, Nepal, Srilanka, South Africa and the latest working class struggles and political turmoil in Russia, convincingly proves that the struggle and resistance of the working people against the devastating effects of Capitalist Globalisation and IMF-World Bank prescriptions are breaking out almost all parts of the globe and the last election results in various Western Counties including that of Sweden and Germany, also in Japan in the East convincingly confirms the fast growing dissatisfaction of the people against the disastrous effects of globalisation and their search for an alternative.

In Europe, Australia and America unprecedented unity struggles are breaking out against IMF-World Bank WTO. i.e the entire process of globalisation. The militant mass demonstrations in Seattle causing collapse of WTO conference in November 1999, vigorous mass protests in Washington in April 2000 against World Bank IMF meet huge mass demonstrations in Melbourne on September

11 2000, against World Economic Forum meet mammoth working class and mass demonstrations in Prague from 24-26 September 2000 against IMF meeting castigating globalisation and demanding moratorium debts of the third world countries indicate a new dimension of global struggle against the disastrous globalisation.

5

Compulsions of Foreign Direct Investment

Foreign direct investment implies the creation of new enterprises abroad, or the acquisition of substantial stakes in existing foreign enterprises. This form of investment has grown at an unprecedented pace for two decades, with only a slight interruption during the recession in the early 1990s.

The growth in international investment of the past decades has been due in large part to increased liberalisation brought about by reduced barriers to trade and investment and discriminatory subsidies. The 1990s also witness the removal of domestic impediments through widespread regulatory reform and privatisation. At the moment, more firms, and in more industries and countries, than ever before are expanding abroad through direct investment.

At the microeconomic level, far-reaching organisational change is taking place as a result of e-business and new technology, which are transforming the value chain for many industries. Today, some 60,000 parent companies worldwide have established over 500,000 foreign affiliates in countries other than their own, with the amount of inward FDI stock valued at roughly $4,000 billion. These foreign affiliates are estimated to have generated total gross output of more than $2,600 billion and total employment of over 35 million in host countries.

While about 90 per cent of all parent companies are located in OECD countries, a little more than half of all foreign affiliates are in operation in non-OECD countries, providing a major source of industrial production and employment in a number of emerging and developing economies.

The significant increase in FDI flows towards developing and emerging economies, and concerns about the practices of MNEs have contributed to the resurgence of both theoretical and policy debates regarding the impact of FDI on the process of economic development. On the one hand, FDI is an important source of financing of domestic capital needs and compared with other forms of private capital flows—e.g. portfolio equity and debt flows—FDI is more stable. FDI also allows the transfer of technology.

Multinational enterprises—the main drivers of FDI—are a powerful and effective means to disseminate technology from developed to developing countries, and are often the only source of new and innovative technologies that are usually not available through the market.

Technology disseminated through FDI generally includes the 'entire package' including experts, skills and the financial resources to exploit the technology appropriately. Other potential benefits of FDI for host countries include increased competition in input and product markets and human capital enhancement. On the other hand, there has been growing public concern that these benefits still have to be demonstrated and, where benefits exists, that they are not being shared equitably.

Some of the potential costs associated with FDI could include increased unemployment due to restructuring and increased market concentration. In addition, many factors account for differences in the level and range of benefits accruing to recipient countries, including exogenous factors such as size and proximity to markets or endowment of natural resources.

Institutional, legal, and regulatory frameworks, along with policy coherence, the availability of skilled labour and infrastructure also impact upon a country's ability to attract and capture the benefits associated with FDI. The impact of FDI on economic growth and productivity via technology transfer. The growth of world FDI in recent years has been exceptional and the last two decades have seen the worldwide production and consumption of goods and services become increasingly internationalised.

FDI has become strongly oriented towards the services sector. In 1999, more than half of OECD FDI outflows involved this sector, with banks and other financial institutions accounting for the bulk of these investments. However, FDI in electricity, gas and water, and telecommunications saw the most dramatic increase, reflecting the massive privatisation and deregulation of these public utilities in the past decade.

In recent years, an increasingly large part of FDI flows has been through mergers and acquisitions, rather than through the establishment of new enterprises. Whereas mergers and acquisitions have become the main mode of entry worldwide, in developing countries greenfield investment remains dominant.

The vast majority of world investment still takes place amongst OECD countries. More than 90 per cent of world FDI outflows originates in OECD Member countries, and in recent years OECD countries have received around three-quarters of world FDI inflows as well.

OECD outflows to non-OECD countries are also highly concentrated. Though OECD FDI outflows to developing countries have accounted for only a small part of their total FDI flows, from the developing countries' perspective this FDI has been of great importance. FDI has become the most important source of external financing for certain developing countries, overshadowing other capital flows such as official development assistance (ODA) or export credits.

While at the beginning of the 1990s OECD FDI flows to developing countries accounted for around 30 percent of private capital flows to developing countries, by 1999 this had risen to as much 80 percent. While ODA in real terms has declined in recent years from its peak in 1992, on the whole it has remained relatively stable in comparison to private flows.

Non-FDI private flows have been rather volatile, but overall are playing an increasingly larger role since the early 1990s in the total financial flows towards developing countries. Not only is FDI to developing countries overshadowing other capital flows such as ODA, also in relation to GDP it is becoming more important for developing countries.

The non-OECD countries that rank among the top twenty recipients of total world FDI outflows have, in most cases, seen high inflows in relative terms to the size of their economies. Diversification of investment flows spreads the risks that are related to a large dependency on a few countries or sectors. The growth in international investment of the past decades has been due in large part to increased liberalisation brought about by reduced barriers to trade and investment and discriminatory subsidies. This improvement in the investment climate in the 1990s was influenced in part by the recognition of the benefits of FDI.

Of the almost 1000 changes in FDI regulations undertaken worldwide in the 1990s, 94 percent were aimed at creating a more favourable environment for FDI. Instead of barriers, many countries now employ incentives to attract FDI. Indeed, incentive based competition for FDI has become a widespread phenomenon, involving governments at all levels in both OECD and non-OECD countries.

Examples of such incentives include tax holidays, preferential access to (government) credit, subsidies and the reduction of import duties for goods needed for production. These incentives are meant to reap the maximum benefits associated with the activities of MNEs e.g. knowledge, management skills, technological advantages, etc. However the cost-effectiveness of such incentives is questionable since they usually attract primarily short-term profit-orientated or cheap cost-motivated FDI.

Furthermore, evidence suggests that competition for FDI results in no net gain in those countries FDI market shares. The 1990s also witness the removal of domestic impediments through widespread regulatory reform and privatisation. The OECD public enterprise sector is currently estimated to be less than half the size it was at the beginning of the 1980s.

The privatisation movement was in large part induced by dissatisfaction with the performance of state-owned enterprises, and the increased capital investment needed to upgrade infrastructure, especially in the public utility sector. Privatisation offered the opportunity to restructure and introduce competition in sectors previously dominated by state monopolies, to increase investment, and to improve productive and allocative efficiency, all of which benefit consumers and the economy as a whole.

However, in many emerging markets and economies in transition, the benefits from the change in ownership have sometimes proved disappointing, due to weaknesses in the legal, institutional or market environment. While the investment environment has improved considerably in the past decade, barriers to investment have not disappeared and many countries remain reluctant to undertake full liberalisation commitments, even where they are actively encouraging FDI. In order to retain national 'control' over the economy some countries still do not permit FDI in sectors considered "strategic".

Restrictions on foreign ownership also provide an important barrier to entry and prevent the market for corporate control from functioning efficiently. Other examples of remaining restrictions include reciprocity and discretionary liberalisation i.e. where sectors are opened to FDI but on a case by case authorisation basis.

Some countries use measures that are more specifically tailored towards a single goal, like the use of screening procedures to select FDI projects which they consider best serve their country's needs or the imposition of conditions on FDI in an attempt to ensure that technology is transferred.

Finally, a lack of political and economic stability and predictability can also act as a barrier to investment, as can a lack of transparency of regulations, corruption, weak protection of intellectual property rights, and arbitrary application of regulations and laws. One of the most direct ways in which FDI affects development is through adding to the host country's savings and investments, thereby enlarging the production base at a higher growth rate than would have been possible if a host country had to rely on domestic sources of savings alone.

But FDI is much more than just a flow of capital. In particular, the inflow of foreign direct investment can bring new technologies, which usually are not available through the market. These technologies may enhance the productivity of foreign affiliates and, through spillover effects, that of domestic firms as well.

Before turning to the overall impact of FDI on growth, this section therefore will first examine one of the primary ways in which FDI contributes to growth i.e. through the transfer of technology to host countries. Multinational firms are among the most important players in the world responsible for creating and controlling technology. They facilitate putting tangible and intangible resources available in different countries to their most productive uses.

As part of the global profit-making operations of multinational enterprises, FDI, by its nature, involves the transfer of capital, technology and knowledge from home to host countries. Using better technologies offers possibilities to increase productivity and hence economic growth and development. Hence it is not surprising that many countries view investments by those MNEs as one of the most important means to acquire technology and knowledge to upgrade their own production base.

However, it is difficult to paint an unambiguous picture as to how FDI can transfer technology, and how this technology is going to contribute to development. It is not a priori clear that every type of technology transferred is appropriate, and not every investment made is by definition beneficial to host country development. Though FDI is only one of several ways by which firms can transfer technology it remains the most important one, especially for developing countries.

First of all, an investment not only comprises the technology itself but also includes 'the entire package': the complementary resources such as management experience and entrepreneurial abilities. Unlike trade in goods, where developing countries have to try to imitate and learn from 'backward engineering', FDI involves the explicit transfer of technology. This may be especially beneficial for countries with underdeveloped local capabilities.

Secondly, by their mere entry and presence, MNEs disturb the existing equilibrium in the market forcing domestic firms to innovate in order to protect their market shares and profits. This alone is likely to lead to productivity increases in local firms. Another benefit of FDI in transferring technology versus other modes of transfer is that the typical features of a MNE, for example, scale economics, capital reserves, or marketing and sales experience, can contribute significantly to exploiting the technology in a profitable manner.

MNEs also offer brand names and access to regional and global markets. However, these possible benefits are accompanied by possible costs. A highly efficient MNE affiliate may lead to a fall in the number of local firms if the less efficient local firms are forced out of business. Though this may increase overall resource allocation in the long term, the short-term consequences for local employment and market concentration may be severe.

For example, if MNE affiliates are very strong, in the absence of an appropriate competition policy framework they may abuse their monopoly power, with consequentially harmful effects. Other costs include the repatriation of profits with consequences for balance of payments and exchange rates, and the avoidance of taxation through transfer pricing.

The 'whole package' that often comes with FDI also has a reverse side, particularly for countries with relatively high local capabilities and that are able to exploit the technology themselves. Instead of relying on the MNEs expertise, local firms in these countries may prefer to obtain the technology through licensing, though this option may not always be available if the MNE chooses not to license the technology.

Knowing that FDI is important in transferring technology does not however explain how this transfer and consequent spillovers take place. There are four channels by which technology transfer through FDI can occur, either directly or indirectly through spillovers. For some time now it has been recognised that MNEs may benefit the host country via the backward and forward linkages they generate. Backward linkages are relations with suppliers, forward linkages refer to relations with buyers—either consumers or other firms using the MNEs intermediate products as part of their own production process.

Linkages are more pronounced the larger the size of the host market and technological capabilities of local suppliers and when intermediate goods are used intensively. However, when addressing the impact of linkage creation it should be taken into account that MNEs only improve welfare if they generate linkages beyond those that are generated by the local firms they displace. As regards backward linkages, MNEs can contribute to raising the productivity of their supplier firms in various ways.

MNEs can provide technical assistance or information to raise the quality of the suppliers' products or to facilitate innovations. MNEs usually do not hesitate to train local suppliers. However, if suppliers are forced to meet the higher quality standards without any training or assistance, this could lead in the short term to suppliers failing to meet the necessary requirements, leading to firm failures and job losses. Other spillovers from backward linkages include assistance in purchasing raw materials and intermediary goods, training in management and organisation, and assistance with diversification of customers.

Generally, these linkages are extended over time, which could be a consequence of technology transfer. Forward linkages occur with firms' buyers. This can be distributors, which can benefit from the marketing and other knowledge of the MNE, or downstream firms who can benefit from intermediate goods with lower prices or better quality, or both. Downstream firms can also benefit from lower prices arising from increased competition in their supply market, and consumers thus also benefit from lower-priced final products.

Related to the issue of vertical linkages, is the diffusion of technology through horizontal 'linkages' i.e. to competitors of the MNE affiliate. This diffusion of technology takes place through either demonstration effects—when the exposure of local firms to the superior technology of the MNE leads local firms to update their own production methods—or competition effects. These two effects are difficult to disentangle, since they both occur at the industry level, and may reinforce each other, for example when FDI expands the set of technologies available to local firms, it also usually increases competition.

The effects of increased competition are usually seen as beneficial. Increased competition encourages both productive efficiency and a more efficient allocation of resources. This may be especially the case when MNEs enter industries where high entry barriers reduced the degree of domestic competition. Though in theory competition improves efficiency and welfare, however, entry by an MNE may not always increase competition.

Concerns have arisen that strong foreign MNEs out-compete local firms, or at least force local firms to merge, and the increased industrial concentration can result in market power. The abuse of market power by the MNE (and possibly local firms) would then result in a decrease in allocative efficiency. Empirical evidence suggests that FDI is likely to lead to higher concentration in most host countries, and there is a larger risk that MNEs crowd out local firms in developing countries than in developed countries, because of their greater technological advantages.

One study finds that this correlation disappears once other determinants of concentration are taken into account, and that MNEs do not cause concentration but are instead drawn to concentrated industries. Another way through which technology may be transferred and disseminated in a host country is through labour migration.

Workers employed by the MNE affiliate acquire knowledge of its superior technology and management practices. By switching employers or setting up their own business the technology is spread. MNE affiliates usually try to avoid this kind of spillovers by paying an 'efficiency wage', a premium in order to keep employees from switching jobs to domestically owned competitors.

Multinational firms are among the world most important creators of knowledge and technology. Many of these firms concentrate their R&D activities in their home country or other developed countries. Developing countries only account for an estimated 6% of global R&D expenditures. And even among those developing countries, expenditures are very concentrated.

UNCTAD calculated - taking US firms as a proxy - that the top four developing economies accounted for 77% of total R&D expenditure in developing countries. The centralisation of R&D is one of the large policy concerns of developing countries regarding MNEs. In the case where R&D is transferred to foreign subsidiaries this has basically been in relation to adaptive tasks, drawing on a few local resources to better serve the local market.

MNEs are often blamed for failing to adopt their technologies, that are designed for industrialised country wages and capital costs, to the factor prices prevailing in developing countries. In those cases where R&D is performed in developing countries, the expenditures have been found to generate significant efficiency gains, both within and across industries in the R&D performing country.

The inflow of foreign investment can foster growth in the host economy by easing the shortages of capital, foreign exchange, technology and skills. The growth process can be further sustained if backward and forward linkages emerge from MNEs to the domestic economy and if FDI contributes to raising the profitability of domestic investment.

One of the important questions concerning FDI and growth therefore is whether FDI contributes relatively more to growth than domestic investment. In practice, however, the growth-enhancing effects of FDI may depend in part on whether FDI "crowds out" or "crowds in" domestic investment. Also, its impact may depend crucially on the absorption capacity of a host country, as the efficient use of new technology requires a minimum threshold of human capital on the recipient side.

Looking at the impact of FDI on capital accumulation and productivity growth, de Mello finds that foreign investors increase productivity in host countries and that FDI is often a catalyst for domestic investment and technological progress. The estimated regressions are also modified accordingly in order to check whether the impact of FDI on growth is contingent upon the level of educational attainment, economic development or financial development in the recipient country. They find no significant impact of FDI on growth, though they do find that FDI has a positive impact on capital accumulation. However, these results do not mean that FDI has no effect on growth, but only that FDI goes hand in hand with growth.

Even where countries have successfully integrated it's not clear that they are benefiting to the maximum extent possible. Despite multiple efforts at reform, the majority of the least developed countries failed to grow and to integrate into the global economy as rapidly as other developing countries. Market openness clearly is not a sufficient condition for economic growth. The diverse experiences of developing countries suggest that the positive effects of FDI are not automatic, but may be affected by various host industry and country characteristics.

Domestic conditions and certain threshold levels of development such as technological capabilities, human capital or the development of financial markets seem to play an important role on the effect of FDI on growth. Many have also argued sound macro-economic policies and institutional stability are also necessary, as is social stability. With weak institutions, poor governance (both public and private) and unsound policies, market reforms can fail with great costs, especially to vulnerable groups in society.

Acknowledging that such beneficial effects are likely to depend on the skills of the domestic labour force, FDI is interacted with a measure of human capital development (i.e. secondary school attainment). The authors find that FDI contributes to growth although the magnitude of this effect depends on the stock of human capital available in the host economy. In particular, they find that FDI raises growth only in those countries where the labour force has achieved a minimum threshold of education.

FDI is a source of growth only for countries already at a relatively high level of development and that low-income countries lack the necessary capabilities needed to absorb the FDI-related technology transfer. Such a relation holds not only true between countries, but also between different industries within countries.

Spillovers should be easier to identify empirically when the technological attributes of local firms match those of the MNE affiliates. Besides the relative difference in the technological capabilities of the host MNE and the local firm, the absolute level of absorptive capacity is also important.

A possible explanation is that the absorption of MNEs technology by host countries requires a relatively high level of human capital. Most LDCs do not meet the human capital threshold required for recipient countries to benefit from technology spillovers.

Recent studies find that FDI contributes positively to growth in countries where financial market are sufficiently developed and that imperfect and underdeveloped financial markets are likely to penalise domestic firms in favour of MNEs.

Driven by increases in international investment flows and by changes in government policies—liberalisation, regulatory reform and privatisation - national economies have become increasingly integrated into one global one, with the exception of a number of least developed countries.

For developing countries in particular the internationalisation of economic activities poses both opportunities and challenges for development and economic growth. Multinational firms, the main drivers of FDI, are among the most important actors in the world responsible for creating and controlling technology.

These technologies can make important contributions to increased productivity and economic growth in developing countries. It is not surprising therefore that many developing countries want to attract FDI. International investment contributes to economic growth by both increasing the capital base and by increasing productivity.

The latter is perhaps the most important for development, and is mainly influenced by improvements in technology, including managerial knowledge and skills. Though FDI is not the only way to transfer technology, it is the most important one.

Technology transfer from FDI, both direct and indirect, can occur through vertical and horizontal linkages, labour migration and through the internationalisation of R&D. The effects of technology transfer and spillovers on productivity and economic growth have been studied by many.

While the results are not unanimous, the majority finds that these effects have a positive impact on productivity and economic growth. However, the hoped-for positive effects of FDI do not come automatically. Since the results differ by country and industry, it is expected that various host industry and country characteristics may influence the outcome of technology transfer for development.

One of the most prominent is the 'technology gap' between the technologies used by the foreign MNE affiliate and the local firms. Capturing the benefits of FDI seems to require that host countries reach a certain threshold of development, as reflected in the local technical capabilities of its firms and the general level of human capital and education.

Financial Globalisation and Child Well-being

A central characteristic of the world in the twenty-first century is the increasingly free movement of merchandise and capital across national boundaries, with all countries now bound together by global markets. The rapid growth of private capital flows over the past decade presents an opportunity for poor countries to access a global pool of savings, technology and management skills; but at the same time it presents new policy challenges in terms of securing sustainable development and poverty reduction. The linkages between financial globalisation in general—and financial crises in emerging markets in particular—and the well being of children in developing countries are thus always complex and often ambiguous. This section focuses on the analysis of the effect of financial crises on labour markets, the incomes of poor families, and the consequences for child wellbeing. These are the origins of financial integration and instability; the scale of the financial collapses and their wage/employment consequences; and the nature of the recovery process.

Financial Integration, Stability and Poverty

The rising supply of private capital from developed

countries to developing countries (or more precisely, the rising demand for emerging market assets) is mainly due to the scale and scope of modern production systems that has led to the rise of 'multinational' corporations which can locate and articulate their activities on a global basis so as to source local and overseas markets. However, the increasing complexity and competitiveness of financial markets in developed countries themselves have led to a demand for high-yield risky assets combined with a more sophisticated approach to the management of that risk. This has increased the willingness to invest in emerging market assets that are both liquid and possess a low covariance with the rest of the portfolio. This process has generated international bond, equity and credit markets of considerable size; markets which have facilitated by advances in telecommunications and information technology.

The supply of suitable financial assets for foreign investors to acquire has also increased markedly due to the process of market liberalisation in developing countries. The combination of difficulties in long-term international bank borrowing, domestic interest rate liberalisation and strict monetary policies has led to a dramatic expansion of the government bond market. Finally, the opening and expansion of domestic securities markets led by privatisation flotations has encouraged domestic firms to raise funds by issuing shares and bills. The ability to access international capital markets has been enhanced by improved telecommunications technology and changes in these markets themselves. International bond issues by both governments and large firms from developing countries have become routine; while the spread of depository receipts has permitted the quotation of developing country equities on the main global markets.

However, international capital markets suffer from a number of systemic inefficiencies which lead to 'market failure'—that is a situation where otherwise profitable investments cannot find finance. In particular, a shift in external market sentiment can cause a sudden (possibly excessive) reversal in the both risk appetite and perception of uncertain future returns, destabilising the economy. The integration of capital markets has also increased the ease by which nationals of developing countries can move their assets abroad. Of course, portfolio diversification can be micro-economically efficient in itself, and indeed many developing country companies have become to emerge as 'southern multinationals' in their own right, while intra-regional investment flows are becoming more important. None the less, the scale of 'capital flight' from developing countries is legitimate cause for concern because it implies potential investment foregone—particularly in crisis situations.

With an open capital account, the cycle of foreign capital flows tends to be highly pro-cyclical with countries' economic conditions, rather than acting to stabilise the economy. This model also encourages pro-cyclical government policy—increased spending in booms and cutbacks during recessionary outflow periods—and hence increased macroeconomic volatility. The management of capital inflows has costs in terms of increased instability of government finances and the macroeconomy more generally, and also unstable real exchange rates if sterilisation is adopted. The result of this overshooting may be the widespread failure of corporate and banking sector institutions: indiscriminate failures which destroy sound as well as unsound banks and corporations may jeopardise the institutional basis of a future economic recovery.

However, recovery of consumption levels was also relatively rapid in most cases, which has generated some optimism among international financial institutions. However, these financials shocks also have serious consequences for corporate finance and thus on productive investment and sustainable employment. This problem is exacerbated in many developing countries by the especially weak position of small and medium enterprises (SMEs). Affiliates of foreign multinationals by their very nature are largely exempt from local financing constraints.

Large domestic companies or groups generally have preferential access to bank credit, and are thus relatively protected from capital market fluctuations. SMEs are the most vulnerable then to capital outflow-induced shifts in credit availability, and the concomitant impact on the poor can be strongly negative. Financial crises in a number of leading emerging markets in the latter half of the 1990s and early 2000s caused widespread concern about the premature liberalisation of financial sectors in developing countries, before a solvent fiscal structure, a robust regulatory system and a competitive business sector had been built up. In a number of cases large inflows of short-term funds led to overheating of the domestic economy, excessive credit expansion (and a decline in savings rates), real estate bubbles and over-valuation of the exchange rate.

The large outflows of funds once the cycle turned, the collapse of investment and output, the rise of unemployment and the fiscal retrenchment; have had serious consequences for poverty and development and tend to create 'contagion' for neighbouring countries. Capital account liberalisation is seen to act at a general level, through the effects on overall growth and on macroeconomic instability; and more specifically, through the effects on poverty of changes in government budgets, access to credit and industrial performance.

— That it remains to be seen whether the overall growth impact of capital account liberalisation is positive, and the case in lower-income countries is particularly weak. There is no evidence of positive growth effects.

— That the benefits accrue primarily to international financial markets and domestic capital holders, i.e. the relatively wealthy, but eventually to the poorer through improved investment quality (and hence—at least potentially-employment).

— The impact on investment quantity, however, which may be more significant for employment, is unproven; there appears to be no long-term positive impact, although possibly a one-time, short-term boom in investment may occur.

— There is a danger that the impact of increased macroeconomic instability—which has been shown to have damaging negative effects on both the level and quality of investment—will outweigh these benefits and lead ultimately to reduced employment.

— While the most obvious winners are likely to be located in urban areas, with easy access to financial institutions, any competitive effects which lead to branch closures in already under-provided rural areas have clear negative consequences for agricultural industry and poverty.

The first two are negative—at least in the short to medium term—while the third may have differing effects, depending on the extent of possible increases in capital flight and the (output-related) tax base. Government budgets are reduced then, with two effects of particular importance for the poor.

— Social spending will suffer in real terms if not relative to the total budget, and the longer-term impact of reduced health and education provision falls particularly on the poorest.

— Longer-term spending—i.e. infrastructure investment programs—may be significantly cut, and as well as limiting the country's development directly the resulting instability will also reduce the extent to which private investment can be crowded in. The possibility of greater government spending on building up reserves and other measures to protect the currency will compound these effects.

Recovery of output from the immediate post-crisis level is almost complete in most countries in crisis during the 1990s; but the longer economic and social consequences may be considerable. This is due to the large and sudden redistribution of assets and liabilities between domestic and foreign agents, between the public and private sectors, and between the rich and the poor. This redistribution clearly depends on the form that the rescue package takes; but in most cases this has involved the assumption of large new liabilities by the public sector in the form of new external borrowing and the taking over of bad loan books of domestic banks long. This in turn implies future fiscal retrenchment with inevitable social consequences. Much of the problem of addressing this issue arises from the absence of a clear and agreed framework for analysing the effect of macro-financial shocks on poverty, and thus child well being. The poverty effects of adjustment programmes are shown to be inevitably negative in the short run, but to be positive in the longer run insofar as private investment accelerates. This latter problem is particularly acute in the case of financial shocks. The labour market is somewhat crudely modelled in these models, and wage stickiness exacerbates poverty by reducing employment through the price-elasticity of the demand for labour.

Nonetheless, these models do show that the poverty effect of external shocks depends to a great extent on the nature of the macroeconomic policy response. In particular, the adjustment can take the form of a relative price shift (i.e. devaluation) or a demand reduction (e.g. fiscal contraction) and the poverty effect depends upon the balance of private and public expenditure in the wellbeing of the poor—in other words, on the particular country case. None the less, it is very clear from these models that financial liberalisation exacerbates the effect of adjustment on the poor, because of the shift of private wealth out of domestic investment (which creates employment) into foreign assets—that is, 'capital flight'—reflecting the relative immobility of labour. The underlying trend under trade and financial liberalisation is one of rising earnings differentials between skilled and unskilled workers—that is, between employment in the modern corporate sector on the one hand and employment (or under-employment) in the urban informal sector and the rural sector on the other.

However, during the crisis periods the pushing of workers into informal self-employed activities was more critical in explaining the rise in inequality. In particular, the changing employment structure mainly explains the shifts in inequality both in boom (positively) and recession (negatively) periods. However, the change in the average remuneration explains most of the increase in poverty incidence in the recession and crisis periods, and of its reduction during the liberalisation period. In sum, the labour market effects of financial crises are clearly central to understanding the poverty effects of financial crises.

Child Wellbeing under Financial Instability

The World Bank in the Global Economic Prospects and the Developing Countries devotes a whole chapter to 'External Shocks, Financial Crises, and Poverty and Developing Countries' that concludes somewhat optimistically that recovery has been rapid in cases where countries have pursued 'sound policies'. Targeted social support in the form of 'safety nets' has worked well. In particular, it asserts that health and education have not suffered as a share of government expenditures and have even increased in some cases; though naturally per capita spending has declined with GDP and fiscal retrenchment. A similarly optimistic story emerges from Indonesian village-level data which seems to suggest that sectoral experience may differ, particularly where large real devaluations affect traded good producers positively. This contrasts rather sharply with the more recent World Bank view in WDR 2000/01: Attacking Poverty that affirms that boom and bust economic cycles prevent countries from consolidating progress in poverty reduction, because it is the poorest who are most vulnerable to these swings. In the most recent Global Development Finance the Bank takes a more cautious position on capital account liberalisation, hopefully due to the impact on the poor.

Although the literature on child poverty in developing countries is extensive, rigorous studies of the effect of financial crises is scarce. Collect a number of papers on health, nutrition and economic crises which make the point that as most health and nutrition delivery is by women, the impact of crises on mothers and older sisters will be transmitted to children. In particular, if labour market disruption and low incomes force women to work more away from home, then child care in all its forms will suffer—even though mothers tend to spend a larger proportion of their income (and time) on their children than fathers do. Moreover, even though the initial impact of financial crises on children may be reversed as the economy recovers relatively quickly, the failure to invest in early childhood as having a longer-run impact on adult well-being and income earning capacity far beyond the original welfare loss itself.

In one of the few longitudinal studies of health and child nutritional status at a time of economic structural adjustment in Zimbabwe during the mid-90s there was a diversification of income sources and (counter-intuitively) a decline in subsistence production. Safety nets did not reach the poor, and in any case household expenditure on health care, school fees and household durables were all cut. The effect on child welfare in general and stunting in particular was considerable despite the declared intention of both government and aid agencies to protect the poor. The fact that children are forced onto the labour market in times of financial crises may not be as negative as it might appear.

There is not a simple conflict between a child's paid work and education: because children work anyway, but are usually unpaid, a chance to get monetary income increases their bargaining strength within the family, and their nutritional status is actually protected thereby. Turning to micro-evidence on the recent financial crises, much has been written on the social impact of the down-swing, particularly on the Indonesian poor, but unfortunately not on the experience of recovery in more recent years. It is difficult to determine, therefore, how permanent the effects may be.

Enrolment rates fell in Indonesia by 3 percent for primary and 11 percent for secondary schools. Rural primary enrolment fell more than urban, but the reverse was true at the secondary level: Real spending on education fell by more than a third in the two years after the crisis. The long-term consequences are serious because education has been the main factor in reducing poverty. UNICEF that the social impact of Krismon was particularly great on the health status of poor children because the public health system, based on primary clinics was thinly spread and very fragile. Between early 1996 and early 1999 the proportion of population living below the poverty line rose from 18 to 27 percent.

The urban poor were hit more than the rural: the urban formal sector was hit hardest, and though rural sector suffered less, there were more people competing for same jobs. Official household surveys found that between 1997 and 1998 per capita household expenditure fell nationally by 24 percent: 34 percent in urban areas and 13 percent in rural. Forced sales of assets mean that the real income effect may be even greater. But children were not generally withdrawn from school. However, the proportion of children using government health facilities fell from 26 to 20 percent, due to not having money for fees, the deteriorating service and lack of drugs.

Attendance by children under five went down from 47 to 28 percent.

The key problem appears to be in the community clinics, where local volunteers (mainly women) withdrew in order to earn money elsewhere. Government safety nets worked fairly well in food and education, and though they could have been better targeted on the poor, broad coverage may have defused social tensions. Common sense tells us that [child poverty, homelessness, malnutrition etc] must have been exacerbated by Indonesia's crisis. But it would be wrong to assume that these problems will automatically recede as the monetary situation improves.

Macro-economic improvement has not trickled down to restore Indonesians to their pre-crisis standard of living. Even if it had, economic recovery alone would not be enough to tackle the unseen and under-estimated human vulnerability that existed long before the crisis. Financial instability in general and financial crises in particular can place an excessive burden on poor and vulnerable members of society in emerging market economies. The poor are not in general the main beneficiaries of the upswing in an asset price boom, as employment and wages tend to rise in the sectors requiring skills such as banking and construction. However, if the subsequent downturn involves a sharp fall in aggregate output and severe fiscal retrenchment, vulnerable groups are likely to experience serious income decline. Sustained poverty reduction requires long-term growth and substantial public investment in social infrastructure, both of which conditions are negatively affected by financial crises.

The consequence of currency collapse for levels of output, and thus employment, can be dramatic. The result of large nominal devaluations, at least in the short term, has been a decline in imports (i.e. reduced absorption) rather than an increase in exports (i.e. resource reallocation); and thus of domestic economic activity. Real wages fall sharply, an effect that is maintained into the medium term if the real exchange rate is to be depreciated and the traded sector stimulated.

The decline of public investment in crisis periods can have long-term employment consequences, while the effect of financial instability and business uncertainty on private investment can be even more serious. Short-term capital inflows, and the resultant macroeconomic instability, have a number of important consequences for domestic industry. What is particularly significant here is the asymmetric impact of increased levels of macroeconomic uncertainty on firms. In financial crises banks tend to restrict credit to all but preferential borrowers (e.g. large firms).

The dominance of small and medium enterprises (SMEs) is greater in developing economies, where larger firms are fewer and SMEs provide much of the employment. Since smaller firms tend to more labour-intensive and less capital-intensive, their employment contribution is relatively greater and thus their credit starvation in financial crises can have serious social consequences.

Transmission of Financial Shocks to Child Poverty

Households are affected by real macroeconomic shocks

through the level of employment and wages on the one hand, and the availability of government services and bank credit (particularly for residential construction and consumer durables purchases) on the other. To a great extent, therefore, the impact of short-term capital flows on households will reflect the consequence of the response of the fiscal and firms sectors to external shock.

— The negative effect of these flows on public investment stability, and thus on the effective provision of social infrastructure; leading to a reduced supply of and effectiveness in health and education services, public transport systems and urban services.

— The asymmetric effect of these flows on the volatility of corporate output, and thus on the level of current 'formal sector' employment and, through the level of investment on longer term employment.

— The negative effect of these flows on capital market and exchange rate volatility, and thus on the level of private investment; with long-term consequences for the level of sustainable employment and thus income distribution.

However, the most significant negative consequence on welfare is probably—as in the case of trade liberalisation—felt through the long term consequences for private investment, because this (rather than low wage rates or even labour skilling) is the main source of sustainable long-term employment. None the less, the broader effect of capital flows on the real exchange rate is of considerable interest, because this affects the level of aggregate employment in the economy as a whole (including the small-scale sector) and the level of real wages through relative prices.

The mechanics of this boom often take the form of banks extending consumer credit backed by the short-term capital inflows; rather than extending it to companies as in earlier model. This boom is not sustainable, however, and to remain consistent with market expectations of solvency the current account should be closed again in the subsequent period and imports should fall sharply again even if the capital inflow is not reversed.

In practice, halting an import-and-credit boom generated by short-term capital inflows is very difficult. This is partly for the technical reason that reducing credit levels to consumers implies rapid repayment of debt which cannot be achieved by selling the corresponding household assets (e.g. houses or consumer durables); and partly for the political reason that the euphoric sense of economic success is difficult to abandon. In consequence, it is not surprising that the authorities seek to sustain the boom in the hope that further short term capital inflows can be attracted. However, when foreign investors reach the conclusion that the deficit is unsustainable, the reverse process starts. Capital outflows require that the domestic economy generate a large surplus on the current account of the balance of payments. When drastic reductions in domestic demand have caused widespread bankruptcy and household distress, to borrow heavily from international financial institutions in order to - in effect—acquire the domestic assets of non-resident investors. The aggregate impact of these sudden shifts in corporate sector activity affect both wages and employment directly.

An outflow of capital forces wither a sharp decline in GDP as imports fall or a depreciation of the currency, which mitigates the import decline with an export stimulus. Of course, most crises involve both these effects as the capital outflow both reduces liquidity to the domestic market and reduces the price of domestic currency assets. A nominal devaluation only becoming real if nominal wages do not move up proportionately. There is thus a trade-off between real wages and employment levels in the adjustment process.

However this does not arise from the price elasticity of demand from labour, but rather from the impact of the external sector which drives the domestic macroeconomic equilibrium. In the case of a capital inflow, an active monetary policy would involve some domestic inflation in order to force up (i.e. devalue) the real exchange rate and allow output to rise, which may well be politically unattractive. This may be the reason why in Latin America there has been a tendency to allow exchange rates to appreciate during periods of short-term capital inflow, due to the recent experience of high inflation. In Asia, with less inflationary experience, there is more willingness to allow domestic prices (and thus the real exchange rate) to adjust. On the outflow of short capital, exactly the reverse situation should hold; but as nominal prices are more or less rigid downwards in practice, it is much more difficult devalue the real exchange rate than to revalue it, so that a forced reduction in output is much more likely. In sum, an inflow followed by an equal outflow is likely to have an asymmetric character: the real exchange rate falling (i.e. appreciating) with the inflow, and output falling on the outflow. This analysis of the response of the real exchange rate and aggregate demand to short term capital inflows and outflows also reveals asymmetric implications for wages and employment.

The real exchange rate rises on the inflow, but does not fall proportionately on an equal outflow; so that aggregate demand falls more on the outflow than it had risen on the inflow. To the extent that real wages will rise with the inflow but employment will remain the same. With the outflow, real wages would not fall but employment would decline. As a key problem of income distribution is the balance between the incomes of the employed and those of the un- (or under-) employed; fluctuations in external capital flows can be expected to have a negative effect on income distribution.

The effect of the collapse of labour incomes in the corporate sector on the rest of the economy is the key to the welfare effect - this effect being transmitted through expenditures on goods and services from the urban informal sector, and from there out to the rural sector. The key insight here is that urban informal sector employment and incomes are determined by the expenditure of corporate sector employees. The effect on the urban poor of a change in the corporate wage rate is thus different from that of a change in corporate employment, even though the expenditure effect is similar, because the latter involves a change in competition in the informal labour market. Further, migration from rural to urban areas tends to equalise incomes at the margin; so that any shift in urban per capita incomes will affect the migratory process and can even reverse it in a crisis.

With sustained expansion of the corporate sector in a boom period, then both urban and rural incomes rise and poverty rises, even though a minority of migrants to urban areas get jobs in the corporate sector. When this mechanism is reversed in a financial crisis, poverty increases in both rural and urban areas. The model shows that the effect on the rest of the economy of a corporate sector decline depends very much upon whether there is a decline in wages or a decline in employment. The latter is much more disruptive than the former on the rest of the economy, and to the extent that employment loss by the head of household has a more traumatic effect on children than the loss of income, then this finding has significant implications for child well-being.

An adjustment of 10 per cent in the corporate sector activity level due to a financial shock can be expressed either as a 10 per cent fall in employment or a 10 per cent cut in wage rates. In the first case, the employment decline in the corporate sector (keeping real wages steady) has a violent effect on urban informal employment (down 16 percent) as incomes fall and the newly unemployed enter the urban labour market driving wages down and forcing migration back to rural areas, where the workforce rises by 6 per cent and wages are also forced down. In the second case, cutting corporate wages by 10 percent (but maintaining employment) reduces urban informal employment due to the reduction in demand for informal goods and services, but by less because there is no competition in the urban labour market; and less workers are forced back to rural areas so wages there do not fall by so much. In short, the poverty effects in the first case are much greater than in the second case.

Financial Policies for Reducing Child Poverty

The arguments and evidence set out above imply that employment and investment stability are the key to maintaining and improving child welfare in emerging market economies. This has significant consequences for the management of capital flows, exchange rate doctrine and international financial cooperation. First, both theory and experience indicate the desirability of scheduling capital account liberalisation after a successful domestic financial liberalisation. Allowing foreign investment in domestic financial markets and foreign borrowing by domestic banks and corporations calls for minimum levels of both market efficiency and institutional and regulatory capacity to safeguard stability. In consequence, many emerging market governments have begun to consider the re-imposition of capital controls as a means of insulating their economies from the potentially destabilising effects of short-term capital movements. These new controls tend to be 'market based' and range from taxes varying with asset maturity to prudential constraints on foreign borrowing by domestic banks and firms. Indeed, the OECD countries themselves only gradually dismantled controls on capital flows over several post-war decades.

Second, the exchange rate affects both the level of domestic activity (and thus the employment level) and the real wage, and is thus a key determinant of the welfare of poor households and their children. A full float clearly leads to employment and wage instability when the economy experiences exogenous shocks, while hard pegs tend to lead to overvaluation and destabilising speculative attacks. Some form of exchange rate management is unavoidable for small open economies with high trade coefficients and shallow domestic capital markets. Although it is clearly desirable to achieve both real wage and employment stability, the analysis in this chapter indicates that both cannot be attained simultaneously so that if child welfare is the criterion, employment stability (and thus real exchange rate variability) may be preferable to real wage stability. Third, the international financial community must recognize the systemic problems faced by countries whose financial markets are still at an intermediate stage of development.

Their financial systems require some protection from external shocks that might otherwise lead to excessive fluctuations in liquidity. As they are not sufficiently integrated to global markets to rely on permanent access to private financing, they must have flexible access to official financing for counter-cyclical borrowing in order to sustain employment levels through the cycle. Thus emerging market economies should be free to choose the exchange rate regime that they judge best for their circumstances, and international support should not be made conditional on the adoption of a particular regime. Further, for any exchange rate regime to be sustainable for these economies with diversified trading and investment patterns, it is essential that G3 exchange rates (i.e. between the dollar, euro and yen) should not be too unstable. Fourth, emergency financial 'rescue packages' clearly need to be underpinned by strong social policies: providing safety nets without excessive fiscal strain and actions to make sure that the needs of the poor are given proper consideration. As the longer-term development of children can be harmed by household unemployment and loss of health and education access, even if only for a few years. Increased social and economic stability will not only help households cope with shocks and build the political consensus in support of government policy that prevents social conflict from worsening, and thus help restore private sector confidence more quickly.

Fifth, creditors should thus accept greater public intervention in the economy for social protection during a financial crisis, so long as it is consistent with fiscal stability over the cycle as a whole, so as to maintain domestic investment and employment levels. These mechanisms may include public works schemes to create employment, maintenance of bank credit to small firms and the 'ring fencing' of fiscal expenditure on primary education and basic health systems. More long-term funding should also be made available from multilateral development banks to strengthen social infrastructure provision.

Sixth, the international community must thus recognise that for the new International Financial Architecture to be viable, it must be underpinned by sound social protection systems in order to both protect vulnerable groups—above all children—in emerging market countries and maintain political consensus on sound economic policy.

Globalisation, FDI and Growth

Foreign Direct Investment (FDI) has been one of the defining features of the world economy and globalisation over the past twenty years. It implies the creation of new enterprises abroad, or the acquisition of substantial stakes in existing foreign enterprises. This form of investment has grown at an unprecedented pace for two decades, with only a slight interruption during the recession in the early 1990s.

The growth in international investment of the past decades has been due in large part to increased liberalisation brought about by reduced barriers to trade and investment and discriminatory subsidies. The 1990s also witness the removal of domestic impediments through widespread regulatory reform and privatisation. At the moment, more firms, and in more industries and countries, than ever before are expanding abroad through direct investment. At the microeconomic level, far-reaching organisational change is taking place as a result of e-business and new technology, which are transforming the value chain for many industries.

The structure of multinational enterprises (MNEs) is evolving, as are their FDI strategies. Today, some 60,000 parent companies worldwide have established over 500,000 foreign affiliates in countries other than their own, with the amount of inward FDI stock valued at roughly $4,000 billion. These foreign affiliates are estimated to have generated total gross output of more than $2,600 billion and total employment of over 35 million in host countries. While about 90 per cent of all parent companies are located in OECD countries, a little more than half of all foreign affiliates are in operation in non-OECD countries, providing a major source of industrial production and employment in a number of emerging and developing economies.

The significant increase in FDI flows towards developing and emerging economies, and concerns about the practices of MNEs have contributed to the resurgence of both theoretical and policy debates regarding the impact of FDI on the process of economic development. On the one hand, FDI is an important source of financing of domestic capital needs and compared with other forms of private capital flows - e.g. portfolio equity and debt flows - FDI is more stable. FDI also allows the transfer of technology.

Multinational enterprises - the main drivers of FDI - are a powerful and effective means to disseminate technology from developed to developing countries, and are often the only source of new and innovative technologies that are usually not available through the market. Technology disseminated through FDI generally includes the 'entire package' including experts, skills and the financial resources to exploit the technology appropriately. Other potential benefits of FDI for host countries include increased competition in input and product markets and human capital enhancement. On the other hand, there has been growing public concern that these benefits still have to be demonstrated and, where benefits exists, that they are not being shared equitably.

Some of the potential costs associated with FDI could include increased unemployment due to restructuring and increased market concentration. In addition, many factors account for differences in the level and range of benefits accruing to recipient countries, including exogenous factors such as size and proximity to markets or endowment of natural resources. Institutional, legal, and regulatory frameworks, along with policy coherence, the availability of skilled labour and infrastructure also impact upon a country's ability to attract and capture the benefits associated with FDI.

The growth of world FDI in recent years has been exceptional and the last two decades have seen the worldwide production and consumption of goods and services become increasingly internationalised. The US dollar value of world FDI inflows reached a record US$1.3 trillion in 2000 from just over US$200 billion in 1993. In 1980, the FDI stock represented the equivalent of only five per cent of world GDP, while this percentage had almost tripled to 14 per cent by the end of 1990s.

FDI has become strongly oriented towards the services sector. In 1999, more than half of OECD FDI outflows involved this sector, with banks and other financial institutions accounting for the bulk of these investments. However, FDI in electricity, gas and water, and telecommunications saw the most dramatic increase, reflecting the massive privatisation and deregulation of these public utilities in the past decade. The share of FDI in the primary sector fell steadily between 1985 and 1995, but large investments in the extraction of petroleum and gas reversed this trend in 1999. The share of manufacturing on the other hand increased steadily between 1985 and 1995, but witnessed a relative drop in 1999 due to the surge in services related FDI.

In recent years, an increasingly large part of FDI flows has been through mergers and acquisitions, rather than through the establishment of new enterprises (greenfield investment). While it is difficult to estimate the share of FDI that is accounted for by M&As, the growth rate of M&As has outstripped that of FDI throughout the entire 1990s . Whereas mergers and acquisitions have become the main mode of entry worldwide, in developing countries greenfield investment remains dominant.

Still, in recent years, M&As are becoming an increasingly important in developing countries as well. This trend partly reflects the large-scale privatisation programmes implemented in many parts of the world during the 1990s: foreign investors acquired previously state-owned enterprises in former centrally-planned economies and in other emerging markets. Still, in terms of value, developing countries continue to account for less than ten per cent of global M&A deals.

The vast majority of world investment still takes place amongst OECD countries. More than 90 per cent of world FDI outflows originates in OECD Member countries, and in recent years OECD countries have received around three-quarters of world FDI inflows as well (UNCTAD, 2000). OECD outflows to non-OECD countries are also highly concentrated. Two-thirds of total OECD FDI flows to non-OECD countries are directed towards Latin America and Asia. In addition the top 10 non-OECD recipients account for just over 50 percent of total OECD FDI outflows to developing countries and throughout the 1990s the countries on this top-ten list have been broadly the same.

Though OECD FDI outflows to developing countries have accounted for only a small part of their total FDI flows, from the developing countries' perspective this FDI has been of great importance. FDI has become the most important source of external financing for certain developing countries, overshadowing other capital flows such as official development assistance (ODA) or export credits.

While at the beginning of the 1990s OECD FDI flows to developing countries accounted for around 30 percent of private capital flows to developing countries, by 1999 this had risen to as much 80 percent. While ODA in real terms has declined in recent years from its peak in 1992, on the whole it has remained relatively stable in comparison to private flows. Non-FDI private flows have been rather volatile, but overall are playing an increasingly larger role since the early 1990s in the total financial flows towards developing countries.

In relation to GDP, FDI is becoming more important for developing countries. Not only is FDI to developing countries overshadowing other capital flows such as ODA, also in relation to GDP it is becoming more important for developing countries. The non-OECD countries that rank among the top twenty recipients of total world FDI outflows have, in most cases, seen high inflows in relative terms to the size of their economies.

The growth in international investment of the past decades has been due in large part to increased liberalisation brought about by reduced barriers to trade and investment and discriminatory subsidies. This improvement in the investment climate in the 1990s was influenced in part by the recognition of the benefits of FDI. Of the almost 1000 changes in FDI regulations undertaken worldwide in the 1990s, 94 percent were aimed at creating a more favourable environment for FDI.

Instead of barriers, many countries now employ incentives to attract FDI. Indeed, incentive based competition for FDI has become a wide-spread phenomenon, involving governments at all levels (national and sub-national) in both OECD and non-OECD countries. Examples of such incentives include tax holidays, preferential access to credit, subsidies and the reduction of import duties for goods needed for production. These incentives are meant to reap the maximum benefits associated with the activities of MNEs e.g. knowledge, management skills, technological advantages, etc. However the cost-effectiveness of such incentives is questionable since they usually attract primarily short-term profit-orientated or cheap cost-motivated FDI. Furthermore, evidence suggests that competition for FDI results in no net gain in those countries FDI market shares.

The 1990s also witness the removal of domestic impediments through widespread regulatory reform and privatisation. The OECD public enterprise sector is currently estimated to be less than half the size it was at the beginning of the 1980s. The privatisation movement was in large part induced by dissatisfaction with the performance of state-owned enterprises, and the increased capital investment needed to upgrade infrastructure, especially in the public utility sector.

Privatisation offered the opportunity to restructure and introduce competition in sectors previously dominated by state monopolies, to increase investment, and to improve productive and allocative efficiency, all of which benefit consumers and the economy as a whole. However, in many emerging markets and economies in transition, the benefits from the change in ownership have sometimes proved disappointing, due to weaknesses in the legal, institutional or market environment.

While the investment environment has improved considerably in the past decade, barriers to investment have not disappeared and many countries remain reluctant to undertake full liberalisation commitments, even where they are actively encouraging FDI. In order to retain national 'control' over the economy some countries still do not permit FDI in sectors considered "strategic". Restrictions on foreign ownership also provide an important barrier to entry and prevent the market for corporate control from functioning efficiently. Other examples of remaining restrictions include reciprocity and discretionary liberalisation i.e. where sectors are opened to FDI but on a case by case authorisation basis.

Some countries use measures that are more specifically tailored towards a single goal, like the use of screening procedures to select FDI projects which they consider best serve their country's needs or the imposition of conditions on FDI in an attempt to ensure that technology is transferred. Finally, a lack of political and economic stability and predictability can also act as a barrier to investment, as can a lack of transparency of regulations, corruption, weak protection of intellectual property rights, and arbitrary application of regulations and laws.

One of the most direct ways in which FDI affects development is through adding to the host country's savings and investments, thereby enlarging the production base at a higher growth rate than would have been possible if a host country had to rely on domestic sources of savings alone.

But FDI is much more than just a flow of capital. In particular, the inflow of foreign direct investment can bring new technologies, which usually are not available through the market. These technologies may enhance the productivity of foreign affiliates and, through spillover effects, that of domestic firms as well. Before turning to the overall impact of FDI on growth, this section therefore will first examine one of the primary ways in which FDI contributes to growth i.e. through the transfer of technology to host countries.

Multinational firms are among the most important players in the world responsible for creating and controlling technology. They facilitate putting tangible and intangible resources available in different countries to their most productive uses. As part of the global profit-making operations of multinational enterprises,

FDI, by its nature, involves the transfer of capital, technology and knowledge from home to host countries.

Using better technologies offers possibilities to increase productivity and hence economic growth and development. Hence it is not surprising that many countries view investments by those MNEs as one of the most important means to acquire technology and knowledge to upgrade their own production base. However, it is difficult to paint an unambiguous picture as to how FDI can transfer technology, and how this technology is going to contribute to development. It is not a priori clear that every type of technology transferred is appropriate, and not every investment made is by definition beneficial to host country development.

Though FDI is only one of several ways by which firms can transfer technology it remains the most important one, especially for developing countries. First of all, an investment not only comprises the technology itself but also includes 'the entire package': the complementary resources such as management experience and entrepreneurial abilities.

Unlike trade in goods, where developing countries have to try to imitate and learn from 'backward engineering', FDI involves the explicit transfer of technology. This may be especially beneficial for countries with underdeveloped local capabilities. Secondly, by their mere entry and presence, MNEs disturb the existing equilibrium in the market forcing domestic firms to innovate in order to protect their market shares and profits. This alone is likely to lead to productivity increases in local firms.

Another benefit of FDI in transferring technology versus other modes of transfer is that the typical features of a MNE, for example, scale economics, capital reserves, or marketing and sales experience, can contribute significantly to exploiting the technology in a profitable manner. MNEs also offer brand names and access to regional and global markets.

However, these possible benefits are accompanied by possible costs. A highly efficient MNE affiliate may lead to a fall in the number of local firms if the less efficient local firms are forced out of business. Though this may increase overall resource allocation in the long term, the short-term consequences for local employment and market concentration may be severe. For example, if MNE affiliates are very strong, in the absence of an appropriate competition policy framework they may abuse their monopoly power, with consequentially harmful effects. Other costs include the repatriation of profits with consequences for balance of payments and exchange rates, and the avoidance of taxation through transfer pricing.

The 'whole package' that often comes with FDI also has a reverse side, particularly for countries with relatively high local capabilities and that are able to exploit the technology themselves. Instead of relying on the MNEs expertise, local firms in these countries may prefer to obtain the technology through licensing, though this option may not always be available if the MNE chooses not to license the technology. Local firms in this case have to acquire the technology through FDI, which can be an expensive alternative to acquiring the technology through licensing.

Knowing that FDI is important in transferring technology does not however explain how this transfer and consequent spillovers take place. There are four channels by which technology transfer through FDI can occur, either directly or indirectly through spillovers. These channels include vertical linkages, horizontal linkages, labour migration and the internationalisation of R&D activities.

For some time now it has been recognised that MNEs may benefit the host country via the backward and forward linkages they generate. Backward linkages are relations with suppliers, forward linkages refer to relations with buyers - either consumers or other firms using the MNEs intermediate products as part of their own production process. Though linkage creation does not per se imply that technology or knowledge is transferred or spilt over,

Blomström et. al. show that in general it is unlikely that MNEs are able to fully appropriate all the value of these explicit and implicit transfers with their host country business partners. Linkages are more pronounced the larger the size of the host market and technological capabilities of local suppliers and when intermediate goods are used intensively. However, when addressing the impact of linkage creation it should be taken into account that MNEs only improve welfare if they generate linkages beyond those that are generated by the local firms they displace.

As regards backward linkages, MNEs can contribute to raising the productivity of their supplier firms in various ways. MNEs can provide technical assistance or information to raise the quality of the suppliers' products or to facilitate innovations. McIntyre et. al. found that

MNEs usually do not hesitate to train local suppliers. However, if suppliers are forced to meet the higher quality standards without any training or assistance, this could lead in the short term to suppliers failing to meet the necessary requirements, leading to firm failures and job losses.

Other spillovers from backward linkages include assistance in purchasing raw materials and intermediary goods, training in management and organisation, and assistance with diversification of customers. Many empirical studies have found evidence of the creation of such backward linkages; Wanatabe; UNCTC and Behrman and Wallender, though recent studies are scarce. Generally, these linkages are extended over time, which could be a consequence of technology transfer.

Forward linkages occur with firms' buyers. This can be distributors, which can benefit from the marketing and other knowledge of the MNE, or downstream firms who can benefit from intermediate goods with lower prices or better quality, or both. Downstream firms can also benefit from lower prices arising from increased competition in their supply market, and consumers thus also benefit from lower-priced final products. Aitken and Harrison find that spillovers from forward linkages are important in most industries - and in fact they argue that the downstream effects of FDI are generally more beneficial than the upstream effects.

Related to the issue of vertical linkages, is the diffusion of technology through horizontal 'linkages' i.e. to competitors of the MNE affiliate. This diffusion of technology takes place through either demonstration effects - when the exposure of local firms to the superior technology of the MNE leads local firms to update their own production methods - or competition effects. These two effects are difficult to disentangle, since they both occur at the industry level, and may reinforce each other, for example when FDI expands the set of technologies available to local firms, it also usually increases competition.

The effects of increased competition are usually seen as beneficial. Increased competition encourages both productive efficiency and a more efficient allocation of resources. This may be especially the case when MNEs enter industries where high entry barriers reduced the degree of domestic competition.

Though in theory competition improves efficiency and welfare, however, entry by an MNE may not always increase competition. In fact, entry may lead to increased concentration. Concerns have arisen that strong foreign MNEs out-compete local firms, or at least force local firms to merge, and the increased industrial concentration can result in market power. The abuse of market power by the MNE would then result in a decrease in allocative efficiency.

Empirical evidence suggests that FDI is likely to lead to higher concentration in most host countries, and there is a larger risk that MNEs crowd out local firms in developing countries than in developed countries, because of their greater technological advantages. The vast majority of studies mentioned in the WTO paper find a positive correlation between foreign entry or presence and seller concentration in host country industries. However, one study finds that this correlation disappears once other determinants of concentration are taken into account, and that MNEs do not cause concentration but are instead drawn to concentrated industries.

As regards the demonstration effect, Blomström et. al.find that studies that compare new technology adoption by foreign owned and domestically owned firms tend to conclude that new technology is frequently introduced sooner by foreign owned affiliates.

As regards competition effects, the authors find that competition spurs quicker adoption of innovations by both domestically owned and foreign owned firms. The first statement seems to be confirmed by a study of Haddad and Harrison, who showed that foreign firms exhibit higher levels of TFP growth.

Still, some other papers have found negative results regarding the spillover effects of FDI on purely domestic enterprises, e.g. Djankov and Hoekman for the Czech Republic. However, when foreign firms bring more efficient production methods, in the short run it is not surprising that local firms suffer. Positive impacts such as improved resource allocation take time.

Another way through which technology may be transferred and disseminated in a host country is through labour migration. Workers employed by the MNE affiliate acquire knowledge of its superior technology and management practices. By switching employers or setting up their own business the technology is spread. MNE affiliates usually try to avoid this kind of spillovers by paying an 'efficiency wage', a premium in order to keep employees from switching jobs to domestically owned competitors. If disclosing secrets to local managers would create unacceptable risks, e.g. due to managers' tendency to switch jobs to competitors, the MNE may consider using expatriate managers rather than local ones.

Multinational firms are among the world most important creators of knowledge and technology. Many of these firms concentrate their R&D activities in their home country or other developed countries. Developing countries only account for an estimated 6% of global R&D expenditures. And even among those developing countries, expenditures are very concentrated. UNCTAD calculated - taking US firms as a proxy - that the top four developing economies accounted for 77% of total R&D expenditure in developing countries.

The centralisation of R&D is one of the large policy concerns of developing countries regarding MNEs. In the case where R&D is transferred to foreign subsidiaries this has basically been in relation to adaptive tasks, drawing on a few local resources to better serve the local market. MNEs are often blamed for failing to adopt their technologies, that are designed for industrialised country wages and capital costs, to the factor prices prevailing in developing countries.

In those cases where R&D is performed in developing countries, the expenditures have been found to generate significant efficiency gains, both within and across industries in the R&D performing country. It has been argued that R&D by foreign affiliates is better than local R&D expenditures, since MNE affiliates have access to the aggregate knowledge base of the parent company and can use the parents firm's R&D facilities.

The inflow of foreign investment can foster growth in the host economy by easing the shortages of capital, foreign exchange, technology and skills. The growth process can be further sustained if backward and forward linkages emerge from MNEs to the domestic economy and if FDI contributes to raising the profitability of domestic investment. One of the important questions concerning FDI and growth therefore is whether FDI contributes relatively more to growth than domestic investment. The answer to this question seems to be less controversial in theory than in practice.

FDI is an important vehicle for the transfer of capital, technology and knowledge to host countries, and for promoting local competition, thereby generating higher growth opportunities than domestic investment. In practice, however, the growth-enhancing effects of FDI may depend in part on whether FDI "crowds out" or "crowds in" domestic investment. Also, its impact may depend crucially on the absorption capacity of a host country, as the efficient use of new technology requires a minimum threshold of human capital on the recipient side.

Looking at the impact of FDI on capital accumulation and productivity growth, de Mello finds that foreign investors increase productivity in host countries and that FDI is often a catalyst for domestic investment and technological progress. Alfaro et. al. estimate a model whereby FDI induces higher growth directly by increasing production in the MNEs sector and indirectly by increasing production in the domestic sector via spillovers. The authors examine the relationship between FDI and domestic investment and find that FDI increase total investment more than one for one, reinforcing the claim that FDI affects growth through domestic investment.

Foreign investment contributes relatively more to domestic productivity than domestic investment. Baldwin et. al., for example, found that domestic technological progress is aided by foreign technological progress. They cite the study of Eaton and Kortum who find that domestic productivity growth is mainly related to foreign innovation rather than domestic innovation. On the other hand, some studies suggest that the effects of FDI have not always been beneficial for local firms. Haddad and Harrison, find no positive results for Morocco in the late 1980s, and Aitken and Harrison, though finding a positive correlation between foreign presence and TFP growth conclude that this may be wrong if MNEs are attracted by the more productive sectors in the first place.

Carkovic and Levine, employing a new World Bank data set on FDI, also found negative results. Their study includes 72 countries over the period 1960-1995 and examines the impact of FDI on income growth, productivity growth and physical capital accumulation. In their regressions, the authors attempt to control for domestic conditions that are likely to affect the composition and growth of FDI. The estimated regressions are also modified accordingly in order to check whether the impact of FDI on growth is contingent upon the level of educational attainment, economic development or financial development in the recipient country. They find no significant impact of FDI on growth, though they do find that FDI has a positive impact on capital accumulation. However, these results do not mean that FDI has no effect on growth, but only that FDI goes hand in hand with growth.

But despite these outcomes, most empirical studies find a positive relation between FDI, productivity and growth. Markusen and Venables find that FDI has a positive effect on domestic firms' productivity. They claim that increased competition associated with the entry of an MNE upgrades the efficiency and product quality in national firms, and opens up possibilities for export. Xu also finds that FDI contributes to total factor productivity growth in recipient countries. Studies by Borensztein et. al. and OECD find that not only does foreign direct investment stimulate growth but that it has a larger impact than investment by domestic firms. As regards the Mexican manufacturing sector, Blomström and Wolff find that the spillovers in the Mexican industry were large enough to help Mexican firms converge towards US productivity levels during the period 1965-1982.

Despite the overall positive results of the studies cited above, many of the poorest developing countries have not been able to integrate successfully into global markets and to participate in the growth-inducing benefits of FDI. Even where countries have successfully integrated it's not clear that they are benefiting to the maximum extent possible. Despite multiple efforts at reform, the majority of the least developed countries failed to grow and to integrate into the global economy as rapidly as other developing countries. Market openness clearly is not a sufficient condition for economic growth.

The diverse experiences of developing countries suggest that the positive effects of FDI are not automatic, but may be affected by various host industry and country characteristics. Domestic conditions and certain threshold levels of development such as technological capabilities, human capital or the development of financial markets seem to play an important role on the effect of FDI on growth. Many have also argued sound macro-economic policies and institutional stability are also necessary, as is social stability. With weak institutions, poor governance and unsound policies, market reforms can fail with great costs, especially to vulnerable groups in society. One should, therefore, assess whether any necessary pre-conditions or thresholds have to be met in the host economy for FDI-driven growth to materialise.

Developing countries need to have reached a certain threshold of development before being able to capture the benefits associated with FDI. De Mello provides a selective review of the econometric literature that deals with the impact of FDI on growth. The major findings emerging from this review point to the different roles played by FDI in fostering growth in technologically advanced countries versus developing countries. Recipient countries' technological capabilities determine the scope for spillovers from foreign to domestic firms. Hence, the growth impact of international investment tends to be limited in technological laggards.

For example, the magnitude of the contribution of FDI to growth may depend on human capital development. Borenzstein et. al. address the technology-gap question by developing a model of economic growth whereby FDI contributes to technological progress through capital deepening, i.e. through the introduction of new varieties of capital goods. Acknowledging that such beneficial effects are likely to depend on the skills of the domestic labour force, FDI is interacted with a measure of human capital development.

FDI contributes to growth although the magnitude of this effect depends on the stock of human capital available in the host economy. In particular, they find that FDI raises growth only in those countries where the labour force has achieved a minimum threshold of education. the positive impact of FDI on growth vanishes when limited to lower income developing countries. They argue that FDI is a source of growth only for countries already at a relatively high level of development and that low-income countries lack the necessary capabilities needed to absorb the FDI-related technology transfer.

Besides the relative difference in the technological capabilities of the host MNE and the local firm, the absolute level of absorptive capacity is also important. Keller for example states that access to foreign technologies alone is not enough to increase growth rates if, for example, the country's stock of human capital remains unchanged. Evidence for this argument is given by inter alia Xu. Using data on outward investment from the US to forty countries, Xu finds that technology transfer associated with FDI contributes to productivity growth in developed and middle-developed countries but not in the least developing countries.

A possible explanation is that the absorption of MNEs technology by host countries requires a relatively high level of human capital. Most LDCs do not meet the human capital threshold required for recipient countries to benefit from technology spillovers. Haddad and Harrison find similar evidence. When they divided sectors into high-tech and low-tech, they found that the effect of FDI was more positive in the low-tech sectors than in the higher-tech ones. The authors interpreted this result to be an indication of the lack of absorptive capacity of local firms in the high tech sector. Besides relative and absolute technological capabilities, the development of domestic capital markets can also effect the exploitation of benefits from FDI. Recent studies find that FDI contributes positively to growth in countries where financial market are sufficiently developed and that imperfect and underdeveloped financial markets are likely to penalise domestic firms in favour of MNEs.

6

Globalisation and Economic Reforms

The purpose of this chapter is to assess the differential impact that the radical economic reforms implemented since 1989 have had on Argentina's industries and firms both in the country as a whole and in one of its provinces: Mendoza. The foreign trade and investment trends underlying the surge in Argentine economic growth in the early 1990s indicate a less than optimal role for the country and its firms in the world economy. Exports are expanding rapidly, but a disproportionate share of the growth since 1989 is accounted for by products with a relatively low value-added content, and by markets in Mercosur—the customs union linking Argentina with Brazil, Paraguay and Uruguay—and the rest of Latin America at the expense of the more sophisticated markets of North America and Europe. The implications which these trends hold for the future competitiveness of the country are potentially severe. One might argue that Argentina once attained high levels of wealth precisely by drawing on its natural resources and traditional sources of comparative advantage to produce and export low value-added goods.

Infact, Argentina grew rich during the late nineteenth century and the first third of the twentieth century by exporting primary agricultural products, mostly to Europe. One should be reminded, however, that the development of Argentine agricultural production and export income between 1880 and World War II was far from smooth. International demand for its products was subject to sharp crises such as those taking place around 1890, 1910, and 1921 as well as during the early 1930s and the early 1940s. Conflicts between those situated upstream at the relatively less profitable stages of the value-added chain and those closer to the market (e.g. cattle ranchers versus meat-packers, or crude oil producers versus refiners and distributors), became quite virulent during the 1920s and 1930s. Thus, well before structuralist or dependency critiques flourished, and before populist—nationalist economic policies became the norm, Argentina suffered from recurrent balance of payments crises as a result of its reliance on export earnings from low-value, volatile commodities to cover imports of consumer and capital goods and to service its foreign debt.

In a world dominated by bilateral trade deals, Argentina had large surpluses with Britain (its main export market for beef) and huge deficits with the USA (its major source of inputs, machinery and consumer goods), a triangular pattern that proved unmanageable during the 1930s and late 1940s as the British economy and Sterling declined. In a world economy tending towards globalisation, efficiency-based competition, and a mix of multilateralism and trading blocs, the product composition of exports relative to imports is not as important as the value-added content of the exports and how it interacts with patterns of comparative advantage. It is well known that some countries have been able to develop economically on the basis of natural resources, by triggering investments in basic and capital-goods industries (e.g. Australia, Sweden, Finland, Norway). A country rich in natural resources ought to build on those advantages and direct its export effort towards sophisticated markets by focusing on such value-adding activities as product development (if not research), quality enhancement, marketing know-how, and upgraded worker skills.

The Argentine industrial exports have not built upon the country's natural resource advantages, are not principally destined to the more sophisticated markets, and are growing less rapidly than exports of lower value-added content. We also analyse in depth the experience of one of the country's provinces, Mendoza, which, in contrast to Argentina as a whole, has been successful at developing a capital-goods industry with high export growth. However, similar to the national trend the province has seen a dramatic reduction in agro-manufactures in favour of primary agricultural products.

Market Reforms in Argentina

By the mid-1980s pressures to reform the Argentine economy became paramount. The country was falling further and further behind the rest of the world, with a string of years of negative real growth rates. Argentina's share of world exports had fallen from a high of 3.0 per cent earlier in the century to 0.3 per cent by 1990, even though the country produced more than 1.1 per cent of world output. Among the issues which needed to be addressed were a state structure which employed nearly 20 per cent of the economically active population of the country, a system of subsidies on which much of the private sector depended, hyper-inflation, an exploding foreign debt, an ageing infrastructure, and a coefficient of trade openness of only five per cent. With the failure of the Austral Plan to reduce inflation still fresh, Menem correctly understood the need to force changes in state finances and labour negotiations as well as to implement a sound currency stabilisation programme.

The year 1990 witnessed further in roads in public deficit reduction, but inflation success eluded him once again in spite of the harsh therapy of the bank deposit-bond conversion plan. It was not until the implementation of Domingo Cavallo's convertibility plan of March 1991 that inflation finally subsided. Menem's reforms affected virtually all aspects of the economy, but those which had a significant impact on the internationalisation of economic and business activity can be classified into three broad areas : monetary policy, fiscal policy, and trade and regulatory policy.

Monetary Reform

Of all the reforms adopted by the government since 1989, the one which has received the most attention and has served as the foundation for the other reforms is the Convertibility Law. It represented a major change in both the exchange rate and monetary regimes of the country. On the one hand, the Law fixed the currency to the dollar on a one-to-one basis and required that the Central Bank fully back the monetary base in the form of foreign assets. The goal was to reinstill confidence in the currency, which had been severely weakened following a decade of hyperinflation, as attested to by the growing dollarisation of local transactions. However, in addition to bolstering the credibility of the Argentine currency, the Convertibility Law played a second more critical role. It formally laid out the primary objectives of the Bank: above all to preserve the value of the peso, and only secondarily to regulate the amount of money in the economy, to control the banking system, to administer reserves, and to act as the financial agent of the government.

This change in mission accompanied by the freeing of the Central Bank from the auspices of the executive branch (particularly the Ministry of Economy), making it accountable only to Congress, reduced the ability of the Central Bank to be used by the government as the lender of last resort, thus forcing a *de facto* coordination between fiscal and monetary policies. It is precisely this constraint on the Treasury, with its implications for fiscal stability, that lies at the core of the success of the Law. It is difficult to quantify its overall impact on the economy, for in addition to the direct impact on inflation it also had the indirect, but perhaps more important, effect of lending credibility to the reform process as a whole. As such, the success of subsequent reforms cannot be judged indepedently of the Convertibility Law. There are, however, certain aspects of the economy on which the Law had both a direct and immediate impact. The most visible of these was the inflation rate, which by the end of the 1980s had spiralled to levels never before seen in Argentina, reaching a peak of nearly 5,000 per cent in 1989.

Following the change in monetary policy in 1991, however, inflation plummeted to an annual rate of 84 per cent in 1991 and 17.5 per cent in 1992. The drop in inflation resulted in a rapid increase in the money supply, due in large part to the return of capital which had field abroad in the previous decade. By some estimates, the amount of investments held by Argentines outside the country during the 1980s exceeded $50,000 million. Loans to the private sector increased from $14,300 million in June 1991 to just under $55,000 million in December 1994. This increase in lending was due in part to the direct effect of the reduction of inflation on the return of capital to the country and indirectly to the increased confidence in the financial system that it instilled and which allowed for the reduction of bank reserve requirements from 79 per cent on checking account deposits to 43 per cent. As such, from the point of view of the firm, one of the most immediate impacts of the drop in inflation was an increase in the amount of capital in the domestic financial system available for loans.

However, while the level of capital in the economy has increased, the ability to access it varies dramatically by firm. The opening of the capital markets has been accompanied by a shift in their composition. Government banks are playing a smaller and smaller role, being replaced by private lenders, both domestic and foreign. The cliente which these private banks serve, however, tends to be different from that of the government banks. Small and medium-sized firms depend on government banks to a much greater degree, while larger and international firms tend to be customers of private banks. As such, changes in the capital markets appear to have benefited larger firms at the expense of smaller ones. In addition to its economic impact, the reduction in inflation has had organisational effects on the way in which firms operate.

Over the previous decade firms were forced to operate in an environment in which relative prices between capital and labour were constantly changing as a result of differential inflation rates. As such, even if firms were able to access funds during this period the decision on whether to invest them in labour or physical capital was not clear cut. As such, the result was that even firms which were able to access capital refrained from domestic investments. The inflationary environment of the 1980s forced firms to be short-sighted for fear of increased future instability. Following the stabilisation of prices, however, firms were able more accurately to determine relative prices and as such make the investment decisions which had previously been unclear.

Fiscal Reform

On the fiscal side, two key laws were enacted to bring about structural reform. The first of these, the Economic Emergency Law, suspended virtually all subsidies to the private sector and reduced extraordinary government expenditures (e.g. industrial promotion arrangements, regional subsidies). The result has been a balancing of the budget which in turn has aided the reduction of interest rates. The second of these laws, the Government Reform Law, set up the regulatory framework for the transfer of firms and assets from the public to the private sector. In addition to replenishing the coffers of the government and reducing the need for subsidies, it was hoped these privatisations would help raise the level of productivity of these enterprises and the economy in general. While this was not always the case, the general level of labour productivity of the economy increased by an impressive 26 per cent from 1991 to 1994, due in part to lay-offs and capital investments and in part to the application of better organising practices.

Trade and Regulatory Reform

In the realm of trade policy many changes have been undertaken to open up the economy to foreign markets. In addition to the completion of the Mercosur agreement, which liberalised trade between Argentina, Brazil, Uruguay and Paraguay, there has been a general trend towards reduced protectionism in recent years. As one can also see, however, while the general trend has been one of reducing protectionism, this has not always been linear in its evolution, particularly in the case of the statistic tax. As such, while the economy is much more open today than in the late 1980s, signs of hesitation in tariff policy may have discouraged even further investment in the economy. In addition to trade liberalisation, many of the internal markets in the country have also been deregulated, including energy, communications, and transportation. While changes in all three have had an impact on the competitiveness of the country *vis-a-vis* foreign markets, that which seems to have had the most immediate impact for exports is deregulation of the transport sector.

With the privatisation of many of the road systems and the opening up of markets to competition, land transportation costs have dropped substantially. Furthermore, ocean freight prices have also fallen dramatically, in part as a result of a depressed international shipping market, but also as a result of deregulation of the port system. Taxes were reduced, ports privatised, and competition opened. This has resulted in reductions in ocean freight charges of over 50 per cent in many instances according to the Comite!de Conferencias de Fletes. The impact of monetary, fiscal, trade and regulatory reforms has begun to be felt. From 1990 to 1994 the economy grew by over 30 per cent, a growth rate outpaced only by China and Thailand. Furthermore, gross investment as a share of GDP increased from under 15 per cent in 1989-90 to 21 per cent in 1993. Concurrent with these results have been increased levels of inward FDI, challenging Mexico as the largest Latin American destination.

The impact on internationalisation

The reforms discussed above have had a significant impact on the level of internationalisation of the Argentine economy. While still far below the level reached 60 years ago, the coefficient of openness of the economy has increased to nearly 9 per cent from a low of five per cent in early 1989. During the 1989-94 period, Argentine exports increased 65 per cent to reach levels of $15,000 million, and are projected to have reached levels of more than $22,000 million in 1995. More dramatically, imports increased from $4,200 million in 1989 to $21,500 million in 1994 (an increase of 413 per cent), due in large part to the release of pent-up demand following the dropping of tariff barriers and the growth of the domestic economy. While increased exports were one of the desired objectives of the market liberalisation programmes, the aggregate trade figures tend to mask certain underlying structural changes, which affect not only Argentine exports, but also the overall make-up of the economy. Among the most important changes since the opening of the economy in the late 1980s has been a redistribution of resources within the country towards what are generally considered to be lower value-added products.

As a result, the nation has seen a disproportionate growth in the exports of primary products and energy in lieu of higher value-added agro-manufactured and industrial products. Whereas in 1989 products with relatively low value-added contents accounted for roughly 25 per cent of exports, in 1994 they had grown to account for 34 per cent. This trend is even seen within each general category. In energy exports, for instance, which are dominated by YPF (the formerly state-owned oil company), there has been a shift from refined products to crude oil exports and natural gas. Whereas the latter represented 26 per cent of exports in 1992, by 1994 that share had grown to over 61 per cent. It is perhaps too early to tell whether this is a long-term trend, as there are signs that it may be moderating.

Nearly 45 per cent of this recovery in industrial exports, however, is attributable to the sale of motor vehicles and parts to Mercosur, a trade promoted by a special regime requiring balanced exports and imports between the trade pact signatories. Unfortunately, the backward linkages into the general economy which the auto sector provides are relatively weak, as it is dominated by foreign players, whose Argentine facilities are for the most part production and assembly oriented.

The research and development and other higher values activities of these firms are located outside of the country, thus reducing the potential benefit normally associated with industrial exports. Furthermore, an additional 15 per cent of the increase in industrial exports is due to a growth in precious metals and their transformation, a sector with relatively low levels of industrial value-added. Much research has pointed to the level of value-added of a country's exports as a sign of the degree of economic development. Countries which are dependent on the export of raw materials and commodities not only miss out on the potential to capture value-added rents, but are also subject to the higher degree of volatility found in commodity markets. Using cross-national data for the 1970-89 period.

In the case of Argentina, this is an issue of central concern, given the high degree of dependence on relatively low value-added exports. While it may be claimed that Argentina is simply adhering to a path dependency argument by exporting products based on its natural resources, it should also be noted that the country has the best educated population in Latin America, a resource which such exports do not exploit. Furthermore, even if path dependency is applicable, the point being made here is that these are changes that should be monitored as they can have a significant impact on the future structural composition of the economy. In addition to the change in the composition of exports over the past five years, change in the destination of those exports has been in evidence, largely in part due to the growth in importance of Mercosur. Whereas in 1989 Mercosur accounted for 15 per cent of Argentina's exports, by 1994 that figure had doubled to 30 per cent, with Brazil accounting for the lion's share. While this growth in trade with its neighbours was part of the purpose in establishing the bloc in the first place, it also entails potential drawbacks.

The main threat is the fact that while Brazil is a large market with strong growth potential, it does not possess the sophisticated demand present in the United States, Europe or Japan. As such, competing in the Brazilian market does not necessarily force local firms to confront the leading edge in global competition. This trend is eventually self-reinforcing, for the longer one stays out of the leading markets the harder it will be to enter them in the future—particularly in the area of industrial exports in which technological advances are fastest. One already sees that, while in general Mercosur countries import more lower value-added products from Argentina than the developed economies, the one exception is industrial products. Again, much of these industrial exports relate to intra-firm transfers of the auto industry. And, while the developed markets still represent 39 per cent of Argentina's exports, that share has been decreasing with the growth in trade since 1989. Although one should not ignore the economic incentives which compel firms to increase sales within Mercosur, one should also be conscious of what is occurring outside the bloc.

One approach is to adopt a tapping procedure of selecting more advanced markets. By directly participating in these markets one can extract knowledge and information which can then be used to improve one's position in home and bloc markets. Such an approach differentiates the role each market serves in the firm's overall strategy. The importance of Europe, the USA, and East Asia, therefore, may not be due to their overall market size potential, but rather the learning which can arise through operating in those markets. It is for this reason that withdrawing from the more advanced markets could be harmful in the long run. Certain researchers, including some economic growth theorists, claim that regional trading blocs can serve as testing grounds for eventual global integration, as they allow firms gradually to develop internationalisation skills. In many ways this argument is similar to the infant industry protectionist argument, in which barriers are used to protect domestic industries until they develop the skills necessary to compete internationally.

Unfortunately, such policies have a fairly poor record in Latin America. The same potential fate could lie in store for firms operating under the protection of Mercosur, wherein their level of competitiveness is confined to the demands and pressures of the Mercosur market, rather than the global one. While it is still too early to tell whether firms are in fact viewing Mercosur as a launching pad, interviews with managers do not reveal such tendencies. Another trend which has intensified over the past five or six years is the increased concentration of exports in the hands of a smaller number of firms. This is due in part to the general increase in concentration in Argentine industry as a result of enhanced, efficiency-based competition. However, the degree of consolidation in the export markets far surpasses that of the economy as a whole, implying that the trend towards concentration has been much more prevalent in the tradeable sectors. For the economy as a whole, the largest 500 firms' share of GDP increased from 23.4 per cent in 1990 to 30.4 in 1994. By contrast the proportion of exports controlled by the 30 largest exporters increased from 32.6 per cent to 55.0 per cent during the same time period.

One of the potential explanations of exporter concentration is that while the economy is in the process of opening and exposing its firms to competitive forces to improve quality and costs, it is not a pressure which is felt uniformly throughout the country. There are still many sectors, insulated from the direct stimuli of tradeable markets, which have been slower to reform. The competitiveness of the non-tradeable sector, however, also has implications for the tradeable sector, as it provides many of the service inputs. As such, lack of integrated reform may inhibit the ability of the tradeable sector to expand its exports in the future. A second reason for the rising concentration of exports is the disproportionate growth of primary and energy exports, which are typically accounted for by relatively few and large firms. The top 30 exporting firms are involved in one of four areas : petroleum, foodstuffs, steel products or motor vehicles. In most cases, little value is added to the raw material being exported, with the only exceptions being certain steel products (e.g. seamless tubes), and motor vehicles and parts, whose recent export booms have much to do with a new requirement that imports be compensated by exports.

With the exceptions of YPF and the vegetable oil producers, the top 30 exporting firms are either controlled by foreign capital or by diversified local groups, in many instances with the assistance of foreign partners. The important trade in agricultural commodities, for instance, has become increasingly dominated by business groups and foreign multinationals because of their access to export market information and cheaper financing. Local business groups have clearly benefited from the process of economic reform. Their ability to take advantage of market, information and financing imperfections and to capitalise on their project execution capabilities, as suggested by the established theories of business group success in developing countries, has probably been enhanced, at least temporarily.

New opportunities have become generally available, but business groups have found themselves in a better structural and financial position to exploit them. Most importantly, they have entered into numerous alliances with foreign firms, frequently as a result of becoming partners in privatised companies. Overall, 40 per cent of privatised equity has gone to foreign firms, generally in conjunction with an Argentine business group acting as the local partner. These and other renewed contacts with foreign firms have helped the groups acquire technology, equipment and organisational and marketing know-how. Not surprisingly, they are ardent supporters of the new, overtly liberal regulation (or lack thereof) concerning foreign investment. The groups have seen their shares of total Argentine exports surge from about 15 per cent in the mid-1970s to more that 25 per cent in the early 1990s.

They are also among the most active Argentine firms in terms of outward foreign investment. Unfortunately, several of the groups are active in low value-added activities such as oil or agricultural commodities, while those active in manufacturing consumer goods are trying to reorganise and refocus. Some firms such as Techint (steel and seamless tubes) and IMPSA (heavy machinery), however, have shown that they can be successful at exporting high value-added products. Foreign multinationals have also benefited from economic reforms, but one should differentiate between those linked to natural resources for export and others engaged in manufacturing for the domestic market. Overall, the multinationals' share of total Argentine exports has remained stable at around one third since the mid-1970s.

The average manufacturing multinational in Argentina imports three times as much as it exports.

Unfortunately, only five per cent of their imports have to do with capital equipment, with the rest evenly divided between inputs and final goods for sale inside Argentina. Thus far, economic reforms seem to have failed at stimulating changes in the traditional roles that multinationals have played in Argentina: exporters of low value-added primary commodities or manufacturers of price-inflated goods for the domestic market.

The evidence is that they devote few resources to technology development, worker training, or process and product quality enhancement, as indicated by the few multinational operations in Argentina which have obtained an ISO 9000 certification. It is, perhaps, too demanding to ask either the business groups or the foreign multinationals to totally revamp their long-standing managerial and organisational practices within three or four years of the inception of reforms. However, point is that the changes in the economic behaviour of business groups and foreign multinationals since 1991, with a few exceptions, could constrain the long-term well-being of Argentina in the world economy.

Internationalisation of the Mendozan economy

They are more clearly identified at the provincial level : differences in geographic specialisation that might confound the results are reduced. Furthermore, there are a number of other advantages to not focusing solely on the national level, which tends to be dominated by Buenos Aires. The first benefit stems from the fact that the economic mix of Mendoza is more representative of the typical region in Latin America than is that of Buenos Aires. Firm size in Mendoza is also more characteristic, in the sense that the majority of the economy is comprised of small to medium-sized firms. Given the growing concentration of exports in the hands of fewer and fewer firms, it is important to understand how these smaller firms are adapting to changes in the market and the regulatory environment. The Province of Mendoza occupies over half of the Cuyo region at the foot of the Andes to the North of the Colorado river, and accounts for about four per cent of Argentina's population and GDP.

The City of Mendoza's one million inhabitants make it the fourth largest in Argentina. Founded in 1561 by Spanish colonisers arriving from Chile, it lies about 600 miles west of Buenos Aires and 130 miles east of the border with Chile. A class of middle-sized farm and vineyard owners emerged in the second half of the nineteenth century occupying the flat, arid lands stretching east from the Andean sierra. The railroad reached Mendoza in 1885, allowing for increased immigration and improved transportation of goods to the markets in and around Buenos Aires. Wine production increased rapidly at the turn of the century, displacing alfalfa growing and extensive cattle breeding. The provincial government played a key role at this time in establishing the first technical training institutions and chemical testing laboratories for wines as well as improving basic irrigation infrastructure. The first mineral water, soft drink and beer bottling plants were established in the 1890s, while the mechanisation of vineyard and bottling activities resulted in the growth of metal-mechanic repair shops.

New industries developed between the two world wars: processing and canning of fruit, vegetables, and olive oil; petroleum drilling; cement; and industrial alcohols. Glass and tin factories followed in the 1940s. By the 1950s Mendozan agroindustry and railways had generated a sizeable metalworking and machinery industry, which started exporting food-processing equipment by 1960. Contacts made with foreign firms allowed Mendozan firms to improve their designs of machinery. A large petroleum refinery and petrochemical complex and several chemical plants, were established during the years of import substitution. By the mid-1980s primary agricultural activities accounted for a mere six per cent of Mendozan GDP, with industry-mining and services each representing about 46 per cent.

This growth of almost 200 per cent, however, has been somewhat erratic, with exports rising rapidly until 1990, before falling for two years and eventually recovering in 1993. This drop in exports can be partly explained by the upturn in the economy in 1991 and the ensuing increase in domestic demand. In relation to the rest of the country, Mendoza improved its export ranking among the provinces during this period from seventh to fifth place. However, exports are still below what might be expected on the Economic Reforms in Argentina 421 basis of the provinces show of national production. In this sense, Mendoza still lags behind the average, by nine percent when measured on a straight provincial average basis, and by 28 per cent when weighted by GDP.

While there has been an overall growth in Mendozan exports, this growth features many of the same underlying characteristics identified at the national level, among these the shift towards lower value-added products. In the case of Mendoza, this trend has been more dramatic in one sense, but at the same time tempered by the growth of industrial exports. The province has always been, as has much of the country outside of Buenos Aires, an exporter of relatively low value-added products. However, in recent years, this trend has been accentuated still further. Whereas the relative share of low value-added exports has increased by nine percentage points in the country as a whole, they have experienced a growth of nearly 15 percentage points in Mendoza and now account for over half of the province's exports. In contrast to the country as a whole, the province has witnessed a substantial growth in industrial exports, increasing from 19.5 per cent of the total in 1989 to 26.3 per cent in 1995. While this is encouraging news, if one looks behind the figures, one realises that another phenomenon is occurring. Much of this growth in industrial exports can be attributed to the export growth of one or two large firms in the metal-mechanic sectors, and not necessarily to increased exports by the entire Mendozan industrial sector.

On the other hand, the production of these leading firms has been moving towards increased subcontracting. As a result, while these smaller suppliers may not export on their own, they participate in the internationalisation process indirectly through supplying intermediary components to exporting firms. Even though final goods exports may be concentrating, it does not necessarily mean that fewer firms are reaching international standards. In fact, this situation may prove to be a better internationalisation model than one in which all factors try to export, as it allows for greater product specialisation.

Table 1

Level of value added of exports (%): Mendoza

	1989	*1994*
Low value-added	36.7	51.5
Primary products	15.0	22.7
Energy	21.7	28.8
High value-added	63.2	48.5
Agro-manufactured products	43.7	22.2
Industrial products	19.5	26.3

Source : Ministry of Economy.

While industrial exports have grown, the other group of higher value-added products, agro-manufactured products, have witnessed not only a relative but also an absolute decline in exports. From a high of $135 million in 1990, agro-manufactured exports dropped to barely $100 million in 1994, with most of the decline coming from reduced processed fruit and vegetable exports. By contrast, exports of unprocessed fruits and vegetables have increased by a similar dollar amount, implying that the agro-industrial sector in particular has reacted to the market changes of the last five years by moving to lower value-added products, thereby revealing potential weaknesses in the international competitiveness of the sector. Even within agro-manufactured exports there appears to be a move towards lower value-added, witnessed by the growth of table wines over fine wines. The changes in export composition discussed above have taken place in the context of (and in some ways more pronounced) structural changes in the composition of Mendozan GDP.

Since the mid- to late-1980s, the Mendozan economy has witnessed a considerable shift away from industry and mining towards what are generally classified as service industries (commerce, transportation, financial services, and social services). Together they have increased from roughly 40 per cent of GDP in 1986 to nearly 57 per cent in 1993. While agriculture has maintained its share of roughly 5.5 per cent, industry and mining have seen not only their share (from 46 to 29 per cent) but also their absolute value decrease. During the 1989-93 period, the economy of Mendoza grew by 17 per cent in real terms. By contrast, the industrial and mining sector shrunk by 25 per cent and agriculture by 15 per cent. Even though the economy has seen a shift away from tradeable goods, as was mentioned earlier, exports have increased substantially, implying that the export intensity of the tradeable sector has increased even more than might be apparent at first glance.

The export intensity of the agricultural sector has increased by a factor of 1.61 since 1989. Even more revealing is the increase in industrial export intensity, whose level in 1993 was 3.21 times that in 1989. Despite this relative growth in the export intensity of the industrial and mining sector, it still lags far behind that of the agricultural sector.

The implications which follow from this analysis support the conclusions arrived at earlier that the Mendozan economy, while in the process of changing, is still disproportionately dependent on the agricultural sector, and is moving towards lower value-added products for its export performance. An analysis of Mendozan exports by product reveals a greater intertemporal consistency than alluded to when one looks only at the industry versus agriculture split. If one excludes energy, the leading five or six exports have been relatively consistent in their ranking over the last four years. From 1991 through 1994 the leading export of the province was fresh garlic, followed by canned olives and dried plums.

The variability which was mentioned earlier appears to come in large part from non-core exports of the province which have either made temporary inroads, such as crane parts in 1993, or others which have lost importance such as most (unfermented grape juice). Another notable observation is that although the province is the heart of the Argentine wine industry (the world's fifth largest), exports of all kinds of wine products totalled less than $20 million in 1994. Furthermore, the majority of the modest growth during this period came in the form of increased low-quality table wine exports to countries such as Paraguay, as opposed to finer wines whose main export markets are the United States and Japan.

With regard to country of destination for exports, Mendoza is even more dependent on the Mercosur market than the nation as a whole, with 45 per cent of exports heading for other Mercosur nations (versus 30 per cent heading to the United States, Europe and Japan). In contrast to the nation as a whole, however, one sees that many of Mendoza's higher value-added products are sold primarily to more advanced economies, implying that the industrial base which the province has is in fact competitive at international and not just regional levels. While Brazil is the leading importer from Mendoza of a whole host of raw or semi-processed agricultural products, the more sophisticated exports such as machine valves, crane parts, ferrous alloys and other metals have the USA, Japan and Europe as their main markets. Wine is another good example, in which the fine and bottled segments have the USA and Japan as their main markets while the growing segment, table wine, has Paraguay as its leading destination. Given the composition of exports, this trend towards increased trade with Mercosur will only serve to strengthen the shift towards lower value-added products and potentially weaken a currently competitive industrial base.

The objective of this chapter is to probe beneath the aggregated trade statistics and observe the second-order trends whose impacts will be felt later. Until now, the discussion has been focused primarily at the industry and in some cases product level of analysis. However, in order to confirm the trends identified at these levels it is necessary to assess the changes in outward orientation at the firm level. To do so we rely on information from conducted in 1995 by the Ministry of Culture, Science, and Technology of the Government of Mendoza covering roughly 200 firms in the province. The effort to highlight common attributes of Mendozan firms and identify those factors which can impact on competitiveness. Firms from all the major industries present in the province and covered a wide range of issues relating to firm demographics and strategies. Of more than 200 variables, a subset was selected for its potential relevance to a firm's internationalisation capacity.

Two indicators of internationalisation were chosen. The first, EXPORT, states simply whether or not the firm exports any of its production. The second dependent variable, EXPORT%, is used only for the sample of firms which do in fact export, and is a measure of the export intensity of the firm (exports over total sales). The model developed includes three sets of variables thought to affect firm internationalisation behaviour: firm demographic variables, strategic choice variables, and finally government programme variables.

A logistic version of the model was estimated for the first dependent internationalisation variable, EXPORT, and a similar model was then estimated for the independent variable EXPORT% using linear regression. This may be due to the fact that they have a dominant presence in the domestic market and do not see the need to go abroad, while smaller, less domestically entrenched firms see foreign markets as offering greater potential. Alternatively, what are classified as large firms here are in reality medium-sized ones that have neither the scale of truly large firms nor the niche markets of smaller ones.

Another key variable in predicting whether a firm will export is if it is part of the agrosector, in which case it will have a much greater likelihood of exporting. Mendozan-based firms in certain agriculture-related areas do enjoy a comparative locational advantage over firms in machinery, chemicals, or other industries : hence the positive effect. Other variables which tend to have a significantly positive effect on export likelihood include partial foreign ownership of the firm, and participation in government-sponsored commercial missions and management training. By contrast, firms with high percentages of uneducated workers are less likely to export, pointing to the importance of an educated workforce, even in low value-added industries. Two other variables, which are not statistically significant but which appear to be exerting an influence are the possession of quality control measures (NQC) and product research or design (PROPDES) capabilities. As might be expected, firms with no formal quality control systems tend not to export while those with design capabilities do. Taken together, these results tend to support the points highlighted earlier using industry-level statistics regarding the importance of value-added (associated with quality and education-training levels) in a firm's ability to be successful in international markets.

Similar results were found using EXPORT% as the dependent variable. Once again, large firms tended to export less on average than smaller firms, a result confirming the commonplace inverse relationship between firm size and export intensity. Older firms also tended to export less, a finding that reinforces the impression that the more embedded firms are in the domestic environment, the worse their export performance. Furthermore, firms in the machinery industry, if they do export, export more on average than firms in other industries, supporting the hypothesis that certain segments of Mendoza's industrial sector are in fact very competitive at the international level. By contrast, the agro-sector includes many firms which export due to the comparative advantage of the region but not many which export a lot, implying few competitive or firm advantages.

The main argument of this chapter has been that in order to assess completely the impact of a market liberalisation programme such as that which Argentina has undergone, one must look beneath the aggregate statistics and analyse underlying changes in critical market structure and organisational variables, changes whose impact will only be felt in the long term. On the surface, Argentina's liberalisation programme appears to have been quite successful. Comprehensive reforms of the nation's monetary, fiscal, trade and regulatory regimes have been undertaken, resulting in considerable growth in GDP. Furthermore, the objective of reintegrating the country into the world economy appears to be well underway. Trade levels have increased substantially, outpacing GDP growth in the 1990s.

The central argument being made here, however, is that while this growth has been beneficial for Argentina, it has been accompanied by certain other underlying trends which could potentially prejudice the country's long-term development prospects. The two main trends which are of greatest concern relate to the level of value-added being created in the country, particularly with regards to its exports, and the change in composition of its trading partners. As has been shown, there has been a trend in recent years towards greater reliance on exports with lower value-added content. The second trend discussed in the chapter poses a similar threat to the long-term competitiveness of the Argentine economy. Growth in trade with its Mercosur neighbours, primarily Brazil, holds potential drawbacks, the main one being trade diversion away from more developed markets.

The level of competitiveness of a firm is directly related to the sophistication of the demand it serves. By moving more and more away from the leading edge markets, Argentina runs the risk of damaging its long-run competitiveness, as the demand pressures to improve quality and performance are weaker in these secondary markets. Each of these trends was shown to operate both at the national and provincial levels in Argentina. Furthermore, firm level data provided additional support for the claim that those sectors which rely primarily on comparative advantage in natural resources are more likely to participate in foreign markets. The case of Mendoza also provides encouraging news in that its high-value added sector does in fact appear to be competitive at the international level. However, the challenge it will encounter, and one which the country as a whole has been failing to meet, is whether in the fact of changing trading pattern it will continue to maintain its level of competitiveness.

Neoliberal Globalisation

Neoliberal globalisation constitutes the dominant trend in the world economy at the present juncture. It is driven by a wide-spread push towards trade and capital account liberalisation, increasing internationalisation of corporate production and distribution strategies, intensification of technological change that is rapidly dismantling barriers to the international tradability of goods and services and extraordinary mobility of capital. Most commentators would accept that the process of globalisation offers enormous benefits in the form of more rapid economic growth on a worldwide basis due to the accelerated pace of technical change and the associated increases in production, international trade and investment. It is also recognised that the globalisation process poses a novel set of challenges. Hitherto, the critiques of neoliberal globalisation have focused primarily on the extremely uneven nature of the integration process, drawing attention to the fact that the benefits of the growth are likely to be distributed on a highly unequal basis between different countries, as well as between different social groups or regions within the individual country itself. It is anticipated that growth will be concentrated heavily within the "core" and certain segments of the "semi-periphery", the so called "emerging markets", with large components of the Third World, notably regions, such as Sub-Saharan Africa, being left largely outside the scope of this expansionary process.

Countries in the semi-periphery posses the advantage of relatively large internal markets, a considerable base of human and physical infrastructure and comparatively low wages in spite of significant expansion of manufacturing activity. These advantages, in turn, act as a magnet for large inflows of foreign capital. The uneven distribution of the benefits of globalisation on the developing world is accentuated by the fact that the globalisation process itself undermines the redistributive capacities of the nation state which would otherwise even out the resulting income disparities, at least to a certain extent. Critiques of globalisation have, therefore, naturally drawn attention to the social tensions on dislocations that would be associated with rapid economic expansion, tensions which would inevitably manifest themselves as conflicts over ethnic or religious identity in a variety of national contexts. Anti-globalisation perspectives have also singled out the problems of ecological dislocation and have emphasised the major trade-offs that would emerge involving the two key objectives of material expansion, on the one hand, and a clean, pollution-free environment on the other. In retrospect, it is clear that both sets of arguments are essentially a reflection of concerns about the negative side effects of globalisation on income distribution, with one focusing on income distribution within the current context, whilst the other draws attention to income distribution over time and the welfare of future generations. What has been striking until recently is the intense optimism surrounding the potential benefits of globalisation in terms of the magnitude of overall growth, an optimism which help to relegate its intrinsically uneven character into the background.

A series of successive currency crises during the 1990s culminating with the widespread Asian crisis of 1997, the Russian crisis of 1998, and the possibility of an impending crisis in Brazil during the early months of 1999, have been instrumental, however in dismantling the early unqualified optimism concerning the expansionary potential of the world economy in the context of a particular form of globalisation. Enormous flows of short-term speculative capital have emerged as the principal element of systemic fragility, posing a major threat against the sustainability of growth in the first place, regardless of its income distributional or environmental consequences. A generalised deflationary bias has been injected into the world economy resulting from successive currency crises, notably in the semi-periphery of the global system, and the subsequent attempts by the key institutions at the centre of the system, namely the International Monetary Fund, to deal with these crises primarily, if not exclusively via fiscal and monetary contraction. This, in turn, poses a central threat to the sustainability of economic growth in the context of a globalised competitive market system which is under-regulated both in the domestic and the global sphere.

The need for effective intervention or regulation at the national and the supra-national levels emerges a key precondition for overcoming a major market failure in the system, namely the dislocations caused by the uncontrolled expansion of the short-term, speculative capital flows. Whether the institutional or political capacity exists to create effective forms of regulation at the level of nation state or at the supra-national or global levels is another matter. A paradox of neoliberal globalisation is that the powers of the nation state vis-a-vis corporate actors are reduced considerably through a process of intense financial and capital account liberalisation at a time when the need for effective regulation emerges as a major requirement for the proper functioning of the system. Furthermore, the degree of inter-state cooperation and the associated institutional infrastructure necessary to deal with major global challenges such as successive currency crises appear to be weak and underdeveloped. To substantiate our broad thesis, we present a stylised comparison of the three major financial crises in the current era of financial globalisation, namely the Asian crisis of 1997 and the Mexican and Turkish crises of 1994.

The conventional wisdom regarding the origins of currency crises draws attention to the two key factors in precipitating a possible crisis: a weak underlying economic structure (poor fundamentals) and speculative behaviour on the part of economic agents. According to the orthodox perspective, corresponding to the position of IMF for example, at least prior to the outbreak of the Asian crisis, a weak economic structure is typically associated with poor macroeconomic management on the part of the government. A combination of fiscal instability, high inflation and inward-oriented trade regime are commonly identified as key ingredients, which would sooner or later contribute to a major balance of payments crisis. The Mexican debt crisis of

1982, which has subsequently generalised in to the rest of the continent with profound económic costs, fits in nicely with the orthodox vision of a prototype financial crisis.

The natural corollary of this perspective is that a country which achieves sound fundamentals, notably fiscal discipline and open outward-oriented trade regime is likely to be immune to a possible speculative attack leading to a major currency crisis. Some of the more recent financial crises, notably Mexican crisis of 1994 and the Asian crisis of the 1997 have raised serious doubts concerning the relevance of the orthodox perspective. There is no doubt that countries which are characterised by high degree of fiscal instability, as the case of Turkey in 1994 testifies, are countries which are highly prone to a crisis and to a speculative attack on their currency. Yet, in retrospect, one of the key lessons to emerge from the more recent financial crises is that a major speculative attack is perfectly possible even in countries where the underlying macroeconomic fundamentals, notably the fiscal indicators, appear to be quite sound.

In fact, both Mexico in 1994 and the Asian group of countries in 1997 enjoyed a fiscal surplus and low inflation. It would be extremely misleading to identify the public sector or the government accounts as a direct contributor to the crisis in both of these cases. Furthermore, the sound fundamentals argument applies even more firmly to East Asian countries, in the sense that these countries have traditionally enjoyed extremely high savings ratios, a pattern which continued to characterise their performance in the context of the 1990s. These countries also managed to attract unusually large magnitudes of foreign direct investment, which most commentators would unambiguously regard as a vital input to long-term economic development. The observation that the crisis economies displayed sound fundamentals in certain key respects, however, requires a serious qualification in the sense that the economies concerned typically manifested important structural deficiencies, which were amplified over time in the context of the 1990s. What is striking, in retrospect, is that these structural deficiencies are not the type of deficiencies, which have typically been emphasised by the conventional wisdom or the IMF perspective, at least until very recently, significantly in the aftermath of the Asian crisis.

The comparative analysis highlights a structural characteristic which applies to all crisis countries, whether they are characterised by fiscal equilibrium or instability in the first place, namely a mixture of appreciating exchange rates and large current account deficits. In the presence of large inflows of short-term foreign capital, following the liberalisation of domestic financial systems and the drastic opening up of the capital account regimes, the countries involved inevitably experience a loss of export momentum and concurrent expansion in imports, resulting in unusually large current account deficits. Policymakers concerned with the health of the overall balance of payments tend to ignore the fact that this apparent equilibrium is very much a fragile equilibrium, based on large and yet highly reversible inflows of short-term capital, as external actors try to capitalise on high domestic interest rates in emerging markets. When a speculative shock is generated, however, which may originate from a multitude of different sources, and the country experiences a major outflow of short-term capital, the large current account deficit is translated into a major balance of payments deficit. Another striking observation concerning the common tendencies associated with the crises of financial globalisation in the current conjuncture is that the process of globalisation itself has tended to undermine the models of national regulation which had characterised the earlier era of post-war development.

In fact, the present context is a transition from an earlier era of over-regulation and control to a new phase involving under-regulation and demise of national economic management. In retrospect, the very transition from an 'over-regulated' to an 'under-regulated' system may be identified as a major underlying cause of the financial crises in the current historical juncture. This broad inference can be made much more explicit with reference to the case of South Korea; a country, which arguably experienced a deeper crisis, compared with most other Asian countries in 1997 and the ensuing period. It is widely acknowledged that South Korea's hyper-growth during the post-war period, notably from the early 1960s onwards, has been facilitated by an activist state and a specific form of industrial policy designed to increase manufactured exports and build competitiveness in external markets.

A high degree of state autonomy combined with an unusual degree of government collaboration with the large conglomerates has been instrumental in the implementation of successful export-oriented industrial policy. The effectiveness of Korean industrial policy is typically associated with the mix of support and discipline that has characterised the approach of the state and its relations with the corporate sector. Due to a combination of internal and external pressures, a consideration of which is beyond the scope of the present essay, the domestic financial system has been privatised and controls over trade and capital accounts have been dismantled. The process effectively started during the mid-1980s and continued well in the 1990s.

The outcome of this process was a major transformation of the equilibrium characterising the previous pattern of state-business relations, with the corporate sector progressively escaping from the boundaries of effective state control, with direct access to short-term external finance providing a major avenue for establishing corporate autonomy. In the aftermath of financial and capital account liberalisation, the 'support' element underlying government business relations in South Korea continued but the 'regulation' on the 'discipline' element has largely been dismantled. The result was a transition from the developmental state model of the earlier era to a model of "crony capitalism", where cooperation between business and government without effective discipline resulted in the Chaebol pouring profits less into research and development and more to gambling in the stock market and the real estate. Weak corporate governance and corruption, in an environment traditionally characterised by excessive industrial concentration, as well as a poorly managed banking system with a high percentage of non-performing loans have been identified as the overriding structural weaknesses of the South Korean economy in the context of 1990s.

The natural conclusion to draw concerning these structural deficiencies which may be identified as fundamental factors leading up to the crisis, is that it was not over-regulation but inadequate control or surveillance on the part of the state which was at the hearth of the Korean crisis.

The East Asian Financial Crisis of 1997

The roots of the East Asian financial crisis can be extended to the beginning of 1990s. Capital account liberalisation emerged as a global phenomenon during the period, a process that was directly encouraged by the United States and other industrialised countries. The drastic shifts towards capital account liberalisation was also facilitated by the broad environment of the early 1990s, with intense optimism surrounding the future of globalised capitalism following the collapse of the Soviet system. Inevitably, a number of developing countries including Mexico, Argentina, Turkey liberalised their capital account to generate large inflows of foreign capital and in turn, managed to accelerate their economic growth with the help of these inflows. The East Asian countries pursued similar path. They also liberalised their capital accounts, a process that was accompanied by a dismantling of the regulatory role of the state in financial markets. Not suprisingly, financial market and capital account liberalisation combined with a record of outstanding macroeconomic performance were instrumental in attracting substantial inflows of capital into the region.

Annual capital inflow into the region constituted 6 percent of GDP, on average, between 1990 and 1996. The East Asian governments maintained a regime of fixed exchange rate, which helped to reduce risks and contributed further to process of large inflows of capital. Increasing inflows of capital to the region, however, resulted in rapid appreciation of exchange rate in real terms. Another critical turning point in this process was the sharp reversal in the long- term trend involving the Yen's appreciation relative to dollar after 1994. Since, the countries in the region pegged their currencies to the dollar; this meant in effective terms an appreciation of their currencies. Another striking trend in this context involved the rise of China as an important economic power. During the course of 1990s, China embarked upon an export-oriented development strategy and emerged as a major competitor to rest of the East Asian Countries.

China devalued its currency -Yuan - in 1990 and 1994: The devaluation decision, coupled with lower inflation and higher productivity growth relative to its trading partners, meant that the Chinese Yuan became the world's most undervalued currency. The progressive overvaluation of the exchange rates, the appreciation of the Japanese Yen against the Dollar after 1994, the devaluation of the Chinese Yuan were combined with the competitive pressures exerted via Mexico's participation in NAFTA, the devaluation of the Mexican peso and finally the worldwide glut in semiconductor production constituted significant background elements to the East Asian financial crisis. These multiple influences contributed to a deterioration of the export performances of the East Asian countries. Export growth (measured in current US Dollars) began to slow down in the mid-1990s and then dropped sharply in 1996 in every country of the region.

Exports of labour intensive manufactures had constituted one of the principal building blocs of East Asia's growth during the preceding decades. But there emerged a new glut in labour-intensive manufactured exports in the world market. Declining terms of trade for labour intensive products, such as footwear, apparel and consumer electronics led to slower export earnings for the Asian countries. Semiconductor industry, a major export sector, was negatively affected by a global tendency of declining prices with the estimated decline of output in the region as a whole amounting to some 80 percent in 1996. The process was accentuated by the entry of China and Mexico as leading competitors in electronics production. Their entry also contributed to the over-production, excess capacity and declining prices. The American market had played an important role historically in the growth of the East Asian countries and also continues to be the single most important market for the crisis-ridden countries of East Asia in the current conjunctures.

Following the signing of the NAFTA agreement and the devaluation of the Peso in 1994, Mexico emerged as a key competitor to the East Asian countries in the US market. Mexico's total exports to the American market climbed from $52 billion in 1993 to $96 billion in 1996, with the gains concentrating in several areas that directly competed with the East Asian exports including electronic machinery, apparel, and automotive components. A brief survey highlights the fact that the Asian financial crisis is a multi-dimensional process and blame should not be directed against a single factor at the exclusion of other possible determinants of the crisis. Clearly, a number of global forces of a structural nature were in operation escaping the boundaries of control by the individual nation states. It would be unfair, therefore, to place the blame on the East Asian policy makers for factors associated essentially with shifts in global market conditions. It would be misleading to imply, however, that the individual nation states are immune to criticism. In fact, important policy errors could be identified on the part of the East Asian governments. The nation states involved had adopted, in many cases, premature financial liberalisation without adequate safeguards or regulations.

The partial nature of the reform process helped to generate increasingly fragile financial systems. Excessive reliance on short- term foreign debts, rapidly expanding bank credits and inadequate regulation and supervision emerged as overriding characteristics in the region in the aftermath of financial liberalisation. Firms benefited, in the short-run, from these perverse incentives and were rather successful in terms of exploiting the loopholes created with piecemeal approach to financial liberalisation. As a consequence of the weakening of control over the financial sector, domestic bank lending expanded rapidly throughout the region. Thus, observe a profound structural change in the region, involving a new set of relations between banks, corporations and the state, making sharp contrast with the previous model of the developmental state or other possible variants of the interventionist state.

The principles of 'support and discipline' had constituted the central elements of the developmental state model. As a result of the disappearance of 'discipline' element, the productivity coalitions of the earlier decade progressively degenerated into a rent-seeking coalition or to 'crony capitalism'. A number of East Asian countries including South Korea and Thailand, abandoned the regulatory and disciplinary role of the state in parallel to the process of financial and capital account liberalisation. South Korea, for example, largely dispensed with a key institution of the period, the Economic Planning Board, and also discontinued its traditional role of coordinating investment in large-scale industries. The outcome was negative and could be considered as a form of market failure. An increasing share of bank lending was apparently used for unproductive forms of investment. The result was over-investment in some sectors; declining prices and a decline in export competitiveness. As export-oriented manufacturing became less profitable, investors in the East Asia invested in the real estate property and the purchase of equity funds.

Speculation flourished a process that was magnified as foreign currency continued to pour into the countries concerned. It is clear, therefore, that the drastic shifts in the East Asian policy regime, in an environment where capital was available on a massive scale, contributed to the emergence of the crisis by creating perverse incentives for the firms and encouraging a shift away from long-term, productive to short-term, speculative forms of investment. A key characteristic of the East Asian experience during the period in the steady rise in the share of foreign borrowing in total short-run borrowing, with the former emerging as the principal form of short term debt, a phenomenon which is also observed in the Mexican and Turkish crises. A progressive increase in the ratio of short-term debt to foreign exchange reserves in the East Asian context after 1994. This tendency is important in highlighting the inherent vulnerability of countries concerned to a financial crisis, considering that the ratio of short- term debt to foreign reserves is considered by many as a key indicator of financial market stability. Hitherto, the emphasis has been on global structural factors of a real nature as well as on domestic policy errors associated with the demise of previous model of the 'developmental state'.

In contrast to the typical vision of the IMF of a country heading towards a financial crisis, the countries involved manifested a number of favourable trends including high domestic saving ratios, budgetary equilibrium and low rates of inflation. The fact that capital inflows into the region continued right up to the outbreak of the crisis, clearly confirming the fact that the crisis itself was largely unexpected. Once the crisis was initiated, however, it became a self-fulfilling financial panic. The crisis was triggered and amplified by dramatic swings in the expectations of the creditors concerning the behaviour of other creditors. The key conclusion, therefore, is that inherent financial market instability in an era of globalise financial markets is a key determinant in the Asian financial crisis. What is striking in this respect is that in spite of glaring structural weaknesses, a number of macroeconomic fundamentals of these countries could be considered to be sound prior to the crisis. It may also be argued that an over-appreciated exchange rate can be adjusted without experiencing such a drastic financial turmoil. In fact, the panic itself led to over-reaction than necessary.

The recent Asian crisis, therefore, draws attention to the inherent instability of the international financial system and its extreme vulnerability to detrimental panics, with a consequent need to regulate short-term capital flows on a global basis.

The Mexican Financial Crisis of 1994

The origins of the Mexican crisis in 1994 can be traced back to the consolidation and restructuring policies of President Salinas. When Salinas came to the power in 1988, he started out by reaffirming earlier policies as well as by embarking on structural and institutional reforms in a neoliberal direction. The reform package involved a fundamental opening of the economy to international competition, large-scale privatisation, and deepening of stabilisation based on a predetermined nominal exchange rate anchor and restrictive fiscal and monetary policies. During the Salinas' term of office, a broad social and economic agreement, of a neo-corporatist type, between the government, the private sector and the labour unions known as "the Pacto" continued to guide price, exchange rate and wage increases and was instrumental in facilitating a relatively smooth stabilisation and adjustment process.

Mexico benefited from the Brady agreement in the sense that its debt burden was reduced through a major negotiation of the total debt outstanding, the interest payments on debt and the repayment period. Following the Brady Plan, Mexico began to open up its financial sector and to privatise the banks. According to Sebástian Edwards, although the growth performance of the economy was rather modest after the reforms the media, financial experts, academics and the multilateral agencies -including the World Bank and the International Monetary Fund-exaggerated the economic results of the reform programs and reflected Mexico to the public at large as a major success story. The US administration's efforts to persuade the public and congress of benefits of

NAFTA also contributed to an exaggerated representation of the Mexican success.

The opening of financial sector and privatisation of banks combined with the widely held perception that an economic miracle was taking place led to the international capital holders to rediscover Mexico and to lend to the country in large magnitudes. Mexico in the early 1990s was also influenced by the global trend involving the changing course of international capital flows away from developed countries. Mexico was considered as the best hedge by external investors, considering the falling interest rates and continuing recession in the developed world. During the early 1990s, the positive signals provided by the restoration of macroeconomic equilibrium, the liberalisation and privatisation drive as well as the prospects of the NAFTA helped to attract foreign capital on a massive scale to the Mexican economy.

Speculative and short-term investment constituted the majority of the capital inflows. It is estimated that only one fifth of the massive capital flowing into the Mexican economy was in the form of foreign direct investment. A large privatisation program and high Mexican interest rates (three times higher than the US rate) contributed to the process of large inflows of foreign capital. As in the East Asian case discussed earlier, the liberalisation of the capital account, and the subsequent increase in the capital inflows created a pressure for appreciation of exchange rate in Mexico. The appreciation of the currency reflected itself in the real economy as a dual process of export stagnation and import expansion. As a result, the trade deficit increased considerably between 1989 and 1992. As the trade deficit widened, the

Mexican government had to resort to further borrowing to cover the growing current account deficit. At the same time, one of the main sources of capital inflow- privatisation- started to lose its momentum once the bigger state companies were sold off, leaving little to be handed over to the private sector.

The flow of international capital to the Mexican economy slowed down during the course of 1994 largely because of political uncertainty in Mexico due to the Chiapas uprising as well as due to the recovery of interest rates in United states during the second half of 1994. The outcome of this process was a crisis of confidence and a financial crisis in December 1994 signalling a dramatic decline in Mexican reserves and a drastic devaluation of the exchange rate. American investors' interest, membership of NAFTA, as well as the possibility of an international transmission of a crisis of confidence compelled the United States to rescue the Mexico by providing $51 billion to pay its short-term debts. As many commentators would agree, Mexico was rescued as no other country had been rescued. In retrospect, part of Mexico's problem was due to domestic mismanagement Mexico was not able to direct capital flows towards production and investment in tradeable commodities.

The capital attracted to the economy was employed predominantly as a basis for generating a consumption boom. Indeed, a steep decline in private savings accompanied the large inflows of foreign capital after 1990. In one critical sense, however, Mexico appeared to be quite similar to the East Asian cases viewed from a standard IMF perspective. Mexico had managed to restore its budgetary equilibrium after 1992. Fiscal accounts were in surplus and inflation was under control. In an important sense, therefore, the 'fundamentals' were sound and fiscal disequilibrium was not at the heart of the crisis. From a comparative perspective, therefore, the Mexican crisis of 1994 demonstrated that it is perfectly possible to experience a financial crisis in the current global environment, even in a context where a sustainable fiscal position has been established from the outset.

The Turkish Financial Crisis of 1994

Turkey started to implement its neoliberal reforms in 1980. After a decade of fairly rapid economic growth coupled with a significant surge in manufactured exports, the momentum of the reform process was in decline towards the end of 1980s. Under worsening economic conditions, the Turkish government conceived large inflows of foreign capital in a key mechanism to restore economic growth, without focusing on basic structural deficiencies of the Turkish economy, namely large fiscal imbalances and a loss of momentum in the export drive. Turkey, as other semi-peripheral economies under investigation, was hoping to benefit from changes in global financial markets. The rising flows of international capital due to combination of recession and low interest rates in the developed countries was considered as a unique opportunity for overcoming Turkey's financial difficulties. To attract external capital to Turkey, on the required scale, there was a need for liberalisation of the capital account and establishing the full convertibility of the Turkish Lira. The August 1989 measures constituted the final hurdle in the stage by stage liberalisation of capital account in Turkey, a process that had been initiated in January 1980.

Following the introduction of the August 1989 measures, Turkey's financial system experienced a major transition to an extremely liberal capital account even by the standards of advanced economies with highly developed financial markets. The liberalisation of the capital account, indeed, contributed to an acceleration of economic growth in the early part of 1990s. But, it was a type of growth that helped to disguise rather than to overcome the basic structural weaknesses of the Turkish economy. Distributional pressures or conflicts associated with the neoliberal restructuring process emerged as the key driving force in the government's strategy to achieve accelerated growth on the basis of large inflows of short-term capital.

The year 1987 was a crucial turning point in the Turkish economy in the sense that it marked the return to fully competitive politics. Following the referendum of 1987 and the consequent opening up of the political system, distributional demands which had largely been repressed by the military in the early years of the decade, became particularly acute. Hence, the referendum of 1987 intensified the political struggle and placed pressure on the party, in power, to follow policies of 'populist' economic expansionism. Rather paradoxically, however, populist policies failed to prevent ANAP (Motherland Party) to lose the general elections in 1991.

The coalition government represented a coalition of losers from the post-1980 reform process. Powerful political pressures associated with its principal base of support deterred the coalition government from implementing a far-reaching stabilisation program. In short, the populist economic policies following by the referendum of September of 1987 and the subsequent elections of November 1987 continued to characterise the economic stance of governments in the 1990s. The inflow of capital helped, at least in the short-run, to overcome the acute distributional pressures present in the Turkish economy during the period. The economy expanded at a faster rate than would otherwise have been possible and the rising capital inflows provided a way of satisfying the distributional claims of the key groups involved. The final stage of capital account liberalisation and the transition to full convertibility of the Turkish Lira in 1989 resulted in a dramatic increase in the international capital inflows to Turkey.

The rising foreign capital inflow to Turkey created a pressure in the direction of appreciation of the exchange rate in real terms, rather similar to the process that Mexico and the East Asian countries had experienced following their capital account liberalisations. The appreciation of exchange rate, in turn, helped to undermine export growth and encouraged a parallel process of import expansion. The increase in the capital inflows was used to compensate the current account deficit from 1989 to 1994. In fact, lack of constraints over the public expenditures, due to the financing of budget deficit through both domestic and external debt, led to expansion of the fiscal deficit and rising interest payments. Capital inflows to Turkey increased sharply from 1990 onwards. These capital inflows were predominantly in the form of short-term capital.

The surge of speculative capital inflows amplified the magnitude of the existing macroeconomic instability. In fact, investigators found out a strong causal relationship running from net foreign assets to the budget deficit in the Turkish context. Financial liberalisation largely altered the process whereby the public deficits have been traditionally financed. The public sector deficit started to be financed through domestic agents that increasingly borrowed from abroad. The indirect borrowing from abroad realised by domestic agents replaced direct borrowing by the public sector from the international capital markets. The distributional demands of the principal groups were met through the low tax burden; and low cost of imported inputs for the business community due to an over-appreciated exchange rate and rising wages for workers. This process resulted in a higher budget deficit through the 1990s. Almost the whole of budgetary expenditures of the central government were being allocated to current expenditures (mainly wage and salary payments), interest payments on domestic and external debt and transfer payments in 1993, shortly prior to the onset of the crisis. Public investment, arguably a crucial element for long-term economic growth, constituted a very minor component of government's expenditures during the period.

A systematic increase in the domestic debt and short-term domestic borrowing requirements created an upward bias in the interest rates. The financial sector emerged as a major gainer in terms of high interest earnings. Indeed, it became possible to realise annual returns as high as 47 percent on the dollar in 1989, 25 percent in 1990, 18 percent in 1992 and 18 percent in 1993. By the end of 1993, it became apparent that the rapid growth of the Turkish economy in the early years of 1990s had not been based on strong foundations. It was highly difficult to sustain economic growth in an environment characterised by overexpansion of public expenditures and inadequate increases in public revenues. It was clear in retrospect that the rising current account deficit, covered by inflows of primarily short-term capital flows, could not provide a basis for a sustainable growth process. In order to break the vicious circle of domestic borrowing with high interest rates, the government adopted the low interest rate objective and implemented it by relying heavily upon the resources of the Central Bank at the beginning of 1994.

A major component of the base money created by the Central Bank was channelled as bank credit to the public sector. These policies combined with the reduction of the investment rating of Turkey by two major credit rating institutions precipitated the crisis in 1994. This, in turn, generated a major outflow of short-term capital. The financial crisis manifested itself as a major balance of payments crisis leading to massive depreciation of exchange rate in the early months of 1994.

A Comparative Analysis of the Financial Crises

All the crisis countries tried to benefit from the opportunities provided by the international financial markets in the 1990s. Under the influence of the global shift in the direction of neoliberal reforms, they liberalised their capital accounts in order to accelerate their growth rates by capitalising on access to cheap foreign resources. Indeed, the countries concerned managed to attract considerable sums of foreign capital from the international financial markets following the liberalisation of their capital account regimes. At first sight, capital flows appeared to be channelled to diverse sectors of the economy. A closer examination reveals, however, that the capital flows were directed predominantly to unproductive areas, namely spheres of economic activity where the returns from investment or expenditures realised were less than the cost of acquiring capital. Even in East Asian countries, financial resources were directed towards speculative real estate investments. Furthermore, the failure to take into account the regulatory and supervisory role of the state constituted a common feature in the experiences of the 'crisis countries'. When these countries undertook measures to liberalise their capital account regimes, they totally relegated the regulatory dimensions of the reform into the background. Attention was confined exclusively to the potential benefits associated with the market mechanism, without adequate attention being paid to possible problems of economic management originating from the capital account liberalisation. Domestic bank lending expanded in all the crisis countries during the course of the 1990s. This trend was particularly pronounced in East Asia, where banks and the corporations were confronted with an easy access to international capital.

The regulatory, supervisory or disciplinary role of the state, a characteristic of development process in the region for most of the postwar period, was largely absent during this particular conjecture. The opportunities provided by easy access to foreign capital manifested itself as a typical moral hazard problem. Banks continued to expand credit, not caring about establishing prudential limits to their lending process, an approach rationalised on the grounds that the underlining strength of East Asian economies would prevent the emergence of an economic collapse or widespread bankruptcies. A broadly similar pattern was evident in the Mexican case. The foreign debt was incurred by the Mexican government and channelled to the private sector via an expansion of bank credits. A similar moral hazard problem could be identified in the Mexican case, as the relaxed conditions favouring the expansion of domestic credit stimulated a consumption boom and discouraged domestic savings. The state or the public sector, in contrast, was the primary actor in the Turkish context. Although, the rise in the capital inflows were translated into expanding bank credit prior the crisis in Turkey, a major component of these flows were used to cover the budget deficits that were widening due to the income distributional pressures associated with the post-1980 neoliberal reform and restructuring process. Once an extremely liberal capital account regime was established, international capital flows expanded dramatically due to the lower profit opportunities in the center and increasing confidence and optimism concerning the future growth prospects in a limited number of semi-peripheral countries.

The rising international capital flows amplified the demand for domestic currencies and, in turn, led to the appreciation of exchange rates. In fact, the appreciation of the exchange rate was an element common to all crisis countries throughout the 1990s. Appreciating exchange rates combined with the typical government policy of fixing the exchange rate to the US dollar undermined export competitiveness and growth in all the countries experiencing a crisis, following the drastic appreciation of the US dollar from 1987 onwards. In retrospect, the establishment of an extremely liberal capital account regime made it impossible to control the money supply in the crisis countries. The capital inflows to these countries were not associated with increases in productivity, a process which resulted in inflationary pressures.

The governments, in turn, regarded inflation control as a main priority and adopted a policy of exchange rate stability in order to control inflation. This, however, caused a further overvaluation of the exchange rate. This trend became unsustainable as the countries concerned lacked the sufficient foreign reserves to finance the rapidly growing trade gap. All the crises, perhaps with the single exception of the Turkish case, were largely unanticipated and manifested themselves as crises of liquidity rather than solvency. It seemed perfectly rational for the individual creditors to fly ahead of the others and expand credit. But this created a basis for panic and, in consequence, a self-fulfilling crisis.

The apparently rational behaviour on the part of individual creditors, in the short-run, failed to produce desirable collective results in the long run. Looking back, the panic was unnecessary in the sense that the underlining fundamentals could have afforded a much more favourable outcome. The majority of the crisis countries have not sufficiently considered the ramifications of financial account liberalisation in the 1990s. By ignoring the problems of coordination and management associated with financial reforms, the crisis countries typically established fragile, incomplete and under-regulated financial systems. Therefore, we may conclude that despite country specific differences, capital account liberalisation in an environment of incomplete regulation was a major reason for generating the crisis.

Yet, the disastrous effects of a potential panic have been intensified as major inflows of foreign capital poured into a typical crisis country. Hence, the intrinsic instability of the global financial markets, and not only the regulatory failures on the part of the individual nation states, deserves emphasis as an ultimate cause of financial crises experienced in the semi-periphery during the 1990s.

In addition to the similarities emphasised, a number of striking contrast may also be identified with respect to the comparative experience of East Asia, Mexico and Turkey, with the added qualification that 'East Asia' itself is not a homogeneous category. On the whole, the East Asian countries, as a group, appeared to be far more integrated into the international markets compared with the Mexican and the Turkish economies. An examination of foreign trade indicators such as the shares of exports-imports in GNP as well as the size of capital flows clearly testifies this view. This, in turn, suggest that the East Asian countries were much more sensitive to changes in the external economic environment, whereas the domestic markets has been comparatively far more important in the Mexican and the Turkish cases. Prior the crisis, certain key macroeconomic fundamentals appeared to be sound in the East Asian and the Mexican cases in profound contrast to the Turkish case. Both the East Asian countries and Mexico enjoyed low inflation, budget surpluses (or only small deficits).

The emergence of a crisis in those cases was triggered by a speculative attack or a panic and was rather suprising for many observers given the nature of the underlying fundamentals. The imbalances in East Asia were concentrated in the private sector rather than the public. The short-term debts of Mexico and Turkey, in contrast, had been incurred by the governments preceding the crises of 1994. Mexico has been able to sustain a fiscal surplus after, 1992 and channelled the capital flow to the private sector through bank lending as opposed to the Turkish case which involved the financing of fiscal deficit through domestic agents who increasingly borrowed from the international capital markets. The use of the short-term capital inflows provided the Turkish government with an instrument to finance the current expenditures and repayments of interest without undertaking the required tax reform to raise revenues on an adequate scale. In East Asia, weak control and regulation over capital inflows helped to generate a vicious circle of speculative and unproductive forms of investment, rising inflation, appreciating exchange rates and declining export growth, factors that rendered the countries concerned progressively vulnerable to a financial crisis.

The countries exposed to international capital flows have functioned without any attention being paid to constraints imposed by these capital inflows. Mexico has channelled the capital flows to finance a consumption boom without considering the fact that the rate of return on capital should be higher than the cost of capital for the sustainability of the capital flow. Turkey, on the other hand, has utilised the capital inflows to cover the rising fiscal deficits without considering the fact that there would be a need to generate a fiscal surplus to pay back the debt. In the light of the broad experiences of the countries, which experienced financial crises, it seems rational to refer to the presence of both 'market failures' as well as 'government failures' as underlying causes of the crises.

Capital inflows, considered beneficial at the beginning brought about important economic turmoil due to a combination of policy errors and excessive confidence regarding the functioning of markets.

Concluding observations: the limits of national regulation and a possible case for supra-national or global initiatives

A comparative analysis of a series of financial crises, predominantly in the semi-periphery, during the 1990s provides a major challenge to the dominant "Washington consensus" and suggests the need for an active or interventionist state. The empowerment of the state in the developing countries to make it more effective in its supervisory and regulatory functions may well entail wider interventions considered to be unfriendly by the private sector such as antitrust regulations laws to increase corporate transparency, regulations over the banking sector and even the possibility of reducing short-term, speculative international capital inflows via direct controls . It is also abundantly clear that macroeconomic stability, defined in a narrow sense, as fiscal equilibrium, low inflation and high domestic savings ratios is not a sufficient condition for avoiding a major financial crisis, as the Asian cases testify.

Greater transparency and accountability may be achieved by reforms designed to address the micro level fundamentals of the economy such as augmenting the degree of competition in key areas of the economy and improving corporate governance as opposed to simply concentrating on generating fiscal stability at the macro level. It is undoubtedly the case that a major financial crisis tends to undermine the power and independence of the corporate sector and restores the power and autonomy of the state to undertake a more regulatory or activist role in relation to the private sector. A problematic issue in this context concerns the question of how long this enhanced power and autonomy of the state will continue. Stated somewhat differently, is this likely to be a temporary phase which will be shortly replaced by renewed power and influence of the corporate sector, resisting attempts at regulation or reform as in the pre-crisis situation in a liberal financial market and capital account environment? A particularly controversial issue, in this context, concerns the ability of the nation state to institute controls over short-term capital flows. Indeed, there exist striking examples of experiments on the part of individual nation states to impose some degree of control over short-term capital flows.

Malaysia and Chile are typically identified as the two principal cases where such policies have been implemented during the recent period. Other countries in Asia appear to be following on their footsteps. The instruments employed in the two countries differ markedly in the sense that the Malaysian policy makers have focused their attention on instituting controls over short-term capital outflows, whilst the Chilean policy makers have concentrated their efforts on restricting short-term capital inflows. Although it is too early to provide a definitive assessment of these experiences, it is fair to say that their outcomes so far has not been counterproductive. In fact, in the Malaysian case, there appears to be an improvement in the external reserve position of the country following the institution of capital controls. In the long run however, once the crisis conditions are over, it is unlikely that capital controls at the national level will prove to be an effective instrument in a competitive global environment. Countries may well discover that interventionist attempts to regulate short-term capital inflows may generate perverse signals to foreign investors, leading to a reduction in the size of capital inflows of a longer-term nature which are of crucial significance to the development process.

Bibliography

Andrew Herod, Gearoid O Tuathail, and Susan M. Roberts: *An Unruly World?: Globalization, Governance, and Geography*, New York, Routledge, 1998.

Ankie M.M. Hoogvelt: *Globalization and the Postcolonial World: The New Political Economy of Development*. Baltimore, Johns Hopkins University Press, 1997.

Caroline Thomas and Peter Wilkin: *Globalization and the South*, New York, St. Martin's Press, 1997.

Gary Teeple: *Globalization and the Decline of Social Reform*, New Jersey, Humanities Press, 1995.

Ian Clark: *Globalization and Fragmentation: International Relations in the Twentieth Century*, Oxford, Oxford University Press, 1997.

James H. Mittelman: *Globalization: Critical Reflections*, Boulder, Lynne Rienner Publishers, 1996.

Jeff Haynes: *Religion, Globalization, and Political Culture in the Third World*, New York, St. Martin's Press, 1999.

Jeffrey James: *Globalization, Information Technology and Development* (New York, St. Martin's Press, 1999)

Jeremy Brecher and Tim Costello: *Global Village or Global Pillage: Economic Reconstruction From the Bottom Up*, Boston, South End Press, 1994.

Lowell L. Bryan and Diana Farrell: *Market Unbound: Unleashing global capitalism*, New York, John Wiley, 1996.

Mark Lewis: *The Growth of Nations: Culture, Competitiveness, and the Problem of Globalization*, England, Bristol Academic Press, 1996.

Michel Chossudovsky: *The Globalisation of Poverty: Impacts of IMF and World Bank Reforms*, London, Zed Books, 1997.

Oliver Boyd-Barrett and Terhi Rantanen: *The Globalization of News*, London, Sage, 1998.

Priyatosh Maitra: *The Globalization of Capitalism in Third World Countries*, Westport, Praeger, 1996.

Proshanta K. Nandi and Shahid M. Shahidullah: *Globalization and the Evolving World Society*, Boston, Brill, 1998.

R.J. Holton: *Globalization and the Nation-State*, New York, Macmillan press, 1998.

Richard Barnet and John Cavanagh: *Global Dreams: Imperial Corporations and the New World Order*, New York, Simon & Schuster, 1994.

Roland Robertson: *Globalization: Social Theory and Global Culture*, London, Sage, 1992.

Sandra Braman and Annabelle Sreberny-Mohammadi: *Globalization, Communication and Transnational Civil Society*, New Jersey, Hampton Press, 1996.

Victor Segesvary: *From Illusion to Delusion: Globalization and the Contradictions of Late Modernity*, San Francisco, International Scholars Publications, 1999.

William Greider: *One World, Ready or Not: The Manic Logic of Global Capitalism*, New York, Simon & Schuster, 1997.

Zdravko Mlinar: *Globalization and Territorial Identities*, Vermont, Avebury, 1992.

Zygmunt Bauman: *Globalization: The Human Consequences*, Cambridge, Polity Press, 1998.

Index